Also by R. Foster Winans

Trading Secrets:
Seduction and Scandal at *The Wall Street Journal*

THE GREAT
WALL STREET
SWINDLE

THE GREAT WALL STREET SWINDLE

Jim Salim

with
R. Foster Winans

Xlibris

Philadelphia

Order additional copies of this book online:

http://www.xlibris.com/TheGreatWallStreetSwindle

To Lizzy, the love of my life

THE GREAT
WALL STREET
SWINDLE

This is a true story.

We have pinned down most dates and major events, but some share prices, volume, and other figures quoted in connection with trading stories are approximate. Facts, after all, are infinite in number. We have told the truth by selecting those that best illustrate it.

Dialogue was reconstructed.

Whether or not you invest—even if you regard Wall Street with distrust or disdain—we all have a relationship with money. Everyone needs it, has ideas about what it represents, and desires for what it can provide.

This is the story of an unusual man's relationship with an unusual sum of money, and the unusual way he made and lost it. But the lessons passed along are universal and timeless.

Read it and you will never think of your money or Wall Street the same way again.

Contents

Acknowledgments

My sincere thanks to all the men and women who contributed to my Wall Street education: to the late Mel Marks for taking me from the ground up; to David Batchelder for teaching me the takeover game; to the late Charlie Bluhdorn for inspiring me to be fearless; and to the many honest and capable people who have been part of my financial career.

My thanks also go to Jim and Nancy Donegan for showing me what grace under pressure is all about; to Foster Winans, a terrific writer and friend; to my wife, Maryanne Elizabeth Salim, who gave me something I could never make in the markets, true love; and most of all to Doctors Steven Dow and Jim Johnston—and to God—for giving me the gift of life.

Foreword

People have been asking me to write this book for fifteen years. Until now I resisted the urge. A private person by nature anyway, I decided that despite its dark side, Wall Street had been good to me. Why give up for the price of a book what I had paid a fortune to learn?

A couple of experiences came along to change my mind. One of these was a conversation I had one night over dinner and drinks with friends. The stock markets were near their peaks, early in 2000. It was plainly a bubble set to burst. I got to reminiscing about how much the economy and the investing business had changed in the previous two decades.

To illustrate my point, I reminded my companions that the only broadcast coverage of Wall Street in 1980 was a thirty minute public television program aired Friday nights: *Wall Street Week with Louis Rukeyser*. One night Peter Lynch, a smart guy who ran the Fidelity Magellan mutual fund, was a featured guest. Lynch told Rukeyser he managed about $40 million in the fund.

"Today the Fidelity funds manage more than a trillion dollars," I said. "Almost a hundred million Americans own stock. CNBC, which General Electric bought out of bankruptcy for practically nothing, now throws off hundreds of millions of dollars a year in revenue. It's amazing to me that so many people watch it every day. The market has become a national obsession."

One of my dinner companions, a man who manages a fertilizer plant in Louisiana, quickly chimed in, "I can tell you what it is, Jim. The reason we all watch CNBC is we're nervous about our 401ks. And the reason we're nervous about our 401ks is because we know we can't depend on Social Security when it's time for us to retire."

He leaned toward me, his voice rising with emotion. "I'm just an average working guy with a family to support. I would be so grateful if you would write your book and show me how to take care of my retirement. Because I really don't know what to do. It's confusing and scary, thinking about the future and how I'm going to make it. I'm sure millions of people like us would be grateful as well."

That was the first time anyone had begged me to explain the markets for the purposes of self-preservation. As I mulled it over in the following days it did strike me as unfair to hoard the knowledge I had accumulated, especially the knowledge that could save people from being cheated.

Although I had just been cheated myself, my goals were always speculative profit. I knew the risks and took them with eyes wide open. People like this plant manager aren't shooting for the moon, trying to maximize their profits. They just want a fair shake at building a nest egg. I thought, Why shouldn't they have it?

Around this time a friend introduced me to Foster Winans, a former columnist for *The Wall Street Journal* who expressed strong interest in helping me tell my story.

We discussed how to go about writing it. He made it clear from the start that the book could hold nothing back. I had to tell all. That gave me pause. Rattling around in my closet was a skeleton I wasn't sure I was ready to let loose in the world. But after some hard thinking and gentle encouragement, I committed. You hold the result in your hands.

Although the title of this book suggests wall-to-wall scandal—an exposé of all the ways that Wall Street gets you—the market is still the greatest tool the world has ever known for acquiring wealth. For every swindle there are a dozen examples of prosperous companies and their shareholders who were rewarded for the risk they took.

I'm reminded of an old proverb: There is so much good in the worst of us, and so much bad in the best of us. For me, that sums up Wall Street and, for that matter, life itself.

I hope you enjoy my tale and profit from my experiences.

—Jim Salim
Dallas, Texas
May 2001

Introduction

There are no lakes at The Lakes of Arlington. There are only holes where the water was supposed to go. Eleven enormous scars in the earth. Jim Salim tells me that the scale of those holes is best appreciated from a helicopter. But for now, we are limited to what we can see from the front seat of his German sedan.

Some of the holes actually held water at one time, up to 30 feet deep in spots. The shimmering surfaces attracted flocks of ducks, geese, and seagulls, and even a few families of blue herons.

That was the beauty of it. All you had to do was dig the hole. Clear blue water just naturally percolated up from an invisible aquifer and turned that hole into a lake. In Jim's vision the resulting network of lakes would become the jewel in the crown of a glittering Xanadu— The Lakes of Arlington.

Jim was going to build a golden city within the city of Arlington, Texas. In his vision, The Lakes of Arlington would resemble a lush South Florida oasis sprouting from the North Texas prairie. The location had it all: plunk in the middle of a teeming corridor of humanity, freeways, and business campuses known by its soulless nickname, the Dallas/Fort Worth Metroplex.

The property is a five-minute drive from the bustling Dallas/Fort Worth airport, national hub for American Airlines and home to a list of other corporate mammoths as long as your arm. Just down the street sprawls Six Flags Over Texas, the region's prototypical amusement park. A major league baseball field that George W. Bush takes credit for getting built is just a few blocks away. A couple of miles east, glowering down on Interstate 30, squats Texas Stadium, home of the Cowboys.

Jim sighs. "I had my own house lot all picked out, on the island in the big lake. It would have been a sweet place to live."

Jim Salim was going to do something big in Arlington. After more than three decades making his living as an aggressive market speculator and corporate raider, he was going to put his money into building something he could see and touch. It would be huge. It would leave a footprint that would outlive him, his children, and his grandchildren. It would earn him a lot of money. That's the way it was all supposed to work out.

But gazing through the windshield all we can see are mounds of churned-up dirt covered with dead weeds. A surge of traffic from the stoplight in the distance roars by. Jim has pulled over and parked along a local highway that cuts through the middle of an enormous swale of bottomland. He leaves the car purring and makes no move to get out. It's cold today and the view discourages closer examination. The dried stalks of milkweed and wild grasses sigh in the wind. A plastic bag flutters against a fence post.

"There it is. The Xanadu that turned into my Xana-don't!" His laugh is hearty with bravado: "They near destroyed me," I can almost hear him say, "but they couldn't."

The water table runs high along the banks of the Trinity River and the river floods almost every spring. But there are no lakes at the Lakes of Arlington. When work was halted before the project could be completed, the U.S. Army Corps of Engineers deemed the site unstable. The Corps stepped in and installed drainage pipes and dams to prevent the holes from filling.

"The only water you'll see in there now is a bunch of mud holes in the lake bottoms. It's a damn shame, a total waste."

Jim once owned all the land we can see to our right, east toward Dallas. Paid cash for it, too. He could walk five and a half miles along the winding Trinity shoreline and never once step off his property. And then he could walk another four or five miles back around the remaining perimeter without retracing his tracks.

He owned 2,250 contiguous acres—more than three square miles. Real estate experts still talk about it as one the best located chunks of undeveloped dirt in the country.

To the left of Jim's car, across the road, a ridge rises gently from the shallow valley. A cloud of gulls and crows undulates against a matte-gray sky. The scavengers are dining on a monstrous landfill.

"Jim, how did the landfill figure in with the luxury home development?" I have a hard time picturing an American Airlines executive putting down a million bucks to live next to a dump.

"Actually, it was part of the plan," he says, drumming his fingers on the steering wheel. He cracks the window to flick the ash from his cigarette. From hair to shoes he's in black.

"The city needed my dirt to line the landfill. Then they were going to cap it and turn it into a park, part of a green belt that'd connect with The Lakes, and one day reach to downtown Dallas."

For six years during the heart of the 1990s, Jim Salim toiled at his shining vision on this scrabbly, desolate-looking place. It was one of the largest dirt-moving projects ever undertaken in this country—two and a half times the size of New York's Central Park. Part of it had to be scooped out to make the lakes, part had to be raised out of the flood plain. Estimates of the final build-out time stretched to twenty years.

But he never got to pour the first truckload of cement. Instead, a few sharp-eyed investment bankers from New York—"suspender boys" Jim calls them—with visions of bonuses dancing in their heads, suckered Jim Salim into signing away a piece of land that had once been valued at $100 million in exchange for stock in a company that was three heartbeats away from bankruptcy. A couple of thugs in custom-made shirts and Armani suits picked his pockets.

The callousness with which a blue-chip global bank like Credit Suisse First Boston hung him and many others out to dry fascinated me from the moment I first heard the details. As a journalist who used to cover the stock market, it cried out for an exposé. As an author, the tale provided the necessary elements for a gripping suspense novel. It was full of deception, drama, and farce. You could tell the good guys from the bad guys.

But as I got to know Jim, he revealed a life of many layers and adventures. These were the true stories of a shrewd speculator, starting from scratch and learning hard lessons during almost forty years of plunging in the markets. His career was a guide to all the ways that Wall Street picks the pockets of almost every investor.

From modest roots in a small town in Louisiana, he was a millionaire by age 27, and broke at 29. He recovered, going on to set a record for trading the most bond futures in a single day. He'd been a stalker for corporate raiders, and then a raider himself. He'd rubbed shoulders with some of the biggest legends and slyest rogues on Wall Street. He'd been swindled by the best, and gotten the best of swindlers.

Although I'd never crossed Jim's path while covering the stock market, we found our conversations liberally seasoned with moments of recognition. His favorite Wall Street book is mine as well: Edwin Lefèvre's 1923 classic, *Reminiscences of a Stock Operator*. We had taken breakfast and dinner meetings in many of the same New York haunts. It wouldn't surprise me to learn that, one breakfast all those years ago, we'd sat next to each other in the dining room at the Park Lane Hotel.

I had written about or knew of a surprising number of the companies he'd invested in and the people with whom he'd crossed paths. Because of the research I'd done on Wall Street for my first book, *Trading Secrets*, I knew the historical context of almost every tale he told. But I had never heard a version of market history as funny, entertaining, intimate, and above all honest.

As he gradually revealed the heft of his knowledge and experience, it was clear Jim Salim could make a claim that can't be made by any stockbroker, trader, money manager, analyst, journalist, economist, or investor. He has seen and done it all.

Now he's telling it.

From penny-stock scams to hostile takeovers, from cotton to bonds, from venture capital to real estate, from stock options to gold futures, from the "go-go years" of the 1960s to the "new economy" of the late 1990s, Jim Salim has traded virtually every market, every way possible. Since making his first stock purchase at the age of 19, he has shifted billions of dollars of value around the economic landscape. He's made and lost a couple of fortunes, and left a few more on the table.

For a new generation of players, the investor class that first entered the markets in the 1990s, Jim's experiences provide an unvarnished look at how Wall Street really works, how it has always worked, and how most investors get cheated every day—even the smart money. On its most fundamental level, the story of his career is a rich slice of oral history.

Not since publication of *Reminiscences of a Stock Operator* has a character as colorful as Jim Salim stepped out of the shadows to talk about what goes on behind the scenes. Like Jesse Livermore, the legendary stock market plunger whose roguish exploits are portrayed in Lefèvre's popular book, Jim Salim offers a once-in-a-generation account of life as an insider in the fastest lane on Wall Street.

Like Livermore, he has spent his career riding a roller-coaster of gains and losses. Like Livermore, he has chosen to "play a lone hand" and is a master at reading hidden messages in a blizzard of numbers. Like Livermore, when he was ahead, he was never content to sit on his laurels.

Jim Salim has been a millionaire and a pauper, also sharing with Livermore the discovery that he'd chosen a hard way to make an easy living.

"I didn't think of anything," Lefèvre's protagonist explains in *Reminiscences*, "except that I could keep on proving my figuring was right. That's all the fun there is—being right by using your head."

Eighty years later, Jim Salim says, "I never enjoyed spending money as much as I enjoyed making it. I just wanted the satisfaction of knowing I could do it."

Not much has changed in the financial markets since Jesse Livermore's heyday. Fear and greed are still the basic human emotions that grip and guide the herd. Wall Street is still a carnival with its subcultures of rigged games and bogus sideshows. All the government regulation, clever slogans, slick TV commercials, screaming technology, and sober-sounding advice in the world can't change the fact of Wall Street's eternal self-interest. It's them versus you with the prize being your money. Adam Smith, the Scotsman considered the world's first economist, put it plainly enough in his 1776 tract *The Wealth of Nations*: "Everyone intends his own gain."

After a lifetime of expensive lessons and profitable revelations, Jim Salim is talking back to Wall Street, pointing out the hidden but common swindles that line the pockets of insiders every day at the expense of the rest of us. In doing so, he has recorded a thoroughly entertaining portrait of American capitalism in the second half of the twentieth century.

—Foster Winans
Bucks County, Pennsylvania
April 2001

The game taught me the game.
And it didn't spare the rod while teaching.

—*Reminiscences of a Stock Operator,* Edwin Lefèvre

1

Roadrunner

"Dad, I love you, and I appreciate it, and I love the money,
but it's just way too rich for my blood."

Me and Wall Street. It was love at first sight.

The moment couldn't have been clearer if it was yesterday instead of the mid-1950s. I was just a kid, no older than ten, growing up in a drowsy southern backwater with a name only the locals can pronounce. Natchitoches (NAK-uh-tosh), Louisiana, was a town of about 15,000 back then, a small parish capital about midway between two more important towns, Shreveport and Alexandria.

All around Natchitoches, for as far as you could drive in two hours, stretched hundreds of thousands of acres of small farms, cotton fields, and timber stands. Weather ruled our lives. In summer, the breathless heat clamped down like a pot lid. In the spring, you had to watch out for tornadoes. In late summer and fall, hurricanes triggered floods. And in winter, ice storms brought the power lines down.

It was a long, long way from any true city, let alone Wall Street.

Like most other ten-year-old boys, I rode a bicycle everywhere. I can't remember exactly why I pedaled to the grocery store that day. My mother probably sent me to pick up some milk, or maybe I stopped for a bottle of Fanta.

What I do remember is standing astride my bike next to a trash bin outside the store. On top I spotted a discarded newspaper that sure didn't look anything like the *Natchitoches Times*, which my father read. There was something important about it. I could see it was dense with words and numbers. I picked it up and unfolded it. That was the first time I ever laid eyes on the *Wall Street Journal*.

Swear to God, it gave me goosebumps.

I knew nothing about the investing world—I was still just a kid—but I had been earning money since I was eight, mowing lawns. My father set an example of hard work, and I discovered early on that I had a strong interest in making money and a knack for doing it. Maybe it was that immigrant heritage at work. They say the Lebanese have a God-given gift for business.

My dad never encouraged me one way or the other about what to do with the dimes and quarters I brought home. But I grew up tagging along on his trips to the bank each week, and I soberly deposited my earnings in my own account. I'd get my cheek pinched by the lady in the teller cage or my head patted by the manager. I always remembered my "Yes, ma'ams" and "Thank you, sirs." I'm sure they thought I was the cutest thing they'd ever seen.

My father was conservative about money and the main thing he pounded into my head all the time was to go slow. He liked to remind me, "There are no shortcuts to wealth." It came from hard work and being prudent. My father's family had emigrated from Beirut in the 1920s, before he was born. Hard work was a big part of his heritage.

I looked up to him. He'd been a star football player in college, but his real passion had always been flying. He was a commercial pilot and served as a flight instructor during World War II in Pensacola, Florida.

After the war he returned to Natchitoches and went to work for a local crop dusting company. He saved his money for ten years and bought the owner out. The big crop was cotton, and there was plenty of business. Cotton needs dusting every five days during the heart of the growing season, or pests and mold will destroy the bolls.

For a small-town guy, my father made a lot of money, and never owed a cent. Whether it was the experience of the Depression or just natural instinct, he thought walking into the bank for any reason except to make a deposit was a real bad thing. He paid cash for everything: his cars, his trucks, our house, even his airplanes. He had always wanted a farm and waited until he had the money in the bank to buy one.

I admired my father's ethic, even if I couldn't emulate it. In the summer months, when it came time to start spraying the cotton, he was busy all day, every day. The alarm would go off at 4 o'clock and by first light he was at the airfield topping off the tanks of fuel and poison. He flew and dusted cotton fields all day long, until only the last ribbon of pink was left in the sky and he couldn't pick out the horizon and the power lines. He'd be the last of his pilots to land and hangar his plane.

That was his life: diligent, conservative, polite, and honorable. Same as my uncle and grandfather, he prided himself on his good name. And his favorite expression was always "go slow."

But I was a roadrunner. You can't tell a roadrunner to go slow.

I don't remember what it was about that *Wall Street Journal* that caught my eye. But I know I snatched it like a little thief, jammed it in my bike basket, and pedaled home.

I ran up to my room, clutching it in my hand, closed the door, and began to read with a hunger I hadn't known until that moment. I was as mesmerized as my playmates were by their comic books. Every page, every article, had something to do with making money. Those pages spoke to me.

Although I was crazy for sports, especially baseball, and generally enjoyed most things that other children do, I had an industrious streak. Instead of buying stuff with my lawn-mowing money, I understood that I needed to save it for a day when I could use it to make more money.

It's not like I knew anyone who had anything to do with stocks. There wasn't a broker among us or an uncle who was a big player in the market. Something just clicked.

I kept that *Wall Street Journal* until it started to fall apart. I read every word, looked at every table, and then read it again. I checked every trash bin I passed, looking for another. I rifled through the piles of newspapers people left behind on park benches and on the courthouse steps.

The closest thing to a newsstand in Natchitoches was the cigar shop in the lobby of the old hotel. You might have found a single copy of the

New York Times or the *Washington Post* there, but certainly no *Wall Street Journal*. The copy I'd found must have been left behind by a salesman or somebody passing through Natchitoches. And whoever that was, I'm still grateful. When you're raised in a small southern town and you've never seen the world except by watching it on TV, the *Journal* was an eye opener. That was the moment I woke up and realized there was a big, wide world out there full of possibilities.

When I was thirteen I bought myself a subscription, and one to *Business Week* as well. But I never let my buddies know about any of it. In that time and place, reading about investments and business seemed to fall under the same heading as playing with dolls.

My father said nothing to me about reading the *Journal*. He never tried to persuade me to do anything, pro or con. He neither encouraged nor discouraged me from investing. My mother, who kept the books for my father's business, was more supportive of my interest. But she always backed my father up. In our family the environment was always tranquil, never any screaming or shouting. "Go slow," he'd repeat. I think my ambition and determination scared him. I'm pretty sure he thought I was crazy.

My father inherited his caution from his father, who had made his money in real estate and a country store. During the Depression, the people who made fortunes in the South were often those who owned the stores where the farmers took their trade. In bad times, when the farmers couldn't meet their bills, the store owners ended up taking the farms.

My grandfather never did that. He did buy land during the Depression, and, when things got better, he built and sold hundreds of houses. But he told me one time that he could've owned 70,000 acres of good, productive farmland if he'd taken the legal steps he was entitled to. He told me the farmers were just doing the best they could. He couldn't take advantage of their misfortune.

"Your name is everything," he explained.

He was raised in Lebanon, in a Christian family surrounded by a hostile Muslim majority. He arrived in America a penniless twenty-year-old whose first savings went for boat tickets so his wife and first son, my uncle, could join him. He identified with underdogs.

Many of those poor farmers who owed my grandfather money were black. For carrying their debts instead of taking their farms, my grandfather earned a lot of respect in the town's black community. My grandfather's teaching and example went straight to my heart. All my life I have been stirred to act when I've encountered an injustice. And thanks to my grandfather, I've always felt at ease and accepted among African Americans, whether in business, politics, or just socially.

In most other ways I was different from everyone else in my family. My grandfather saw it clearly, even when I was young. When my uncle asked me one day what I wanted to be when I grew up, my grandfather looked up from his newspaper and said, "Whatever it is, it'll be something different from the rest of us."

I dreamed of doing big things. I had hoped to become a professional baseball player, and I definitely wanted to make a lot of money. Unfortunately I wasn't good enough to make it to the majors. The money part of my dream meant what it means to most anyone, having comfort and power. But more than anything, I wanted the satisfaction of knowing I could do it.

You might say that's what I've spent my life at, proving I could do it.

My first plunge in the market came when I went off to Northeast Louisiana University in Monroe. Four times the size of Natchitoches, it was a shipping point on the main rail line between Dallas and the Deep South. It even had a couple of brokerage offices. Monroe also had its share of rednecks. Many of the eight thousand college kids came from rural towns and farms in the sprawling countryside that extended endlessly in every direction.

As a student, I vacillated between unambitious and disinterested. In Natchitoches I'd gone to Catholic schools where the nuns and priests kept the academic standards high, but I found that by cramming for tests I was able to pull out Bs and Cs, just enough to appease my father and mother. College seemed easy by comparison, so I put my energy into baseball, partying, and getting myself elected president of my fraternity pledge class. That's where I got my first taste of politics and caught that bug.

My second taste was bitter but confirmed my interest. The afternoon President John F. Kennedy was murdered—November 22, 1963—I was sitting in the lounge of the student union with a few friends. The public address system crackled to life and a quavering, scratchy voice said the president had been shot and killed in Dallas, and we should all say a prayer for his soul and our country.

Now, if you didn't live in the South at that time, you probably don't know how intensely a lot of people there hated John Kennedy. It was bad enough that he was the son of privileged northerners who pretended they hadn't gotten rich from smuggling and stock market swindles. The president was also helping destroy one of the South's hallowed traditions: "keepin' the niggers down." Louisiana, in particular, was the Jim Crow state that had legalized segregation in 1896, guaranteeing second-class citizenship for African Americans. Kennedy, on the other hand, supported the civil rights movement.

To me and those I counted as friends, that made him a hero. He was tough with the Soviets, always looking out for the underdog, and charismatic. You often see old news clips on television of bewildered young people crying in the streets as word spread that day of his death. I'm sure it was like that in a lot of places.

But in the student union lounge at Northeast Louisiana University a crowd of rednecks sitting in the corner heard the announcement, stood up, and applauded.

In a New York second my short fuse burned from shock to rage. I don't remember a lot of details right after that moment. The adrenaline wiped them out. I'd been lifting weights since I was sixteen and I was big and strong. I thought myself a real Billy Badass. Nobody scared me.

Fists flying, I piled into those boys. A half dozen of my friends followed. When it was over my knuckles ached, the place was a wreck, and people were limping off toward the doors.

I'm not bragging about this. But it was a turning point in my thinking. I knew I wanted to make a difference in the world, but not with my fists. That's when I began to plot a career for myself in politics. I thought I'd make a pretty good governor, from what I'd seen of Louisiana governors.

But first I'd have to make some serious money, enough to be comfortable and support a family. I'd need money to finance my campaigns and to give me the independence to be an honest politician in a state famous for corruption. I knew I could do a lot of good, if I just had the chance.

That chance, at least the chance to get started, came along in short order. One of the reasons my fraternity brothers elected me pledge class president is that I excelled at putting on a party. The other is that I was good at poker, which impressed my classmates once they got over being pissed at me for taking their money.

My reputation got around and I was soon invited into a long-running private game at a table in the back room of a nightclub in town. I had arrived at college with a little more than $10,000 I had saved from all my years working, including summers in the family business. I was young, but I had a stake that would hold me against most anyone I'd find sitting around that table.

One of them was a local doctor who earned a lot of money and was busily losing most of it. When I came into the game, he was down close to $130,000. He had a bad gambling habit and those boys had been plucking his feathers for a long time. After I'd played a couple of nights, he called me aside during a break.

"Are you that good all the time?"

"I'm okay," I said, giving him a guarded glance. I couldn't read where he was coming from. "I guess I do okay more than I don't."

I did know the game well, but I didn't like talking strategy, at least not with casual acquaintances. I'm a cold-blooded player, able to keep my emotions out of it. I just read the cards and study whether the other guy is trying to buy the hand or has the real thing.

The doctor steered me away from the table into the shadows. "I'll tell you what, Jimmy-boy," he said, lowering his voice. "I'll make you a deal. I'm in a bad spot here. I need to get out of my hole. If you're half as good as I think, I'll stake you in this game, and whatever you win you can have 20 percent."

I was intrigued. "And what if I lose?"

He pulled out a handkerchief and wiped his forehead. "You won't lose. But even if you do, I'll eat it."

That sounded like a good deal to me. I wouldn't lose a cent and stood to gain plenty. That's an easy way to gamble, when it's not your own money. We shook hands on it.

Well, within two months I'd won him $180,000. He decided to call it quits after that. He had all his losses back and a little bit more to boot, even after paying me my $36,000. My net worth had suddenly jumped to $50,000, all of it in cash. Just to put that in perspective, when adjusted for inflation it would be the equivalent of about $275,000 in the year 2000.

A few months later, early in 1964, I finally consummated my love for Wall Street. Mike Fettinger, one of my roommates and an upperclassman, had graduated and gone off to earn his credentials as a stockbroker. When he came back to Monroe, he ended up in the Merrill Lynch branch. Mike opened my first brokerage account, and I bought my first share of stock through him. I was nineteen.

Mike and I got along well, and I began passing time in his office. Most of the brokers and many of their customers were only in their twenties and early thirties. I felt right at home, which is the way the brokers wanted it. Active traders would spend part or sometimes all of the market's open hours sitting in their brokers' branch offices, smoking cigarettes, drinking coffee or pop, reading the *Wall Street Journal*, exchanging gossip, and watching the tape.

A good branch office had a clubby feel. It's a shame that tradition has been muscled aside by technology. The same faces showed up many days, and after awhile you got to know people, who owned what, who was trading what, who was making money, and who was full of shit. The brokers liked it because it was easier to talk people into buying or selling—and generating commissions—if they could look them in the eye. But even if some customers just hung around and didn't trade much, the brokers at least knew they weren't out on the streets where they could be seduced by a competitor.

The technology that changed it all was the computer. In 1964, the only place an individual trader could check on the market was in a brokerage office. The tape, the steady stream of stock quotes that we see today on screens in every nook and cranny of society, was then displayed only in brokers' offices on a crawling electric billboard, like the one in Times Square, or the Big Board, as the New York Stock Exchange is known.

In the Monroe office of Merrill Lynch, the billboard hung high up on the wall and ran nearly all the way around the room. Branch offices were often big and open like bank lobbies. The river of quotations flowed around the walls with occasional headlines for major breaking events such as changes in central bank interest rates.

All market news came over the Dow Jones News Service's broadtape, also available to customers only at a brokerage branch. A teleprinter sat in the lobby area and continuously ground out short business items that affected stocks and the market.

The broadtape was just that, a four-inch-wide ribbon of cheap newsprint wrapped around a cardboard core like a large roll of toilet paper and threaded through a small printer. During market hours the machine relentlessly printed out the unfolding details of the markets that day: block trades, commodities prices, company announcements, market imbalances, stock and bond data, government actions, and any other kind of news that might have an effect on prices. Every fifteen minutes or so a clerk would rip off the paper that piled up on the floor, carefully tear it into shorter lengths, and arrange the pieces in chronological order on a long clipboard that hung from the side of the machine.

All day long, customers would walk over and browse the broadtape, or just stand there and watch the news items as they came out of the teleprinter. By the market's closing bell, the clipboard was thick with lengths of paper, and that day's market story of winners and losers had been told.

If you wanted to check the price of individual stocks, Merrill Lynch had the latest technology: a clunky little keyboard with a box containing two tiny computer screens. It was a crude online computer terminal by today's standards, called a Bunker-Ramo for the company that built it. One screen displayed up to a dozen stock quotes at a time, without any details. On the other screen, the broadtape stories scrolled slowly down, line by line, at the same speed as the teleprinter in the lobby. You couldn't control the scrolling speed, and nothing was saved onto a disk. If you missed a broadtape story on the Bunker-Ramo, you had to search for the paper version.

Today, that sounds like the Stone Age, before anyone anywhere had access to interactive, real-time charts and stock quotes could be dialed up on a cell phone in the middle of a cornfield. But for a small-town guy back then, one who grew up reading the *Wall Street Journal* and watching the markets from afar, the immediacy was electrifying.

I was now in the game, with other players who treated me as an equal. I was a roadrunner among roadrunners. I started cutting classes and spending weekdays at Merrill Lynch, reading the tape and learning the ropes.

Mike would tell me each day what Merrill Lynch was recommending to its customers. He said they had analysts up in New York, really smart guys who were wired in to the managements of all the listed companies. These analysts studied the market, studied the industries, and studied the stocks. When they thought a stock was about to break out, they wired a buy signal to all the brokers in all the Merrill Lynch offices across the country. Merrill was then and remains today the biggest wire house in the world. When Merrill flashed a "buy," the power of its hundreds of branches to influence thousands of investors all at one time often gave a recommended stock a nice boost.

I didn't care whether the analyst had gotten it right or not, or if the stock was going to continue up or give it all back. But I noticed that the price pop could last as long as a few days or even a week. The price seemed to ride up for a few days, like a wave building up a head of steam before it breaks. I wanted to get in at the beginning of that wave and get out before it broke.

I made sure to show up at Mike's office long enough before the opening bell each day to read the wires from New York and look for a good candidate. The company I found was EG&G, Inc., a Pentagon technology contractor named for the initials of the three founding inventors: Edgerton, Germeshausen, and Grier. The analyst was pounding the table about how the company was going to profit from accelerated spending on the Vietnam War and new weapons technology. The stock looked cheap, if you believed the analyst's predictions of future business and profits. It sounded strong enough to set off a nice wave, so I jumped on it at the opening, 500 shares at about $20. Sure enough, the stock rode up a couple of points, and I sold it two days later at a nice profit.

You may wonder why I was so quick to pull the plug. The stock did continue to rise after I sold it. I know, as mutual fund guru Peter Lynch has said for years, that if you hold a stock over the long haul, chances are good that one day you'll get a "superior" return. EG&G is a perfect example. If I had held those shares for thirty-five years, my stake of $10,000 would have grown to well over $1 million. EG&G went on to become a commercial technology giant that recently renamed itself after one of its subsidiaries, PerkinElmer.

But I wasn't interested in sitting around watching my investments for decades. And even with the long-term return on EG&G, the stock was essentially dead money during the 1970s when the war was winding down. The biggest chunk of the price gain occurred in the 1990s.

I wasn't interested in going slow. I was determined to figure out how the big boys were making the big money. I learned to do what I have instinctively done all my investing life. I crouched like a cat studying its prey, watching and waiting for a perfect moment to pounce. I studied the tape, paid attention to everything that was being written and said, and listened to what Mike told me about Merrill's recommendations.

Mostly I studied the tape. Some days I sat for hours at a time, eyes locked on the lights flying by overhead, studying every tick and wobble in prices, trying to read the hidden messages. I kept up with the broadtape and read every word in the *Wall Street Journal*.

One of the first patterns I locked onto was in shares of Eastern Airlines, one of the nation's largest carriers and a company that constantly needed to raise money to buy planes. Eastern had a lot of stock out and it was always among the most active on the New York Stock Exchange.

Eastern seemed to be stuck in a trading range between $6 on the bottom and $9 on the top. I bought it on one of its dips and sure enough it worked its way back up over a few weeks and I sold it above $8. I kept it on my radar screen. When it dropped to the low end of the range again, I bought, and again it went up.

I must have traded Eastern fifteen times that way over the years and made a profit each time. If I had known then what I learned later, I would also have sold some stock short at the top to try to catch the money on the return trip. But I didn't know much about shorting stocks then.

Here's the definition of the two principal terms, long and short, most commonly used on Wall Street. If you buy a stock, you are said to be long. If the stock goes up you profit, down you lose. That's pretty simple. If you want to get more bang for your buck, you can go long on margin, as I did with EG&G. That means you only have to put up half of the value of the purchase in cash. The other half is loaned by the brokerage firm. You pay interest on the loan at a modest rate—the broker loan rate. Buying on margin gives a trader leverage. For every dollar spent, you get two dollars worth of stock to speculate with.

A trader who wants to make money on a stock he thinks is going to fall can sell stock he doesn't own, betting that the shares can be replaced later by buying them at a lower price. Shares are borrowed from the brokerage firm's own account, or the firm gets permission from another investor who owns the stock to let him sell it. He owes the firm, or the investor, the stock. He is, literally, "short" of the stock.

Cash from the sale of borrowed stock goes into the short-seller's account, and he or she pays the broker loan interest rate, just as when borrowing cash, although at a more modest rate. He can't touch half of it, which, again, is the margin requirement. If the bet is right and the price falls, he can "buy in" the stock he needs to "cover" the short position and replace the borrowed shares. The short-seller's profit is the difference between the two prices, minus commissions and interest.

However, if a short-seller is wrong and the stock goes up, the risk is theoretically unlimited. As the paper losses mount, the brokerage firm requires the short-seller to pony up more cash to maintain the 50 percent cash margin requirement. That's known as a margin maintenance call.

A legendary example of how badly a short-sale can go is the true story of how an incredibly successful New York investor named Bob Wilson got his clock cleaned shorting Resorts International. Resorts was among the first casino companies in Atlantic City, New Jersey, to go public in the 1970s. Wilson shorted the stock at about $6 soon after the initial public offering (IPO in Wall Street jargon). Then he told anyone who'd listen that only fools and cheapskates would care to gamble in a dump like Atlantic City in the summer, let alone brave the slush and stinging winds of a typical winter at the beach.

Wilson shorted a ton of Resorts and then set out on a 'round-the-world vacation he'd been looking forward to for some time. Resorts shares promptly took off. Wilson's brokers tracked him down in Lon-

12

don, Paris, and India. They begged him to let them buy in the stock and stop the losses as the price soared ever higher. The farther away he got from New York, the worse the damage.

But Bob Wilson was a stubborn curmudgeon. He was dead certain he had it right and every one else had it wrong. By the time he finally caved in and covered his short position, Wilson's wallet was lighter by many millions. He went on to build a personal investment portfolio that, by the time he retired, was estimated at a quarter-billion dollars. But the story of his Resorts debacle became an instant classic among traders.

I could have shorted Eastern Airlines when it reached the top of its range of about $9. But my education in the art of speculating was just beginning. I was discovering that the stock market isn't like poker, where you only have to read the players you can see. There are never more than fifty-two cards in a deck, and a good card counter can often guess the odds with reasonable accuracy.

The stock market has millions of unseen players and an infinite number of potential combinations of transactions and events that could move prices. I was earning my trading education the same way everybody does, by making mistakes and getting hammered on occasion. But, on balance, I made more than I lost. By the end of my junior year I had a substantial grubstake.

I returned to Natchitoches that spring, having learned more of what I would need to know in life by playing the market than I would ever learn in a classroom. The things I cared about were business and my political ambitions, which I kept to myself. No one was ever going to catch me climbing any corporate ladders, working for wages and living for a two-week vacation in Gulfport each summer. Completing school would be a waste of my time. I was pawing to get on with it.

So, with just two semesters left to get my degree, twenty-one years old, and about to marry a girl I met in college, I dropped out. My parents had a fit, of course, but I knew it was right. Quitting meant losing my college draft deferment, so I joined the National Guard and went off to do my basic training. When I was done I found myself at a crossroads. What next?

I could stay in Natchitoches and go into the family business. Flying crop dusters paid big money, $2,000 a day. I'd been in and around air-planes since I was born, started flying when I was fourteen and soloed at fifteen. I had the hand-eye coordination and all the other talents you need.

But it's scary work. Crop dusters earn every penny they're paid. You have to fly right in on top of that cotton, with zero room for error. Coming off those fields, you've got to make tight steep banks, up and off, tight turns coming around, and then drop right smack down on top of that cotton again, making sure you picked the right set of rows to boot.

And there's the tricky business of flying in groups, which dusters often do, swooping down in a staggered formation of two or three planes, to cover a field faster. You can't be dragging ass or you slow everybody down. You have to be quick and make the steep banks right along with them.

Do that all day, from sunup to sundown, sucking up your share of the poison and exhaust fumes along the way, and you've earned your $2,000.

But I decided to give it a try, which delighted my father. I handled just about everything fine, but what got to me were the power lines you could barely see at the ends of the fields. All I could think about as I flew was the next pass I'd have to make over those wires, and what would happen to the plane and me if they got tangled in my wheels.

At the end of the second day I felt like I'd been in a dogfight. My nerves were shot. I landed, taxied over to the hangar, and shut down the engine. My dad met me as I was climbing out of the cockpit.

I pulled off my helmet. "Dad, I love you, and I appreciate it, and I love the money, but it's just way too rich for my blood."

"Everybody starts off scared," he said. "It's like anything else, you get used to it and it becomes second nature. Just give it some time." Go slow.

But I didn't have time to go slow.

2

Go-Go Years

"The new billionaire saw himself . . . as an example to the nation's
youth: 'Somewhere in the United States there's a young man or
woman who will break every financial record I've set!'"
    –*The Go-Go Years* by John Brooks, 1973

I might not have had the nerves for dusting cotton, but I sure knew how
to fly. I also knew there was good money to be made flying corporate
aircraft and commercial airliners, but I needed a commercial license. In
1966, I signed up for a course at Ed Boardman's Flying School at
Meacham Field in Fort Worth, Texas. Boardman's was an institution,
and Meacham Field had been a major pilot training center since the
1930s, when it became home to American Airways, now American Airlines. Over the years Boardman's trained thousands of kids like myself.
    The course took six months. When I finished in 1967, the job mar-
ket was cooking. In fact, the whole economy was smoking hot. In 1966,
the Dow Industrials flirted with the 1,000 mark for the first time ever,
after running almost straight up for three years, an 80 percent rise. A
revolution was taking place in technology and investment. Digital
watches, computers, copiers, color televisions, instant photography, and
business franchising had captured the public's imagination.
    On Wall Street, the cult of the hot mutual fund manager had been
born. The term "a` go-go," borrowed from French, was being slapped
on everything from dancing to investing to make it sound new and ex-

citing. In the stock market, go-go meant aggressive, active, in-and-out trading.

One mutual fund manager who practiced go-go trading with a vengeance and gave it visibility and credibility was Gerry Tsai. He was the first mutual fund celebrity. He had a reputation for being a trading genius. He was as big in his time as Jesse Livermore was in the 1920s. Tsai ran the Fidelity Capital Fund, owned by the same mutual fund outfit that later launched the career of Peter Lynch, author of four investment books, and a frequent TV spokesman for Fidelity.

There were many comparisons made at the time between the 1920s and the 1960s, with all the dire predictions of a crash at the end. But the "experts" said it couldn't happen again. History tells another story.

Going forward another thirty to thirty-five years, the market bubble of the late 1990s was an echo of the 1960s. The parallels were stark. High-tech was the business to be in back then, speculative trading was the rage, and unbelievable stock market valuations were being slapped on anything that breathed. In the 1960s the hot stocks were companies like Xerox and Polaroid.

In the 1990s it was high-tech, day-trading online, the dot-com bubble, and the "new economy." As for the real value of things, how about idiot analysts pinning target prices of $400 a share on money bleeders like Amazon? If you bought into *that* 1999 prediction by analyst Henry Blodget, consider that both Polaroid and Xerox, hot stocks of the go-go years, are dead meat today.

In the 1960s the fashionable growth strategy was conglomeration and diversification. Giants like ITT and Gulf & Western grew by buying up dozens of companies, often in unrelated fields. Gulf & Western subsidiaries made car bumpers and produced *I Love Lucy*. They sold cigars and refined sugar. These days that strategy is called a roll-up, except companies don't diversify anymore. They focus on "core strengths" and look for "synergy." Different words, same hype. But when Wall Street gets on a tear, investors start believing the world isn't round anymore.

That's probably the single most important reason Wall Street has survived and prospered all these years. People forget.

After I quit college in 1966 and went to Boardman's, I continued investing in the market, but only occasionally. I had no spare time for hanging out and reading the tape in any brokerage office. I kept up with the news, reading the *Journal* every day. But I was married now, with one child and another on the way. I had to think about providing.

Once again, I didn't have long to wait. Before the ink on my aviation certificate was dry in 1967, I landed a job flying executive aircraft for Brown & Root, a huge construction contractor based in Houston, Texas. The money was good, $2,000 a month, and nobody needed to explain what a smart move it was to be with Brown & Root. Founders George and Herman Brown had financed the political career of then-president Lyndon Johnson. Johnson was also a Texan who, as a congressman, had steered some lucrative government dam-building contracts their way.

The Brown brothers (Dan Root was a brother-in-law who put up the money) were understandably grateful. When Johnson ran for the U.S. Senate in 1948, it was Brown & Root's cash and airplanes that won him the election. The Brown boys ended up riding Johnson's coattails right into the White House, from his election as vice president in 1960, succeeding Kennedy after the assassination, and winning the presidency in his own right in 1964.

Brown & Root was wired into Washington by the time I came along, with a global government defense contracting business, heavily involved in Vietnam. Things haven't changed much. The company is still a big military contractor, and the last job Vice President Dick Cheney had before he was elected in 2000 was as CEO of Halliburton, the company that now owns Brown & Root. You might say Texans have no trouble figuring out which side of the bread has the butter on it.

I was assigned to fly out of Morgan City, Louisiana, a Gulf Coast town that was smaller than Natchitoches but much wealthier. It was a base for one of the company's other major businesses, building and servicing oil wells. About two thousand Brown & Root employees worked there.

My first assignment sent me to Houston at the controls of a six-seater twin-engine Navajo. My passengers were the head engineer and the safety engineer from Morgan City. I assumed this would be just the sort of trip I'd be making all the time, taking working executives to and from job sites and different Brown & Root offices. I was told I'd be gone a couple of days and expected I'd be sitting around the hotel waiting for these guys to finish their work.

To my surprise, when we landed in Houston a stretch limo was waiting for all of us. We were met by a group of hale and hearty Texans in the pipe business. They sold Brown & Root millions of dollars of pipe every year. Off we rode in the limo to a first-class hotel, where these boys told us to go up to our rooms and get ready; they were going to take us out for a four-star dinner.

Since I was the new kid, I was unsure what was expected of me, except for flying the plane and delivering my passengers in one piece. I figured these Texans didn't actually mean to take me out to dinner with them, but just in case, I waited in the lobby for the engineers to come down. I was bored, so I went to the gift shop for a nickel pack of chewing gum. Standing at the register, I reached into my pocket for change. All of sudden somebody grabbed my hand so quick I thought they were trying to tear my arm off. It was one of the Texans.

His brow was creased. "What're you doing? What're you doing?"

I was stunned and didn't know what the hell to think.

"I'm just gettin' some gum, is all."

"Well, you put that money away right now." He let go of my hand, whipped out a twenty-dollar bill and handed it to the clerk. "You're not paying for anything! Not so long as you're with us."

Well, it just went up from there. They took us all out. They wined and dined us at the finest restaurants. They took us to an Astros game one night, and we even ended up in a strip club. I'm sure those engineers did some work while they were down in Houston, but not two whole days worth. And all of it was on the pipe boys' tab.

After we landed back in Morgan City, I stopped by my desk to complete my paperwork. One of the clerks from bookkeeping walked in and dropped some forms in front of me.

"Fill out your expense report," she ordered.

Like an idiot, I said, "I didn't have any expenses."

Her eyes narrowed in disbelief.

"I didn't," I said, shrugging.

She picked up the expense report forms and left. A minute later the engineers who I'd flown to Houston came over. One of them dropped the blank expense forms in front of me, sat on the edge of my desk, and said, with a grin, "Now Jim, I know you must have had *some* expenses in Houston."

I was beginning to get a sense of where this was going.

"Everybody who travels for Brown & Root has expenses. *Ever'body.*" He pushed the papers toward me and winked. "I'm sure if you think real hard, you'll be able to remember what you spent. You were gone two days, right? So you must have spent, oh, at *least* $75 a day, wouldn't you say?"

That was my first experience with the way big companies get bled white. Brown & Root could stand it because it was making a ton of money. The oil business was recession-proof. But what I saw over the next two years would have made my prudent father dizzy. It taught me a lesson I've tried to remember all my investment life, sometimes successfully: good companies can be ruined from within.

This began my education in the way big corporations work. I met many executives, officers, and even directors with big oil companies like Texaco, Mobil, and Gulf, as well as folks who owned the boat companies and the drilling outfits. But nine out of ten trips I made had nothing to do with business. They were personal favors, flying Brown & Root execs, customers, and suppliers to weddings, funerals, or Las Vegas gambling junkets.

And there were a lot of them. In one year I logged fifteen hundred hours, an average of thirty hours a week. That is a lot of flying, and some weeks were killers. A senior captain for an airline only flies about twenty hours a week. I lived on that airplane, constantly taking somebody somewhere.

Most of my passengers were wealthy. In Morgan City alone there were probably more multimillionaires per capita at that time than anywhere else in the whole country. Business was booming.

I also met a lot of people who were deep into the stock market. Even though I wasn't actively investing, I was picking up a first-class education from the pros. Everyone was at least twice my age, often three times. They had lived a good portion of their lives and been enormously successful. During the course of these trips, passengers would often loosen up and talk shop, talk about business and the market. For them it was like chatting with a taxi driver.

Also, I was eager, a sponge, willing to learn anything and everything and always wanting to please. Older people appreciated that, but especially so back then, when the majority of young people were rejecting business and rebelling against society.

Some of my financial education I got on my own, painfully. On one of those Las Vegas junkets, I took along $1,500 and bellied up to a $10 blackjack table. I decided that if my losses reached $400, I would call it a night.

At 3 o'clock in the morning, I had won $27,000. But instead of getting up and going to bed, I sat there playing until 6 o'clock in the morning and lost every cent. The pit boss, who had been working the table almost the entire time, walked over as I was getting ready to leave. He raised his palms to the ceiling and said, "Jim, he giveth and he taketh away."

Brown & Root's Morgan City base sat in the middle of the oil patch, so many of my passengers knew the oil and oil service businesses inside and out. Sometimes they would say to me, "You know, you ought to take a look at this stock." I made some money on a handful of trades that way.

A few people actually went out and bought the damn stock for me without saying so! On more than one occasion, I got an envelope in the mail, stuffed with cash and a note saying that this or that guy had bought me five hundred shares of something, and it went up five points.

The first few times this happened, I told my boss what was going on and asked him what I should do.

"Take the money," he said.

"But I feel bad about it. I'm just doing my job. I don't do it expecting these tips."

"Listen, if you didn't take the money you'd insult them," he explained. "This is a gesture of appreciation. Besides, you're a little charmer. People like you. They're always telling me that. You make sure they have a good trip, and feel comfortable and secure. They're rewarding you for that. Take the money, Jimbo!"

One time I flew a man and his wife to a funeral, and when I came back to pick them up he said, "Jim, why don't you come over with me to the Petroleum Club? We can catch the game between the Green Bay Packers and the Houston Oilers."

I was flattered, of course, and when we got to the club and settled in with our drinks, he told me to root for Green Bay. So I did. Sure enough, Green Bay won, beating the point spread.

As the clock ran out, this guy turned and said to me, "Well, we won!"

"What do you mean, *we* won?"

"I bet $1,000 on the game for you, Jim. You just won $1,000!"

Such favors came to me all the time. I lived in a fantasy land. There were months during my two years of flying for Brown & Root when I made $8,000 in tips. Besides whatever charms I may have had, I have found that people are just naturally fascinated by flight. On smaller planes, the passengers are right there with you and many of them are scared, even if they won't admit it. They want to bond with the pilot. It makes them feel safe. Passengers tend to see the pilot as someone who miraculously guides them through a dangerous and nerve-rattling experience safely and pleasantly. And they tip big.

I was a good pilot, but it's one of the most overrated things imaginable. It's true that to be a great pilot takes some skills. But no mental skills. Flying is easier than driving a car, because you hardly ever have to worry about someone running into you.

Having said all that, I've had my brushes with eternity. On a trip to Houston, I flew into a thunderstorm that damn near ripped the wings off. The wind was blowing so hard that even after feathering the engines, the storm was still pushing me around at 240 miles an hour.

Another time an ice storm nearly killed me. I was flying to Alabama and, even with the heaters in the wings, ice was building up so fast I couldn't keep any altitude. We were coming up on a mountain range near Scottsboro. I had to break through the undersides of the clouds not knowing for sure where the mountains were. I managed to drop down right into a gorge between two ridges. A half mile either way and my passengers and I would have been a smoking pile of scrap metal in the woods.

The dumbest thing I ever did happened on a flight that followed a couple of days of steady work without much sleep. I took off by myself from New Orleans headed to Shreveport, put the plane on automatic pilot, and decided I would cat nap for five minutes. An hour and a half later, I woke to the sound of sputtering engines.

I was so woolly-headed it took me a long time to clear my brain, get my bearings, and understand that I was running out of fuel. I also didn't know where the hell I was. I had flown so far I was outside all my preflight navigation settings. I had overshot Shreveport and was way up past Little Rock, Arkansas. The plane had extra fuel tanks, and I managed to switch them on in time.

They near flew me to death at Brown & Root, but I made a fortune and got to see how corporations work from within, from the very top. Anytime something substantial was going on, I was there. I witnessed infighting over control and people trying to move up the pecking order. I saw millions of dollars go out the back door in the form of padded expenses and other kinds of nonsense.

For example, one of the top Brown & Root people in Morgan City had political ambitions. He was going to run for state representative. He wanted to build up some political markers with the power brokers and money people who could help him. So, he decided to offer them flying lessons, at Brown & Root's expense.

For this purpose alone, the company paid to get me my flight instructor rating. Then, Brown & Root paid me to teach this executive's cronies how to fly, in company planes. These contacts led to other opportunities for my boss to earn a debt of gratitude. When a huge explosion in a salt mine killed more than two dozen workers, my boss "donated" me and the Brown & Root plane to run some reporters and photographers over there so they could cover it. He was working all the angles.

When one of my passengers tried to lure me away to work in his company, it was a real temptation. Arthur Levy's family owned ships, any kind of ship involved in moving oil for the oil companies, from oceangoing tankers to tugboats. We got to talking about his business on a flight and ended up staying in touch. Before long, Arthur asked me to come work for him and his father. They would pay a fabulous salary and give me an expense account. He promised that in five years I'd be running a $400 million company with a pristine balance sheet and enormous cash flow.

The offer came at a time when I was starting to sour on corporate flying. It was hard work and I had nothing in common with other pilots. Those guys would fly from Dallas to New York and sit in the grubby pilots' lounge at LaGuardia Airport inhaling jet exhaust for eight hours until the CEO returned from Manhattan with a belly full of vintage wine and gourmet food. They were glorified bus drivers. It was the most boring, monotonous, stupid life you can imagine.

As much as I disliked that life, I was equally unimpressed with corporate life. Most young people might read about a Fortune 500 CEO or executive and assume he or she got there by wit and intelligence. I was meeting these people every day and learning that this was not the case, by a long shot. I looked at my wealthy, successful passengers the way I read poker players. I saw their flaws and weaknesses and began to view myself as smarter and more aggressive than they. I can do that. And I can do that better!

In my youthful arrogance I fantasized that I was smart enough to one day become a billionaire. Although I continued to think about politics, I still wanted the money first. I would never surrender my economic independence.

The Levys seemed shocked when I turned them down. I never heard from them again. They probably thought they'd discovered a diamond in the rough, the kid in the mailroom who winds up in the CEO's chair. They were going to make some money polishing me up. I also think they trusted me, which people have tended to do.

In fact, I *was* a diamond in the rough. I have bruised a few egos and done some dumb things along my way through life, but I've tried always to keep my word. I think people like Arthur Levy and his father saw that and were willing to take a chance.

But I wanted my *own* business. I didn't want to rely on anyone else's ideas or have their inhibitions get in my way. The roadrunner was coming back out in me!

In 1969, I had increased my grubstake to nearly $200,000. I quit Brown & Root and returned to Natchitoches, where I saw a chance to start my own flying service. I now knew the business from the bottom up, thanks to my father, and the top down, thanks to Brown & Root. I had gold-plated connections, and no real competition.

I bought a Cessna 150 and began teaching people how to fly. Next, I bought a twin-engine passenger plane and started a charter service. Then I convinced the administration at Northwestern State University in Natchitoches that they should offer students an aviation program. The kids would graduate with the credentials and skills to go right in and pass the test for their commercial pilot's license. I knew they'd get good jobs, which would attract even more students, and that's how the program—and my business—could grow.

The school agreed to a contract guarantee for a minimum number of hours of paid flying time each year. I took that to the local bank, where I'd put my mowing money ten years before, and borrowed the capital for the planes and other equipment, practically on a handshake.

The school and the service were big successes. In less than two years, I owned a fleet of a dozen aircraft and was taking $60,000 a year out for myself, equal to about $260,000 in the year 2000.

He didn't say much about it, but I knew my father was proud as hell and glad to have me back. We were both in the aviation business, so we had plenty to talk about. My family was growing and both my parents loved having grandchildren to spoil.

My quick success at a young age turned some heads in town, especially at the bank, where people treated me with a lot of respect. Where once a kindly teller had patted my head, I now had hundreds of thousands on deposit and more than that flowing through my accounts each year. I paid my bills promptly and ran a profitable business.

One day, as I was making a deposit, the president of the bank invited me into his office for a chat. His eagerness told me he had something on his mind, but he spent a lot of time beating around the bush. He hinted around and hinted around and finally came out with it: one of the directors had resigned and some board members thought I might make a fine replacement. A good example for young people and all that.

Now, in a small town like Natchitoches in 1970 it was a great, great honor to sit on the board of a local bank. There were a dozen or so directors of this bank, almost every last one more than 50 years old, and some of them a whole lot older. They were the wealthiest, most re-spected people in the town, so they practically ran it.

I knew what a compliment it was to be twenty-five years old and even be considered. But I couldn't honestly see enough of a benefit to offset the liability of being on the inside. It was an instinct then, but now I know it from experience. In Dallas in the 1990s I watched as some of the richest men in the city were made to fork over hundreds of millions of dollars to settle claims against them as directors of bank disasters like Republic and Interfirst. Even as a young person, I was aware of this kind of liability and risk.

Another problem: I was financially aggressive in a town of very conservative people. When you have a go-for-broke way of doing things and those around you are "t" crossers and "i" dotters, you don't blend well. I was tolerant and respectful, but, in my heart, I was too full of myself to have respect for them. I'm sure they thought I was arrogant, and they were right. I hadn't gotten my nose bloodied yet.

In my defense, though, some of those men really didn't deserve respect. They flaunted their wealth or were rude and talked down to folks. Some of the nicest people I've ever met are some of the richest people I've ever met. But I've bumped into plenty more who seem to think their wealth gives them the right to be assholes.

Anyway, when I politely declined the bank president's invitation to join the board, his jaw dropped. You'd have thought I slapped the guy in the face, he looked so dumbfounded.

"It's a great opportunity," he said in bewilderment. "Are you sure? Don't you want to take some time to think about it?"

I shook my head. "I've got other plans." They were big ones, too.

3

Big Dog

*"Was my chest ever puffed out! This was the most money
I had ever made in a single transaction.
This does the limit, I thought. My first big lick!"*

I sold my flying service near the end of 1970 for $350,000. I picked a good time to be long on cash. The stock market had come completely unglued after failing the year before to break through its 1966 high, just below the magic 1,000 mark. From there the Dow had crumbled by a third, to a low of about 650. The worst damage by far was to the once hot technology and concept stocks, even those on the respectable Big Board at the New York Stock Exchange. Prices for some companies vaporized, leaving them valued at as little as five cents on the dollar.

What the hot mutual fund managers had been saying about go-go investing turned out to be a load of crap. A Wharton Business School study in 1970 turned up the fact that an investor armed with a fistful of darts and the Big Board stock tables would have made more money than any of the genius portfolio managers.

The world really was round after all.

It was a crash not unlike the one that took the country down in 1929. In 2001 not much has changed, by the way. Anyone with a dartboard can still beat most mutual funds. And the mutual fund business is still one of the more respectable swindles on Wall Street. Arthur Levitt, former chairman of the Securities and Exchange Commission during the 1990's, had that industry nailed when he said, "I don't care if a fund's called the Rock-Solid Honestly Safe U.S. Government Guaranteed Trust Savings Fund, you can lose money in any of them."

By 1970, the country, the whole world, seemed to have come unglued. It had been a year of spiking interest rates and plunging stock prices. Racial tensions remained high following the murder of Dr. Martin Luther King, Jr. Vietnam War protests triggered college strikes and riots. National Guardsmen had killed students in Ohio, and we learned that American soldiers had executed Vietnamese civilians. There was even a bloody confrontation on Wall Street itself, involving protesters with the new environmental movement.

I was as concerned and angry as any young person at what was going on in the country. Sitting on a pile of cash, with no business to distract me, it wasn't long before I got an itch. I was playing the stock market again, and poking around in the political world. It wasn't my first time, but I focused more on my own ambitions.

Although my father had no real interest in politics, his brother did. My uncle had a good friend named Bill Dodd, who was a political animal. He had been Louisiana's lieutenant governor, superintendent of education, and state auditor. My uncle was heavily involved with Dodd and with a state senator from Natchitoches whose son was a friend of mine.

From my uncle I picked up at an early age a love of the way the political game is played: the strategy, the counter-strategy, and all the thought, plotting, and manipulation that goes into it. It's a game not unlike investing.

My first chance to actually participate came when I met a guy in college whose father was the state's public service commissioner and a candidate for governor. My buddy was Walter Fox McKeithen, but we called him Fox, and his father was John J. McKeithen.

The 1960s was an exciting time to be involved in politics, especially in Louisiana. The school desegregation issue was front and center. One of the other candidates was a member of the state's most famous and colorful political families. Congressman Gillis Long was a cousin to the former Governor and U.S. senator Huey "Kingfish" Long, a populist ("every man a king") who ran the state during the Depression like a Mafia don. He was assassinated in the statehouse in Baton Rouge in 1935. Huey's life was the subject of the book and film, *All the King's Men*, by Robert Penn Warren.

Huey's brother, Earl K., served three nonconsecutive terms as governor. Huey's son, Russell B. Long, was elected a U.S. senator in 1948, and remained in the Senate until 1987.

Fox's dad came from the same part of the state as the Longs, the piney hills and small farms of northern Louisiana. He also came from the same folksy political traditions. His plea at every campaign stop was, "Wuncha he'p me clean up the mess in Baton Rouge?" But he started out with very low name recognition, about 6 percent. He faced a second strong candidate in DeLesseps Morrison, mayor of New Orleans.

Fox and I set off on the campaign trail that spring and summer back in 1964, stumping for his dad.

All these men I've mentioned were Democrats. No Republican in Louisiana could have gotten himself elected to clean an outhouse. All the electoral fuss had to do with the primaries, which were held in the fall about a month before the general election. Just about any Democrat who won his primary race went on to win the general election.

Working for a long shot, and friends with his son, I quickly found myself among the inner circle of operatives. I wasn't nailing up posters or ringing doorbells. Because of my skills with money, I was put in charge of rounding up cash from what you might charitably call the less-accountable sources of funding. My real skill turned out to be making sure the cash got passed on to those in the black communities across the state who could be counted on to use it to get out the vote.

Why the black communities? Well, I had connections. Because my grandfather was well-respected in the black community around Natchitoches, he knew the preachers and other leaders, and so I knew them, too. Because of my uncle's involvement in politics, I had an idea of how things worked.

From my connections in Natchitoches, I was introduced to black leaders in other parts of the state. Fox McKeithen and his father understood that to beat the mayor of New Orleans, with so many voters and an entrenched inner city political machine, we would have to make it happen everywhere else around the state. So I evolved into John McKeithen's campaign liaison with the black community.

During the 1964 election, and through several election cycles into the 1970s, it became my role to gather up cash from various sources, stuff it in a suitcase, and drive around the state to parishes where I was known or had an introduction. In each community I doled that cash out to people who would make sure it was spent to get black folks out to vote. Money often went to people no more political than a guy with access to a school bus who needed gas money or an expensive repair. In exchange he would spend the day driving voters to the polls, showing them how to vote, and making sure they got back home.

These were not, in total, small sums. I remember starting out on my rounds one election with about $800,000 in cash.

Against very long odds, John McKeithen won that first election as governor. He won a second term in 1968.

To anyone who's never been involved in rough-and-tumble politics, this may all seem a little shady or underhanded. Certainly, none of it would survive much scrutiny these days. But it's no different than the walking-around money that shows up in any election, whether it's Brooklyn, New York, Miami, Florida, or Bossier City, Louisiana. And whatever we were doing, the other guys were doing it, too. Not to do it was to quit before we got started.

And without trying to justify it too much, in that place and time, without that cash, many African Americans might not have had a chance to vote. This was Louisiana, after all. Only a couple years before, in 1962, a bus company in New Orleans advertised free one-way tickets to any black person who agreed to move to the North. School desegregation and forced busing were hot issues tearing many communities apart. Some candidates had a compelling interest in keeping blacks from voting.

To his credit, McKeithen made a real effort as governor to clean up the mess in Baton Rouge. He promoted reform with a state code of ethics, instituted financial controls on government spending, and created a biracial commission on human rights to find ways to reduce tension.

So, by 1971, at the ripening age of twenty-five, I had begun to build my own political base through my contacts in all these election races, primarily with the money people and the black community. I was especially well-known in the black community, a fact that made me proud. I had markers out here, there, everywhere.

Like investing, politics is a speculative game, and I began to speculate actively about running for governor of Louisiana and maybe for United States senator after that. I enjoyed the process, I loved the campaigns, and I yearned for a chance to govern and help people.

But I still had my financial agenda in front of me.

With Tommy Fussell, a former LSU football star I'd met through my political work, I started buying apartment complexes all over the state. It took us several years but we ended up with about eight hundred apartments. We had between $8 million and $10 million of real estate tied up and heavily mortgaged. We set up our own management company to run the apartments and paid ourselves good salaries. Interest rates were coming down and things were looking up.

Around this time I took a short side trip into show business. Rock and roll has always been a passion of mine and, through a contact I'd made, I decided to try my hand at promoting and managing. Terry Bassett, who owned a big rock and roll management company called Concerts West, agreed to give me some pointers. He took me with him to meet some theater and stadium managers.

Before I knew it, I had a deal to take Blood, Sweat and Tears on a multi-city tour. The group had a best-selling album, a tremendous vocalist in David Clayton-Thomas, and a fistful of hit songs like "You've Made Me So Very Happy," "And When I Die," and "Spinning Wheel."

It took me only a couple of weeks to realize I didn't know what I was doing. The group, as good as it was, couldn't fill seats. I had to pay them a guaranteed minimum. I lost money along with twenty pounds and a lot of sleep. When I regained my sanity, I hurried back to making money doing what I knew best.

As a result of dabbling in real estate, brokers began pitching me land deals. One day, one of these guys brought me a couple of pieces of distressed property. They lay along two rail spurs in different parts of the state, but both were ideal locations for warehouses, and cheap. One was in my home town and I bought it for $80,000. I wanted to make a nice profit, so, full of optimism, I marked the Natchitoches property to the full market value, which was $300,000, and listed it. In no time at all, we found a buyer: Anheuser-Busch's Shreveport office was looking for a distribution center. Without a squawk, they paid my price.

Was my chest ever puffed out! This was the most money I had ever made in a single transaction. This does the limit, I thought. My first big lick, $220,000 on one deal. I was a big dog on the block.

When it came time for closing, I showed up at the title office to discover it was just me and a clerk. This seemed odd after all the paperwork generated from buying and financing the apartment complexes. I expected more fuss over a transaction of this size.

"They already signed all the paperwork, Mr. Salim," the clerk explained, "and the escrow account is already funded." Meaning the deal was done before I arrived.

This took some of the wind out of my sails.

"All you have to do is sign the paperwork and you get your check," she said, smiling. She was an older woman and I could tell she had seen it all before.

As I started signing, she asked, "Would you prefer that the money be wired to your account, or do you want the check? Whichever is fine."

I thought wiring would cheat me out of the thrill and the bragging rights of holding that check, walking into my bank, and depositing all that money. *That* would create a buzz. So I told her she could just give me the check.

When I finished signing, she looked at me with a sly little grin and said, "I think you might find this interesting, Jim. How they paid for this."

"What do you mean, how they paid for this?"

She took the check and held it in front of my face. In big bold letters it said, "Anheuser-Busch, Shreveport, Petty Cash Account."

That was one of the most humbling moments of my investing career. It brought me right back down to earth. *Petty cash*, like they'd just bought a carton of toilet paper!

But my feet didn't stay on the earth long. For the first time, I had broken out of small-time investing. I had a half a million dollars in cash in the bank. I was worth several million dollars on paper because of my stake in the apartment complexes. I became more aggressive with my stock trading and did well in 1972 as the market continued its jagged climb out of the crash pit of 1969.

At the very beginning of 1973, the Dow blasted through the 1,000 mark. Life looked rosy. I was on my way to billionaire land.

And then I got a phone call in the middle of the night.

My partner was on the other end. There had been a fire in one of our complexes. Half the place had been destroyed. I knew we had the insurance to rebuild, but I quickly discovered why people buy business interruption insurance. How often do you lose half your assets in a night?

From that moment we were bleeding $40,000 a month. It was going to take a year to get those apartments rebuilt.

Then, a few months later, I got another phone call. There had been a flood in Baton Rouge. The city sewer system reversed itself and sewage covered the floors of about four hundred apartments we owned.

Lesson number two: this flood, unlike every other source of flooding covered by our insurance policy, was an act of God, and therefore uncovered. We had to spend several hundred thousand dollars ripping out soiled carpeting, cleaning and sterilizing, replacing furniture, clothing, and so on. It was a nightmare for all.

And that's when the manure really hit the fan.

Interest rates kicked up, which pushed our mortgage payments higher and sucked the value out of the properties. The apartment complexes, which I thought had at least a couple of million dollars in equity, sank into the red.

I told myself that at least I could trade in the market and save myself. Thank God I didn't have all my eggs in one basket! Right then I ran into a buzzsaw. The market broke sharply in 1973 after briefly touching a new high at around 1,050. The crash that followed was even worse than 1969. But I refused to believe it, all the way down.

I made all the classic mistakes that unskilled investors make. I fought the tape. I listened to stockbrokers, a 95 percent guaranteed way to lose money. I bought stocks on tips. I had to learn the hard way a fact of the markets that Lefèvre wrote about in his 1923 book. It's as true today as it ever was: "acting on 'inside tips' will break a man more quickly than famine, pestilence, crop failure, political readjustments or what may be called normal accidents."

I held stocks I should have sold, another classic mistake. Taking a loss was admitting a mistake. I held, deluding myself that they would come back.

I was trading big volume, as many as ten thousand shares at a crack. When Avon Products dropped to $30 a share after trading as high as $80, I was certain it couldn't go any lower. I bought a few thousand shares and watched it promptly sink to $20.

I might have been wrong, but I was not in doubt. The market rallied near the end of 1973, flirting again with 1,000. This proved to me that everyone else had been wrong and I was about to be proven right. The bottom was behind us. In a matter of months, the market would break out and sprint to new highs.

But that rally turned out to be another paper tiger. The market resumed its slide. The Dow tried to rally itself one more time, in the spring of 1974. But as it became clear that Richard Nixon was going to be kicked out of the White House for the Watergate scandal, prices fell off a cliff. The stock market hates nothing more than uncertainty.

Mortgage rates climbed above 10 percent for the first time. My stock portfolio drained away. My net worth fell below $100,000 for the first time since my Brown & Root days six years before. In less than twenty-four months, I had swung from paper millionaire several times over, with a half million in cold cash, to being more than $1,000,000 in debt and stone-cold broke. It was a wipeout. My ass had truly been handed to me. I was twenty-nine years old.

The next several years were the most difficult I ever hope to see. As the saying goes, things were so bad even the liars were complaining. I didn't always handle myself well. It's not that I went off the deep end and started hanging out in bars picking fist fights. I was just depressed and stayed that way. To put a face on it, at one point I even had my electricity shut off.

As bad as my smashup was, it would take an event even more shattering—one that cost a man's life—to jolt me into a new direction. But now I'm getting ahead of the story.

Crestfallen as I was, I had the common sense to know that I was never going to be able to pay those debts. Worse, much of it was owed to people who had known me a long time, even from childhood. They knew my family. They had trusted me and I considered them friends.

When my negative net worth bottomed out at around $1.5 million, some of my creditors tried to make me feel better. Ed Pierson, who owned one of the local banks that financed the apartments, tried to convince me it was all right to roll over and play dead.

"Jim," he said, "you need to go and just wipe this out and take bankruptcy. Start over. It's the only way. You aren't the first, and we'll all survive. Ain't nobody gonna go hungry."

But I was stubborn and proud. The humiliation of admitting that it had happened to me, from a family of rock-solid citizens like my father and grandfather, was too much.

This roadrunner had run out of road.

4

Disco Fever

*"Jim, I've been a banker for more than 30 years.
I have never seen anyone do anything like this."*

Somehow, some way, I would get back on my feet. But first, I had to set the record straight. I paid a personal visit to all my creditors after the assets had been liquidated and told them the situation. In their offices, in a coffee shop, on their porches, wherever I found them, I told each one exactly the same thing: "You can go ahead and sue me. I won't contest it, and you can get your judgments. But I don't want to take bankruptcy. If you force me into it, I will do what I must.

"But if you won't sue me, I promise that when I get back on my feet I will repay you 100 cents on the dollar."

Few of those people believed me. The hole was deep. Anyone would have said I was done for good and forever. But I meant what I said.

I had no pile of cash to sit on anymore, and I was downtrodden. But the itch remained. While I sorted out the financial wreckage so I could survive and care for my family, I plunged into politics.

In late 1975 the jockeying for position for the next presidential campaign had begun. When Georgia Governor Jimmy Carter announced his bid for the Democratic nomination, his campaign people tried to recruit me to help with his local efforts. They had heard about my influence in the minority community and thought I could help deliver the state. I passed because Carter seemed like a weak candidate. I didn't want to hitch my wagon to a falling star.

One of the people you had to stroke to succeed in Louisiana politics was Ben Johnson, a wealthy black businessman who lived in Natchitoches. Ben owned funeral parlors and casket companies. He was tremendously successful. If you were black and you died anywhere around Natchitoches, chances were good that Ben Johnson owned the companies that sold your casket, put on the funeral, and carried you to your reward.

Ben had been in every church in the parish more times than anyone could count. He knew who had money and who didn't. He had known the late Martin Luther King, Jr., and spoken with Lyndon Johnson when he was president. Ben was wired.

Before my financial meltdown, I had helped Ben with a real estate project he'd been trying to get off the ground. He owned a vacant, run-down building in the black neighborhood of Natchitoches that he wanted to develop as a shopping center. But in trying to raise the money to fix the place up and attract tenants, he kept running into walls.

He was frustrated and depressed about it. I suggested he open something like a clothing store that didn't require a lot of expensive plumbing and fancy wiring. That would attract another business, and so on. I offered to put up the seed money, and over time the project worked out for him.

The other leader in the black community who became my friend was a high school teacher and athletic coach named Robert Jackson. Unlike Ben, Robert was my age. He was not connected in high places. He was a grassroots political operative skilled in door-to-door combat.

While Ben lived in a big, expensive house, Robert lived in a tiny fixer-upper. While Ben had power in high places, Robert had power at the grassroots level, power that was in ways greater than Ben's.

But they had one thing in common with each other and every other black home I ever entered down there: they all had the same three pictures on the living room walls: John Kennedy, his brother Bobbie, and Dr. King.

Although Ben and I were close, it was Robert and a few of his friends whose company I enjoyed both politically and personally. We spent a lot of time together, talking local gossip and politics. Heading into the 1976 election season, we talked about how to get rid of our crusty old congressman, a fifteen-termer named Otto Passman who liked to say to campaign audiences, "I'm old enough to know, but young enough to go!"

Otto did not represent any black person in his district. He was a rock-ribbed conservative, as far to the right as the most rabid Republican today. He would have been a Republican anywhere but Louisiana.

Robert and I occasionally met for breakfast or lunch at a café in town. These outings always turned heads. In a restaurant full of white people, Robert often was the only black face. It wasn't long before I overheard that I was a "nigger lover."

I didn't care, and neither did Robert. We were youngbloods, unimpressed by worn-out racist crap from a bunch of rednecks and kluckers, which is what we called members of the Ku Klux Klan and their miserable ilk.

With all my political activity and visibility in the black communities, I wasn't all that surprised when I started getting anonymous phone calls. I was working for the challenger in a close race for a state senate seat. We actively courted the black voters and were making real inroads.

No one had an answering machine in those days, or caller ID. I got to hear the messages live: "Y'all step back. Don't get involved, now. Just quit messin' with them niggers, here?" Real elevated stuff.

I ignored the warnings, even when they included death threats. I thought I was bulletproof, that nobody would try anything stupid. I knew these kinds of cowards. They loved to bark but they had no teeth.

One night a short time later, I woke up in the small hours with a jolt. My heart pounded. I felt a sudden premonition of trouble, an instinct that something wasn't right. I got out of bed and went to the living room. The light coming through the curtains shifted strangely. When I looked out I saw why. On my lawn flickered an eight-foot-tall flaming cross.

I don't think I've ever been as angry or sworn as fiercely. I have described my short fuse before. This time it was shorter. I called some friends and they came right over to help me put the damn thing out, drag it down, and cart the debris away. When the sun came up, I didn't want there to be a shred of evidence for my young children to see and remember.

The incident scared the hell out of a lot of people: my neighbors, my wife, and my family. As for me, I had one goal that consumed all my waking thoughts. I was going to find out who was responsible. The local sheriff was well-known as a klucker, so I knew better than to expect any official help. But I was determined that the guilty parties were going to pay. No police, no publicity, no courts. Just pay.

It took me a few weeks but I finally learned that there were three local guys in on it, guys I knew of and knew to be involved with the Klan. They owned a general store outside of town. One day, with two friends for backup, I showed up at their store. With the aid of a baseball bat I resolved the situation to my satisfaction, if not theirs. They lived to tell, but they paid.

I'm not bragging about my behavior. But it was another turning point, or at least the start of one.

My political ambitions moved to the back burner. Three years remained before the next go-round for governor anyway.

Meanwhile, fate stepped in and presented me with an opportunity to finally work myself back from my financial disaster.

I had been to a nightclub in Dallas in 1977. The movie *Saturday Night Fever* opened that year, and the country went wild for disco clubs. This place was the only one in Dallas that played the music and had the dance floor. It was packed.

A friend I went with happened to know the owner of a little company that made lighted dance floors and installed sound systems. Owen was a character and must have smoked a bag of pot a day. He and I got to talking at the bar. I mentioned my investment background and the fact that I was looking for another opportunity. I said it looked to me like there was good money to be made in his business.

Owen said right off, "How about if I make you a proposition, right here and now?"

"Shoot!" I said.

He explained that he hated running a business. He hated tracking down notoriously slippery bar owners to collect his money, hated keeping books, hated all the worry and the bother. It used up all his time when he really just wanted to have some fun. It was a good business, he said. He laid out the numbers, and I thought, if half of what this guy says is true, it's a gold mine.

Finally, he got to the point. "All I want is a thousand dollars a week and a new van to drive and all my expenses," he said. "In return, I'll deed the whole company over to you."

I figured he must be crazy or drunk. But it turned out he just didn't want the baggage in his life. He didn't care about the money. Within a week we drew up the paperwork and I was the proud owner of Sight and Sound, Inc., Dallas-based entertainment contractor.

Owen hadn't lied. It *was* a gold mine. We could build one of those big lighted dance floors, like the one in the film only larger, and install the sound system, all for about $40,000. Bar owners were willing to pay up to $150,000. These were state-of-the-art systems. I hadn't seen *Saturday Night Fever* before I cut my deal with Owen. But when I did, I couldn't believe how ugly and small the dance floor was compared with the Cadillac we were selling.

We managed to crank out two a month, making good money. But then I came up with a wrinkle I thought would earn even more money and make it easier to get more customers. I'd install and lease the system for 50 percent of the door receipts. I figured any time a businessman can defer paying for equipment, he'll do it and happily pay the interest. The bar owners loved it.

I signed long-term contracts with each club. We did every kind of venue: white adult, black adult, gay, teen, seniors, you name it. The installation crews worked like dogs, and we got the business to the point where it was paying me about $100,000 a week. It doesn't take too many weeks like that to get back on your feet.

But it was a fad and started to fade within a year. Receipts fell off. Where I had been getting $20,000 a month from a club, it dropped to $16,000, and then to $12,000.

I had to figure a way to either boost the revenue or get my money out and move on. I didn't want to hang around squeezing every last dollar out of the thing. It was bad enough having to keep head counters at each club to make sure I wasn't being cheated out of door receipts.

When I floated the idea to one of the owners that he buy the system outright, he jumped on it. I looked at all the clubs and realized that if I could pull it off, I'd have a hell of an exit. I called each club and found that almost every one was willing to make a deal. In one fell swoop, in one week, I sold them all—lock, stock, and mirror ball. When it was over, I had netted $2.5 million.

I was back!

I was so back that I could return to Natchitoches and repay all the people who had stuck by me and not sued.

The few who did sue never saw a penny. I made sure of it. I took the steps necessary to legally protect myself so that no matter how many judgments they got, they couldn't touch me.

But to all the others I paid one hundred cents on the dollar, just as I'd promised.

I made these repayments dramatic, not forewarning my creditors about why I wanted to meet them. That way I could quietly hand over their check and have the satisfaction of watching their reactions. These were moments I had dreamed about for four years. This was a time for my redemption.

Every one of them was absolutely stunned. Some people even cried. The fellow that owned the local bank, Ed Pierson, couldn't quit shaking his head in disbelief. He said, "Jim, I've been a banker for more than thirty years. I have never seen anyone do anything like this."

A great weight lifted off my soul.

During my stay in Dallas running Sight & Sound, I found I enjoyed the activity and variety of a real city. I had begun to meet other players in the stock market and in real estate. I was trading stocks again, profitably now. I had started trading cotton and other commodities. I had learned some hard lessons, and I was starting to put them to good use. Financially, I was hitting my stride.

I still had a yearning to govern, but it wasn't as strong as it had been. I was beginning to look outward, beyond the borders of Natchitoches and Louisiana. With more confidence and capital, opportunities seemed to be popping up everywhere.

If I had stayed and run in the 1980 gubernatorial race, I would have put my all into it. But I never got the chance. I threw it away, lost it forever. In the spring of 1979 I carelessly and stupidly agreed to do a favor for an old friend. It blew up in my face. Things went totally off the track. A man got killed. I became estranged from my family and community, and my political future turned to dust.

The story will be told here, but not just yet. For the moment, it is enough to know that I moved to Dallas and haven't set foot in Natchitoches since.

5

Go With What You Know

"Nobody calls a cotton farmer and asks him how his crop is doing or what he thinks about anything. They were flattered. It was the first time it had ever happened to them."

There were several lessons I'd learned about trading by the time I left Natchitoches. The most important was to do your homework, and go with what you know.

If you walk into your local computer store on a weeknight and the place is packed, and it's not the Christmas season, you can hazard a guess that business is booming. It might be time to buy computer stocks. If your mate comes home and complains that their favorite clothing store was empty of customers and full of tired styles, you might have a profitable clue about the future direction of that company's share price.

Well, I knew plenty about cotton, thanks to my father, and quite a bit about oil, thanks to Brown & Root. During the next several years I aimed to make a fortune in both.

My introduction to cotton trading began early in the 1970s, when I had a brokerage account with an E. F. Hutton office in Shreveport. I'd wanted to get some experience speculating in commodities. There was no commodities broker in that office, so they transferred me to their Houston branch, where I was matched up with Jack Reichenthal.

Jack was a broker who mostly ran managed accounts. His customers handed him their money and walked away. He made all the decisions. You have to be a damn good broker to do that. Very few are, but Jack was one of them. His customers got the courtesy of an occasional phone call, and their monthly statement, of course. But that was it.

I knew nothing about trading commodities when I started with Jack, so I opened a managed account. I didn't even know the basics, like the size of a grain contract. I learned that one contract of soybeans, corn, oats, or wheat represents five thousand bushels.

Much like stock options, commodities contracts come with future expiration dates. If you buy a contract of November soybeans in June, at the end of November you can choose to close it out and take your profit or loss. If you don't want to close it out because you think prices are going to rise you can roll the contract forward into the next expiration month, kind of like a certificate of deposit.

You could even take delivery of the soybeans, which meant you'd get a phone call one day to please come down to the rail yard and pick up your boxcar load of beans. Be sure to take plenty of bags.

Brokers will tell you that such a thing could never happen, but I actually met a guy who had the experience. He owned a wholesale beauty products house that supplied grocery and convenience stores. He was speculating in wheat futures and not paying attention. One day he went to open a railroad car shipment he was expecting and found 5,000 bushels of wheat.

The only people who actually want to take delivery are generally shippers, exporters, and processors. Although the vast majority of commodities trades—grains, oil, precious metals, copper, cattle, wool— never result in anyone actually touching a product, contracts are still called "cars," a remnant from the time when the boxcar was a unit of measurement.

Futures contracts, as they are properly known, have been around for two thousand years, ever since merchants in the Middle East had to figure out a way to finance goods being carried all the way to India. It wasn't economical for merchants to wait as long as it took for a camel to cross the deserts and return for payment. So a pay-now, deliver-later system evolved. It became institutionalized during the eighteenth century to finance the growing international trade in rice and cotton, and really caught on in this country after the Civil War.

Today, the trading of futures contracts is an end in itself. Anything can be traded, including currencies and even a commodity as intangible as a stock index.

Between 1960 and the mid-1980s, the number of commodities futures contracts traded in the United States grew from 4 million to 160 million. That represented about $10 trillion worth of stuff, from bacon (called pork bellies) to platinum. But very little of that total represented actual stuff. Contracts are traded over and over again by hundreds of thousands of people who know how to make money in futures but don't know beans about commodities. For most traders, holding a futures contract for five days is a long-term investment.

My first trade was an experiment. I decided I was prepared to lose $25,000, so that's what I gave Jack. If he lost it all, we both understood that he shouldn't bother coming back for more.

The way the first trade went down was a textbook example of why commodities are so seductive. Until the early 1970s, soybeans had traded for decades between $2 and $3.50 a bushel. About the time I took my first plunge, commodities prices were spiking. President Nixon had opened up trade with China in 1973, giving American farmers a gargantuan new market. Soybeans, a staple food product in China, leaped in one year from $3.50 to $9. It was historic.

Daily limits are set by the commodities exchanges on the amount by which futures contract prices can rise or fall. These limits came into being as a result of trading disasters caused by aggressive or unscrupulous speculators. Huge price swings wiped out whole brokerage houses and bankrupted farmers. So, controls were adopted to dampen the gyrations and make it difficult for swindlers to manipulate prices.

For example, the maximum daily move one way or the other in soybean contracts is 20 cents. If, for the sake of argument, the U.S. Department of Agriculture comes out with a crop forecast of a bumper yield, bean prices will fall, and so will the price of futures contracts. If they fall the limit of 20 cents, no bean futures will trade that day for any less. If beans are weak the next day, they can fall another 20 cents, but no more. By the same token, the price can rise no more than 20 cents a day. So, the maximum price swing on any given day is 40 cents.

When a commodity price hits the limit and there is so much buying or selling that it stays there, traders say the price is "locked limit down" or "locked limit up." It just means the price is stuck, and when it's stuck, it can be difficult and even impossible to get out of a losing trade. There are commodities like silver, for example, which have traded during an extended market crisis locked limit up or down for weeks on end.

Just as in any other market, commodities speculators can go long or short. If you think prices are high, you sell short and profit if the price falls. If you think they are low, you buy and profit if the price rises.

One last aspect of commodities futures and you'll be an expert: the leverage is unbelievable. Margin requirements are nothing compared to stocks. For a few thousand dollars in cash, a trader can control huge amounts of value. The mathematical relationship varies from commodity to commodity, but the order of magnitude is always huge. That's known as leverage.

But margin is a tricky business. If you're wrong and prices go strongly against you, your brokerage firm may require you to put up more cash to meet your margin requirement. In a wildly volatile market, this is how aggressive speculators get murdered. That's why I set a limit on my potential losses at $25,000. If it was gone, then I would have been gone as well, and would probably never have considered trading commodities again, which would have been a damn shame.

For the first trade in my account, Jack bought five contracts of beans at $4.80 a bushel. That was 25,000 bushels of soybeans. The margin requirement was $2,000 per contract. I had $10,000 on the line, controlling $120,000 worth of beans.

Beans were trading locked limit down when Jack bought the contracts. A crop forecast was due out within the hour. The market expected a forecast of a bumper crop, which meant supply would swamp demand and prices would fall.

Jack was betting that the market was wrong. He thought the crop report would be bullish. In other words, he guessed that the report would project a smaller harvest than most people were expecting. If demand stayed the same but supply shrank, prices would rise.

Sure enough, the crop report came out showing a sharp drop in the expected harvest. Bean prices shot up the limit to almost $5.20 a bushel. I had captured nearly the whole swing, almost 40 cents. And it all happened in about fifteen minutes. Jack called me with the good news: I had a profit after his commission of $9,800 on the very first trade, almost a 100 percent return!

I had the same reaction any logical person would: I better pay attention here. This was serious stuff. I had never had that happen in any stocks I ever owned, a double in a day. And, frankly, it never happened to me again. I'd had a stroke of beginner's luck, thanks to Jack. I was hooked.

Jack was a real talker. During one of our many conversations I told him about my background, that my dad was a crop duster, I had been around cotton my whole life, knew cotton farmers all over Louisiana, and knew some other crop dusters.

"If I can't figure out how to make money trading cotton, nobody can," I told him.

So, Jack gave me a quick education in cotton futures contracts. Cotton traded 50,000 pounds per contract. A one cent move in the price of cotton was equal to $500. You had to buy a helluva lot of cotton to make real money.

But cotton, like beans, had gone crazy. From a low of 25 cents a pound in 1972, cotton had soared to 87 cents in less than a year. It continued to trade wildly, making huge swings from season to season. Volatility is a trader's best friend. Big swings produce big profits when the leverage is high. And, of course, when you're right.

I opened my own commodities account, unmanaged, and started plunging in cotton, trying to figure out how to use my knowledge to get an edge. At the time cotton traded from a low of about 55 cents a pound to a high of about 95 cents. Margin requirements varied, depending on the market. Generally, it was about $1,000 to $1,250 per contract.

Given a stable domestic economy and world conditions, there are two basic things that move prices: weather and the size of the harvest. You can easily learn how many acres are planted each season in cotton, where the acreage is, and the amount of cotton left over from the previous season. The big commodities trading firms provide you with that kind of information all the time, along with their own crop forecasts.

For two years, before I moved to Dallas, I spent all my energy and emotion trying to understand the cotton market. The Agriculture Department periodically publishes figures giving the number of acres being planted and how much is stored in warehouses. The rest is weather. Commodities traders active in any kind of crop fixate on weather forecasts and weather conditions in the principal growing regions.

My father had more than fifty customers who were cotton farmers. I had gotten to know some of these people well. But to do what I wanted, I needed to know a lot more of them.

So, I set about creating a network of farmers and crop dusters who could tell me as the season progressed what was actually happening in the fields. Just like stockbrokers, doctors, and software designers, farmers have conventions. They invite speakers to talk about mold and worms and soil chemistry and seed. The pesticide companies and equipment makers set up booths and pitch their wares.

I wangled an invitation to one of these conventions in New Orleans. I spent a few days handing out a pile of business cards, talking to farmers and dusters, buying them drinks, and shooting the bull.

"So, are you a cotton farmer or a duster?" they'd ask.

"I'm neither one," I'd say. "I'm going to start trading cotton, and I was hoping you wouldn't mind if I called you from time to time to see how your crop is doing?"

I collected a lot of names and telephone numbers. Cotton is big in the Mississippi Delta, so most of the farmers were from Louisiana and Mississippi. But I also met quite a few from West Texas. There are about fourteen states in which cotton is grown but it's most intensely cultivated in about ten. Cotton needs a five-month growing season, hot weather, with regular rain or reliable irrigation. Most American cotton is grown in the Deep South, although it has spread to irrigated regions of states such as Arizona.

The average farmer in Louisiana can grow cotton, soybeans, wheat, or corn. His land will grow any of them. He's going to plant the crop that makes him the most money. Let's say that last year there was a bumper wheat crop but a terrible corn crop and a disaster in the cotton market. Suppose cotton has spiked to 90 cents a pound.

Those farmers take the land that was in wheat last year and plant cotton. This changes from year to year, and a smart trader pays attention, because it boils down to how many acres have been planted and whether the yield per acre will be one bale, a bale and a half, or two bales. All of this, the reality and the perception, determines the price of cotton at any given moment.

Climate conditions affect whether the farmers can get into the fields to harvest. If the fields are too wet, they can't get the tractors in, they can't pick the cotton, the yield is going to drop, and the price will rise. To be a good cotton trader, I understood clearly that I had to monitor the cycle from start to finish, until the cotton was at the gin.

Once I started trading cotton, I began building my network. I called the farmers whose names I had collected at the convention and I'd ask them for the names of other farmers. Then, I'd get these guys on the phone and they'd say, "Yep, Billy John said y'all was gonna call. What can I do for you today?"

It took me a year before I had 175 farmers around the country who I could telephone and chat with any time I wanted. I made a point to call these farmers year-round so they didn't think I was just using them to make money. I'd call around Christmas and then again in March. I'd call them at planting time to find out if they were getting the seed in all right. From then on it became a monitoring process, calling every two to three weeks. Not a month went by that I didn't speak to every single one of them.

And they loved it. Nobody pays attention to farmers. Nobody calls a cotton farmer and asks him how his crop is doing or what he thinks about anything. It doesn't matter whether he's the biggest cotton farmer in the world. They were flattered. It was the first time it had ever happened to them.

Also, I think they looked on me kindly, a polite young guy just trying to get ahead. The men I was speaking with were often fifty or sixty years old. Their fathers had raised cotton before them. It pleased them that someone gave a damn. They were more than willing, more than happy, to tell me what they thought.

Having said that, I had to take everything they told me with a grain of salt. Farmers love to cry. They like to tell you that things are bad and going to get worse. You have to pay attention to what they're saying, because they like to poor mouth more than anybody I've ever met.

One of my father's biggest customers was a multimillionaire farmer named J. D. Henry. Mr. Henry was very active in Louisiana politics. A famous story about him goes something like this: J. D. was in Washington paying a visit to Senator Russell Long. The good senator greeted him and asked, "How's everything going, Mr. Henry?"

Mr. Henry shook his head sadly and frowned. "Terrible! Just terrible!"

Senator Long, thinking something awful must have happened, asked him what was the problem.

"The cotton crop was terrible," he said. "All we made was 10,000 bales." And he went on down the same trail about his wheat and pecans. It was a long sad story, and Senator Long was starting to get really concerned. After all, J.D. was a big contributor to his campaigns.

Finally, he said, "My God, Mr. Henry, are you going to make it? Why, it sounds like everything is so bad that you may go under!"

J.D. Henry shook his head and said, "No, don't worry, Senator. We made $17 million. It's just we thought we were going to make twice as much."

There was one farmer I met who would always say, "Oh, we got this damn weather front coming through. This son-of-a-bitch weather front. And if it stalls out and goes stationary, we're done for!" There wasn't a single silver lining he couldn't find a cloud attached to.

By the time I got rocking and rolling with my network, I had become an unofficial economist for the cotton industry. Somebody in Mississippi would want to know what was going on in north Louisiana or Arkansas. They would ask me whether I thought they ought to hedge their crops in the futures market. If cotton was 62 cents a pound, they wanted to know if they should short the market in case the price broke before they could get their cotton out of the field. I gave them my advice and discovered I was good at trading cotton.

I started slow and easy. I bought just a few contracts at a time. I wanted to get a feel for the market. I wanted to see how well my trades were being executed by the brokerage firms, if I was getting the best price or being swindled. It was a walk-before-you-run deal.

That's how I've approached most trading opportunities. You've got to test the market first, see how it takes the trades, see how your order tickets are being filled.

Like all investment vehicles, commodities sometimes are overbought and oversold. Periodically, commodities prices will fall so low that the risk of going long is almost nonexistent, or so high that the potential reward in shorting them can be enormous. This happens every few years, depending on the cycle of the particular commodity. If you look at a cotton chart, you will find only five times during the past twenty years when cotton got close to its bottom of 50 cents and four times when it reached a high of 85 cents. Those were low-risk entry points, and still are today.

When I started trading cotton, I didn't have to look at a chart to know what cotton had been selling for the preceding twenty years. I'd heard my father talk about cotton since I was in diapers. If cotton was selling at 50 cents, it was a cinch. It didn't matter how much cotton was planted that year, or how much was left over from the year before, clobbering the farmers with warehouse fees. At 50 cents a pound I knew that the worst case was that all the cotton farmers in the world would be wiped out and wouldn't plant a crop next year, which would send cotton prices soaring.

That's where physical commodities differ from stocks. There are so many stocks that nobody, except the last fool who bought it, cares if one of them is gone tomorrow. Most agricultural commodities are well defined, especially cotton, which depends especially on expertise, locale and weather. If every idiot with a backyard could scatter some seed on the ground and raise cotton, it would be an investment like stocks, where any moron can start a company, or, worse, run a penny stock scam issuing unlimited shares in bogus companies. You can't produce fake cotton, and not just anybody can raise the real thing.

I also knew from my father's business what price farmers had to get for their cotton in order to make it worth planting. I knew how much they needed to make their bank loans, pay their debts, and feed their families. At 40 cents, no bank was going to lend against a cotton crop. The fields will sit idle, or they'll plant something that looks like it's going to pay better, such as beans. This would send prices higher.

I knew that even if the cotton surplus got too big, because of several years of bumper crops, the government would step in and pay farmers not to plant.

So, I would put on a futures position in an agricultural commodity when the price was right and during the growing season between about

May and October. Wheat, corn, soybeans, cotton, oats, coffee—none of them care if Sun Microsystems is going to make its profit numbers this quarter or the Federal Reserve Board is going to lower interest rates.

Even demand isn't much of an influence. People are not suddenly going to start eating twice as much bread or wearing twice as many cotton shirts. If the economy is good or bad, the difference in most agricultural commodities is barely measurable. Weather, acreage planted, and carryover matter. Is it going to be a big crop or a thin crop? Is there carryover from the year before or a shortage in supply?

Where traders make or lose a lot of money is during the growing season, and weather is the fuel that drives prices. Every cloud has potential to nourish, drown, dehydrate, facilitate infestation, and promote disease. Every weather front is studied, every forecast sweated over. Commodities traders keep one eye on CNBC and both eyes on the Weather Channel. A busy hurricane season in the Gulf of Mexico is good for wide price swings. A drought doesn't have as quick an effect in the short run, but, over time, it can send prices soaring.

That's where the volatility is, that's where the potential is for high percentage gains—and losses: during the growing season.

Thanks to my network of farmers, I did well in cotton, with a limited amount of funds. The first time it paid off, the government crop report said 16 million acres had been planted. But my farmers were telling me something different. Cotton was low. They were hedging. "Well, Jimmy, I cut back from 800 acres this year to 600 acres, and planted 200 acres in beans. Looks like beans are strong and the bank's giving me hell about cotton prices being so poor."

I did some math and decided the crop report was high by a good 10 percent. It was time to take the real plunge.

My initial trades were modest, because I hadn't developed faith in my convictions. I was still young and worried that I might be missing something. But as time went on, and I saw confirmation of my estimates, just before the next government crop report I bought everything I could with my limited margin money. I was not in a position to buy one thousand or two thousand contracts like bigger players might. I put on twenty-five cars of cotton, controlling 1.25 million pounds. The margin requirement was $1,250 a contract, so I was on the hook for $31,250, controlling about $700,000 worth of cotton.

Sure enough, the new report came out and the government lowered the forecast dramatically. Over the following week, cotton jumped a nickel a pound, almost a 10 percent move. The $700,000 worth of cotton jumped to about $765,000. I closed the position, and the difference was my profit. It was a lot of phone calls, but I had proved I could do it, and that gave me more confidence.

One year, 1977, I made a lot of money in cotton for the oddest reason. The cotton crop looked like it was going to come in a bumper. That was the latest government forecast. Well into the growing season, the traders had marked the price down accordingly. I had sold all my long positions, and I was out of the market. All that was left was the harvest, and the weather had no remarkable patterns that suggested some last minute disaster. It had been a good year for me, but not great.

For the hell of it, I made one last round of telephone calls to the farmers, to thank them. From the very first call, I heard something that really caught my attention. "I can't get the damn cotton out of the field. It's too wet."

I spent two days on the phone and talked to sixty farmers all across the cotton belt. And each call got my pulse beating a little faster. By the end of the second day I was certain that I had stumbled on a golden opportunity.

Farmers harvest cotton in October or November. First, they hire a crop duster to come in and spray defoliant. The leaves fall off in a day or two, which allows the mechanical harvesters to come in and take the cotton up clean. The harvest is timed to be finished before the big wet season in the South begins in December or January. Heavy rains make the fields impossible to navigate by the harvesting machines and will knock a percentage of the bolls off onto the ground into the mud, ruining them.

This year planting started late because of a rainy spring. That pushed the harvest into November. The winter wet season hadn't started yet, but every three or four days a front had blown through, with some rain. Ordinarily, that's nothing to notice. Warm days and direct sunlight will dry out a field in a day or two.

But the temperatures had been colder than normal, it had been cloudy, and the sun couldn't reach the fields. A good rain in the fall or winter like that won't evaporate for a week. There isn't the heat to draw it out of the ground.

The fields stayed muddy. The farmers couldn't get their harvesters in there to pick. The longer those cotton bolls sat there all opened up and ready to go, the more of them would end up on the ground.

And I was the only one who seemed to know about it.

The government was reporting a record crop. The price of cotton had come down and down. I thought, what's going to happen when everybody wakes up a month or two from now and realizes that it's not going to be a record crop because they lost it in the ground to the rain?

I immediately called a new commodities broker I was using, Roy Price at Merrill Lynch in Lake Charles, Louisiana. I told him the story because he knew a famous commodities analyst named Conrad Leslie. I thought Leslie would like to know what I'd learned. I was damn proud of myself, and there was no doubt I had it dead to rights.

Leslie was to cotton trading back then what Abby Joseph Cohen, the widely-followed Goldman Sachs analyst, has been recently to the stock market. Leslie had similar power to move prices. He had a private forecasting service, and big clients and brokerage firms paid him well for his analysis of the cotton market.

"Roy, you need to tell Conrad!" I insisted. "I'm talking to all these farmers and they can't get the damn cotton out of the fields!" I was all wound up.

"Are you sure?" Roy sounded deeply skeptical.

"I just talked to sixty guys in the last three days, and I'm hearing the same thing all over the place." I was jumping out of my skin, knowing how sure I had it.

I bought the crap out of cotton, everything I could get my hands on. The price sat there going nowhere for about two weeks. Roy didn't call me back and I didn't hear a peep from Conrad Leslie, even though Roy said he'd give him my number.

I would learn as my career continued to evolve that it's a good sign when people start blowing me off. That's when I know I'm on to something.

But I was still learning at this point, and I worried when Roy didn't follow up. I thought about lightening up my position a little. I wasn't getting hurt. Cotton was trading narrowly around 52 cents a pound, moving a penny up or down. If prices didn't pop, at worst I could roll my position over into next year's contract.

Finally, one night after dinner, Roy Price telephoned from his office.

"Jim, I got Conrad Leslie on the other line."

That put me on instant high alert.

"He wants to know," Roy continued, "who told you all that nonsense about cotton?"

"Farmers," I said.

"What farmers? Since when do you know any farmers?" I could tell he was leading me somewhere.

"My *network* of farmers." I chuckled.

"Well, who the heck am I talking to? What do you mean your network of farmers?"

"I have my own network," I said.

"What you got over there, Jimmie, a feed and grain place or somethin'?"

"No, Roy," I laughed. "I told you, my dad is a crop duster. All his friends are crop dusters around the country. I know these farmers and they introduced me to other farmers and I went to this convention and . . . ."

"Well, you little bastard," Roy busted in. "You are dead right. Those fields are gonna come in somethin' terrible."

A month later the final government harvest report came out and cotton jumped ten cents in a week. I had outworked everybody. No analyst had been sitting on the telephone talking to one hundred cotton farmers every two weeks for six months. They wouldn't have lowered themselves to do something like that.

The experience confirmed what I'd known instinctively all along: I should do my own research. I learned to distrust analysts and economists and any other experts who I knew for a fact would not bother to get their hands dirty digging up the truth.

As good as I had become at trading cotton futures, I began to get bored. You could make a decent living but you couldn't get rich. The trading season lasted only five months or so, and my research required hours of telephone time, having nearly the same conversation hundreds of times over.

All that effort and, in a typical season, the spread between the high and low in cotton was at most 20 cents. Unless there was a big weather event or some other disaster, 20 cents was the most I'd get if I were nimble enough to catch the trade at the low and run it to the high, or vice versa with a short position. But, more likely, the spread would end up at only 10 or 12 cents.

Cotton had taught me to trust my instincts, do my homework, go with what I knew. Now I wanted to put all that to work in a speculative market where the leverage and volatility would produce spectacular returns.

I got my chance, and it damn near ruined me.

6

A Rambunctious Time

*"I get my pleasure out of matching my brains against the brains of
other traders—men whom I have never seen
and never talked to—"–Reminiscences of a Stock Operator*

Cotton futures stoked my appetite for leverage and risk. Clearly, real
money, many millions, could be made by a trader who did his homework and plunged into the right market on the right side of the trade at
the right time.

Roy Price told me a story about one of his customers that intrigued
the hell out of me. This guy had turned $10,000 into a million by trad-
ing soybean futures. He never put up a single penny more than his initial investment. Bean prices rose, and he was able to use his paper profits to buy more beans, and the price kept rising, and so on.

I've already described the dangers of holding a position on margin
when the trade starts to show a loss. You have to cough up more cash
collateral to keep from being sold out by the brokerage firm and forced
to take the loss. When a position shows a gain, on the other hand, your
unrealized paper profits add cash collateral to your account. You can
use that collateral to buy yourself a new car or take a cruise around the
world. You can also use those paper profits to buy more futures contracts, or anything else your broker will let you buy on margin. It's the
closest thing you can get to a free ride, and it's called leveraging up. You
pyramid your profits. It works like a charm in a bull market.

Roy's customer had leveraged his $10,000 all the way up to $1,000,000, but one day bean prices broke sharply. His customer's position disintegrated, totally, overnight. Out the window went $990,000, right along with his original cash investment.

That's the kind of leverage that makes trading futures so seductive, and death defying. Trading cotton futures made Jesse Livermore a wealthy man in the 1920s. Trading sugar futures would later break him. I can't remember a single person who stayed in the commodities market who didn't end up self-destructing.

My unscientific observation is that 1 percent of the people who trade commodities make money, and they are the professionals: traders who work on the floor of the commodities exchanges, the brokerage firms who make the commissions, and the local traders. A local is an individual who stands in the pit and trades only for his own account, as opposed to a floor broker who executes trades for the firm that employs him. A local puts his own capital at risk. To be a local, you have to be a real gambler at heart.

On any given day when I used to visit the pits from time to time, I might see Tommy Baldwin, a famous local at the Chicago Board of Trade, make or lose a million dollars in five minutes. I've watched plenty of locals blow up and lose all their money.

The people I knew who traded commodities were looking for a big hit. I saw people in all types of professions try it—medical doctors, university professors, entrepreneurs, businessmen. Every one was wiped out, even some of the brokers who made their commissions whether their customers were winning or not.

"Jim, I went and blew myself up," one of them told me recently. "Lost everything and worse than that, I can't hardly remember any of it."

The biggest commodities crack-up I ever rubbed shoulders with came early in 1980, when the Hunt brothers imploded while trying to corner silver. It's a long story and books have been written about it. Gold had already run up to its all-time peak of $875 an ounce in early 1979. Nelson Bunker Hunt and his brother, William Herbert Hunt, sons of a Texas oil billionaire, inherited their dad's money but not his brains. They had gotten into trouble for violating the limit price on soybeans in

1976. They paid a big fine and were banned from the market for two years.

In 1979 they went in with some rich Arabs and proceeded to buy up half the world's available supply of silver, more than 200 million ounces. That's called a corner, when a speculator or a group of speculators tries to control so much of a commodity they can dictate the price.

Within two months, around the end of 1979, the Hunts ran the price of silver from $10 an ounce up to a high of $50. They technically controlled a trillion dollars worth of silver. Only problem was, the high price of silver brought out all of Aunt Mary's candelabras and Uncle Bert's silver dollars. For that, and a host of other reasons, the bubble burst on January 18, 1980. Within a few months, the price fell back almost to where it had been. The Hunts were wiped out.

The strain on the banking system to cover such an enormous bankruptcy was so severe that the Federal Reserve Bank had to come in and bail out the Hunts. I lived down the street from Nelson Bunker Hunt at the time. One day, on my way into my office, I drove past his mansion in Highland Park, the wealthiest neighborhood in Dallas, and saw a media circus milling around outside. A fleet of limousines lined the curb, and just as I passed, I caught Federal Reserve Board Chairman Paul Volcker stepping out of one of them to face a mob of reporters and cameras.

The economy survived, but the Hunts took personal bankruptcy, lost billions, and disappeared off the face of the earth. At the time, bonds were yielding 15 percent. The Hunts could have taken a billion dollars, bought Treasury bills, and sat there clipping coupons. Instead, they managed to lose it all. Both brothers were convicted in 1988 of conspiracy to manipulate the silver market.

It was a rambunctious time to say the least.

Trading commodities is the hare to the stock market's tortoise, but I still kept up on stocks while I traded cotton. Keeping to my basic scheme of investing in what I knew, and doing my homework, I snooped around in the oil stocks and found the timing was perfect. The stock market had been fighting its way back over the years from the 1972/1974 crash. There'd only been one year of correction out of eight, but many market indices by 1980 were still just flirting with their old highs. However, the Standard & Poor's 500 index had actually broken through, offering some hope that the bear was going into hibernation. Smart traders and people who studied charts began saying it could be just a matter of time before the market would finally break loose, and the bull would come charging out.

In the meantime, there were a host of problems. The world appeared to be falling apart at a good clip. Islamic terrorism dominated the headlines after the hostage-taking by Iranians of American embassy workers in Teheran, Iran.

The Arab oil states were draining the treasuries of the developed world by pushing oil prices straight up for two years. Light crude, which never broke $3 a barrel before 1973 and traded just below $15 in 1978, was less than a dollar shy of $40 early in 1981. Interest rates poked above 20 percent, making it almost impossible for anyone to raise the capital to build or buy anything. Japan was busily decimating our heavy industries by doing everything cheaper and better, nearly bankrupting Detroit.

But a speculator like myself welcomes volatility and extreme conditions. Nothing looks more tempting to a trader than a market that is beaten down to the point where people are practically giving away good companies with solid assets. Or, as in the case of oil at that time, a hot commodity attracts a crowd of cash.

Living in Dallas, I had been drawn into a social scene that kept me running into people from every corner of the oil business. *Dallas*, the television series, had been on the air a year or so. Living in the real town at times felt like inhabiting the fantasy world of the character J. R. Ewing and his richly dysfunctional family. High oil prices had everyone exploring and drilling. That set off a building boom. Texans had hit an economic gusher, and the money poured in faster than they could stuff it in their pockets. While the rest of the country was struggling off its knees, it was Mardi Gras in the oil patch.

At one of these parties, I met a guy in the oil service business who worked for one of the big outfits like Schlumberger or Halliburton. He was talking shop with a group of other oilmen, so I listened. "You should check out Houston Oil and Minerals," he was saying. "The stock's cheap if this gas well we're drilling down Sabine Pass comes in like it looks."

Houston Oil was an independent that didn't drill its own wells, unlike some of the giants such as Texaco or Royal Dutch Shell. This man's company was drilling for them. I knew those drillers were on the front line of oil exploration, and if they thought a well was going to come in strong, that would be big news. They check the seismic readings day by day as they go farther down into the ground. At some point they get a good idea if they're going to have a producing well or a dry hole. Once in a while, maybe once out of a hundred wells, they find a barn burner. With oil at $30 a barrel and up, when these smaller companies made a nice strike in oil or gas, the stock prices jumped.

Houston Oil was unknown to me, so I set about doing my homework. I dug up everything I could about the company and made a point of talking to management, although you almost never get anything useful out of management. But I learned where they were drilling, where they had put most of their money to work. I rented a plane one day and flew over to Beaumont, Texas, on the border with Louisiana, picked up a car, and drove down and across the Sabine Pass, a water inlet that makes the border between the two states. Down a dirt lane off the coast road in Cameron Parish, I found the rig this guy had been talking about.

I dressed that morning in jeans and old boots. I introduced myself to the crew foreman, told him I had an interest in buying the stock of Houston Oil, and asked him how things were going. He was happy to talk with me about prospects for the well. In this case, the news was good. In fact, it was so good he told me a planeload of company executives were flying in the next day to have a look for themselves.

You can bet I didn't wait to reach Dallas to phone my broker. I bought 50,000 shares at about $8. The well came in as predicted, and I rode that stock all the way up to $40. It turned out to be one of my biggest scores to date.

But as the pit boss told me in Las Vegas all those years before, "He giveth and He taketh away." There was an expensive lesson waiting for me just around the bend.

At the time I was riding Houston Oil up the chart, I was reading *Reminiscences of a Stock Operator* for the first time. If I had any doubts about my abilities, reading that book cleared them up. Livermore, presented as a fictional character named Larry Livingston, had traded cotton and other commodities and what he had to say described my own experience and philosophy to a T.

I studied that book closely and decided to put some of his wisdom to work. One of the things Livermore/Livingston said was that if a trade had reached his price objective and he decided to sell, he had no choice but to go on and sell more stock short. This made sense to me. If you believed your trade had reached its high price, then it only followed that the price was now going to fall. Why not catch the profit on the reverse trip?

I had made that mistake with Eastern Airlines years earlier in Monroe, leaving a lot of money behind by not shorting the stock after I sold it. I wouldn't make that mistake again.

After I closed out my position, Houston Oil moved higher. I shorted 30,000 shares at $46. When it sprinted on up to $52, I put out another 30,000 shares.

This has always been the way I work my trades. Instead of sitting there moaning about how my first trade was $4 a share under water, I put away another block of stock and lowered my cost. Now I was short 60,000 shares at $49. If you believe you're right, no sense beating around the bush.

Now, no stock or commodity or any freely traded financial instrument goes straight up day after day, at least not under normal circumstances. Some days are up, some down. Doesn't matter how strong a bull market might be. Just as the old saw goes, the market climbs a wall of worry. As greed battles fear, prices move in sawtooth fashion.

Being a short-term investor, if a stock is going against me but I'm convinced I'm right, I'll average my cost as close as I can to the market price. That way, if the stock should have a pop or hit an air pocket, I'm more likely to have a chance to get rid of it at a smaller loss or even a profit.

But when Houston Oil reached $59, I couldn't take the pain any longer. I had been wrong. I bought in my shorts at a loss of $600,000, giving back to the market more than a third of my profit. It hurt like hell, especially when I added in the $650,000 I would have made had I kept my itchy finger off the trigger in the first place. The experience taught me a lesson that has saved me tens of millions in my trading life. I've never been good at picking tops, so I don't try. It's much easier for me to pick a bottom, where the potential for loss is a damn sight lower.

There are times in the markets when reality counts for nothing. Consider the dot-com craze of the late 1990s. It wiped out so many traders who believed there was no reason for stocks like AOL and Ebay and Pets.com to trade where they were, even when they were just starting to really take off. Logic screamed to short those stocks, just as logic screamed to Bob Wilson decades earlier to short Resorts International. But the prices of those companies kept right on inflating. Thanks to Houston Oil, I never bought or shorted a single share of a dot-com.

After I grew bored trading cotton, I began trading gold and silver futures. The volatility and the leverage suited me better. A contract of gold controlled a hundred ounces. If gold rose or fell $5, that was a move of $500 per contract. Ten dollars translated into $1,000 per contract.

Silver traded in 5,000-ounce cars. A one cent move in silver produced a $50 move per contract. In two weeks gold or silver would move more than cotton moved in a whole season. In gold, I had the chance to make a lot of money fast, and I did. Gold flailed around a lot during that turbulent period of high inflation. You can't make that kind of money in silver and gold today. As I said, it was a rambunctious time and would get even more so for me.

By 1981, I was swinging a big line in the markets. The Houston Oil trade, before the short position trimmed me back, had been my biggest success so far. The whole trade netted me about $1 million in profit. In one trade!

My plunging became very active, a full-time job with an office and a secretary. I had trading accounts at several brokerage firms, including Kidder Peabody, E. F. Hutton, and Merrill Lynch. I was always on the lookout for brokers and firms I could trust. I had discovered that brokers and the trading desks at their firms had a dozen ways to swindle me out of some of my money.

I'll get into the whole world of stockbrokers and trading desks a little later. For now, I'll tell you that I've fired about sixty brokers and traders in my career, including the head stock trader for Merrill Lynch.

Along the way, I found a few great brokers and traders and have stayed with them.

One of these was Jim Donegan, a broker in Kidder Peabody's Los Angeles office. At the time, I was trading an unusual and little known speculative vehicle called Rule 144 stock. The average investor would never run across something like this, but there was money to be made if you liked risk and you thought you could make some money by doing your homework.

Just about anyone who worked for a dot-com in the late 1990s knows about Rule 144 stock, as do nearly all officers and directors of public companies. These people often received some of their compensation in company stock. But they usually have to wait a year from the date they receive it before they can actually register and sell it in the open market, according to Securities and Exchange Commission rule number 144. Stock issued with restrictions on trading is known as Rule 144 stock, or restricted shares that must be registered with the SEC before they can be sold.

Well, a lot can happen in a year's time, both to a company's stock price and to the person who receives restricted stock. Ask any dot-com employee who got stock priced during the market bubble, only to watch it deflate over a year to a 95 percent loss.

Like anything of value, the boys at Kidder Peabody had figured out a way to trade Rule 144 stock off the market, and I was making money that way. If a vice president of a solid, profitable, ongoing public company needed to raise some cash to buy a house or cover a debt and couldn't wait a year, he could sell his restricted stock at a discount, often steep, from the market price. If a trader did his research and picked a good company, he could make a nice profit when the 144 stock was finally free to trade.

I met Donegan through some other brokers who were big in trading 144 stock. Donegan was a big player himself, a commodities broker.

Donegan was one of the earliest brokers to understand and deal in what were then called financial commodities, but are now known as derivatives. He was one of the first to trade S&P 500 index futures when they became available in 1984, and he was on the cutting edge selling portfolio insurance before the 1987 crash.

Up until the brokerage industry cooked up these financial futures or derivatives, a commodities futures contract covered a real commodity, a carload of rice or potatoes or coffee, a set quantity of gold or oil. A futures contract meant there was a pile of something out there somewhere that somebody someday was going to actually get their hands on.

By 1981, some very smart people had figured out a way to trade futures contracts on financial commodities like U.S. Treasury bonds. Donegan had been a silver trader before he was wiped out in the Hunts' silver crash. He sat helplessly by while he and his customers were cleaned out as the price of silver locked limit down for thirty-two days in a row. As a result, you couldn't sell an ounce of the damn stuff for anything.

Donegan and I got along from the start because, like me, he was a roadrunner. He loved leverage. And like me, he had made a lot of money and knew what it was like to lose it. We spoke the same language, but with different accents. He was an urban cowboy, raised in a working-class suburb of Philadelphia. Charming but direct, generous but competitive, he, like I, spent most of his time thinking outside the box.

Soon after we met, Donegan started badgering me to take a plunge in this new thing called bond futures. He didn't have to try all that hard. I figured this much right off: bonds don't give a rat's ass about the weather, so I didn't have to talk to 175 good old boys a dozen times a year to figure out whether to buy or sell. And I would never find myself in a position of wanting to buy or trying to sell enough bond futures that the market couldn't take it in the blink of an eye.

I like to trade big liquid markets. I don't want to be limited to what I can buy for fear of not being able to get out of a position without knocking down the price. Many commodities markets are highly illiquid compared to bond futures. Look what lack of liquidity in silver did to the Hunts!

As for my homework, I knew a lot about the economy by now. I'd been reading the *Wall Street Journal* nonstop for almost thirty years. I'd been learning the markets and the economy from the bottom up under seven presidents, counting Ronald Reagan, who'd just been elected. I knew all the players, events, and factors that lift interest rates up and push them down.

I'm not talking about big economic theories, the kind that look at whether inflation is coming back and what effect that might have on the stock market and tax revenue, and how interest rates will be affected. That's the kind of research an investor does to justify a large long-term trade. That's the level of complexity of the research I had to do to trade cotton profitably.

Forget about all that. I had just stepped into the big leagues.

Five days is as long as most traders will hold a bond futures contract. Most speculators like myself trade for half a point or a quarter of point or even for a single tick or two. Futures contracts trade in increments of 1/32s, called a tick. In other words, the next price above $97^{31/32}$ is 98. Those amounts are just as small as they sound. But they get multiplied by millions, which turns them into serious profits and losses.

Commodities traders sometimes describe or think of themselves as investors, but they're only investing for thirty minutes at a time, continuously. Commodities traders are thoroughbreds, Donegan and I agreed one day. When he took me to New York for my first visit to the floor of the New York Stock Exchange, he said, "Let's go see what the turtles are up to."

Bond futures quickly became my favorite commodity.

I had found the ultimate trading vehicle. I understood it plain as pudding. Trading was completely liquid. The leverage was huge. There were frequent violent market moves. You could make or lose half your capital in a day.

A Treasury bond futures contract has a face value of $100,000, equal to ten government bonds each with a face value, called par, of $10,000. Price quotes for bonds are expressed as a percentage of par value. The Treasury bond was at about 80 when I first began to try my hand at trading them. At that time the coupon interest rate was 8 percent. That means that if the price of the bond was exactly $10,000 or par, the interest the U.S. Treasury would pay the holder came to eight percent a year.

I don't intend to give a detailed lesson here on how bonds trade. But, put as simply as possible, if interest rates are generally rising, the price of the bond will fall. The opposite is also true: if interest rates are falling, the price of the bond will rise. This is because the dollar amount of the coupon payment stays the same.

If a bond pays 8 percent interest at par (100), and interest rates go up, money will naturally seek higher yielding investments. Traders will therefore pay less for the bond, which mathematically raises the bond yield, which keeps it competitive with other interest-bearing investments.

If interest rates are falling, the bond that pays 8 percent at 100 becomes more attractive, and the price rises to generate a yield that is closer to other investments.

So, if you think interest rates are going to fall, you buy bond futures. If you think they are going to rise, you short bond futures. It's simple, on paper anyway.

When I first started trading bond futures, the price was about 70, and the bonds were yielding around 11 percent.

I had been trading bonds for about two years when several events came together to send me off on a bond futures trading frenzy.

The year was 1984. President Reagan was running for reelection, and interest rates, after plunging in 1982, had spiked again. The stock market had started its long bull run two years earlier, in August of 1982, but had lately hit an air pocket.

The Treasury bond was trading at below 70, yielding about 12 percent, unthinkable in 2001 when the bond was yielding less than 5.5 percent. But in 1984 inflation appeared to be out of control and the economy was staggering along at best. The Chairman of the Federal Reserve was still Paul Volcker, the cigar-chomping giant who had stepped in to bail out the Hunts.

I looked at the situation and decided that, even though the recession was brutal and the pundits were giving Reagan low odds to win a second term, I could see there was a fierce determination by both Reagan and Volcker to cram interest rates back down. Volcker was going to kill inflation at all costs, even if it meant a severe recession that bordered on or even tipped over into a full-blown depression. Even if it meant costing Volcker his job and Reagan the election.

What happened to stock prices made no difference. Only the direction of interest rates mattered. We weren't, I was sure, going to become a banana republic. We weren't going to tolerate 15 percent inflation forever. And if I was right, when inflation was brought under control, interest rates would drop like a rock. Bond prices would soar, and bond futures contracts would fly to the moon.

Everybody on the face of the earth seemed to be shouting the opposite. Gold was going to $2,000 an ounce. Crude oil was going to $50 a barrel. The world was coming to an end, and we were about to go through a decade of hyperinflation. The experts, the analysts and economists, were banging their desks to get their customers to buy precious metals, real estate, art, and anything else that might benefit from inflation.

I listened to all this and I thought, wait a minute. We're the superpower of the world. This is not going to stand. The president and Volcker are going to do whatever it takes, even if it means throwing 50 million people out of work. I knew for a fact that interest rates were going to fall.

When I looked at the bond chart, the price had plunged off a cliff since the start of the year. It was just a free fall. There was no base being built, just a few blips up and down, one or two bounces off of 64. So I thought that was a good entry point. That looked like the place where the bond would make its last stand against the bears and then come out fighting.

Although I lacked professional knowledge at that point, I knew I was right. I knew it was an incredible opportunity and I had to act. This was going to be my biggest score yet, a piece of ripe fruit just hanging there overlooked, waiting for me to pick it. Everyone else saw worms. I saw juice.

The first trade I put on 100 contracts, which controlled $10 million worth of bonds, a large sum of money for a one-man band like myself. I wanted to create a core position of 300 bond contracts, which would have controlled $30 million in bonds.

The margin requirement per contract was $2,500. My first trade required me to put up $250,000 in cash. Just like clockwork, bonds started to sink. It happens even to hard-core traders.

But I was a hard-core trader, I knew I was right, so I began to load the boat. I bought another 200 contracts at 63. The price sank, and I doubled up. And it sank and I bought, and it sank some more and I bought some more.

Now, I was carefully reducing my cost, using my tried and true strategy. But I also was starting to get daily margin calls as I sank deeper and deeper. At one point I bought a huge position of puts, which are low-cost options that would increase in value if the bonds really went down the toilet. I was getting nervous because I had passed the $1 million mark in red ink.

Before I knew it, the bond position had completely taken over my life. At one point I was trading about 1,000 contracts a day. That's $100 million worth of bond futures! My commission cost me $15 a round turn, meaning a matched buy and sell. So, I was shoveling out $15,000 a day just trading the things, $75,000 a week, a minimum of $300,000 a month.

Next, I had to hire a clerk to fill out the Commodities Futures Trading Commission disclosure forms required for large trades. The clerk came in at 10:30 in the morning when the mail arrived and sat there until 2:30 in the afternoon filling out forms, five days a week. I was trading gold, bonds, and stock-index futures. But the 800-pound gorilla was the bond futures action. Each month I traded tens of thousands of contracts.

If this insanity had lasted for a month or two I might have weathered it, kept my focus, and rode out the storm. But it went on and on. A day turned into a week, a week turned into a month, a month turned into nearly a year. And on top of the commodities, I also was actively trading stocks.

When you trade commodities aggressively and in such large amounts, you don't talk to regular brokers anymore. You deal with institutional brokers on stocks and directly with the floor on commodities. I had hotline phone connections, always open, to the trading floors at Merrill Lynch, Kidder Peabody, and GNP, a Chicago-based commodities firm where I sent a lot of business. I only had to pick up the phone and my contact was there. I had similar phone connections in my home.

Gold trades twenty-four hours a day somewhere in the world. So, if there was a major move during the night in gold, the traders had instructions to wake me up. I had detected a regular trading pattern that I began to exploit. If gold closed at $400 in New York, it seemed to rise during the night by $5 or $10 an ounce. By morning it would have settled back to $400 at the opening in New York.

The Europeans must have been more bullish on gold than Americans. So, I would buy big on the New York close and give orders to the trading desk in New York to sell at night as the price drifted higher around the world. I must have pulled that trade two dozen times, making hundreds of thousands of dollars.

After awhile, the pattern went away, as patterns always do. No doubt other people had spotted it and word got out not to chase gold in Hong Kong and London.

During this period I threw a Christmas party in my home in Dallas and invited a group of people I knew in the commodities business. One of these was Gary Monieson, co-founder with his brother, Brian, of GNP Commodities.

During the party, Gary commented on the incredible volume of bond contracts I had traded that year. I'd paid his firm a huge amount in commissions. I was a big customer for a lone wolf. I wondered, how big?

"What's the most bond contracts any one person ever traded in a single day?" I asked him. A bizarre idea began to form in my head.

"I don't know for sure," Gary said, "but Tommy Baldwin is the biggest individual trader in the bond pit. I'm sure he's traded several thousand contracts in a single day."

"Well, here's my New Year's resolution, Gary. Next year I'm going to set a record as an individual for trading the most bond futures in a single day."

Gary laughed. I'm sure he thought it was just the liquor talking.

But the idea took root. A few weeks later, I called Gary in Chicago and asked him to meet me at O'Hare Airport in a couple of days.

"That's great, Jim. Always glad to see you. What's the occasion?"

"I'm coming to set a record in the bond pit, just like I promised."

Gary and the person who handled all my business at GNP, an amazing trader named Bunny Donagan, thought I'd lost my mind. I assured them no matter how bad it got, I wouldn't blame anyone but myself.

The morning after I arrived in town I showed up bright and early at the Chicago Board of Trade to make my mark. This is the same trading pit seen on television whenever the financial news programs report changes in Federal Reserve Board interest rate policy. But you can't feel on television the size of the place. It's on the scale of Madison Square Garden. But instead of the Knicks or Rangers and their loyal fans, its filled with thousands of traders, brokers, and support staff shouting and milling about like a pack of hungry jackals. The New York Stock Exchange is a funeral chapel by comparison. It's crass versus class.

You also don't get a sense of the atmosphere from television. It's hard to convey what a place like that does to the heart of a speculator like myself. Imagine dropping an 18-year-old boy into a whorehouse and you have a clue what a thrill it was to be there.

On the opening bell I gave my orders to the GNP floor traders. Because I wasn't officially a trader myself, I couldn't enter the pit. For the first part of the day, I was just a guest of GNP, standing off to the side by the telephone banks. Nobody else took much notice of me.

But as time passed and the number of contracts I traded grew, the traders in the pit became interested in what I was doing. I was buying and selling at a furious pace, making and losing only pennies per contract.

At some point the floor traders figured it out. One of the GNP traders must have let it slip that this idiot customer had gotten a wild hair to set a one-day record. The most amazing thing happened: everyone tried to help me!

If I found myself with a big position that slipped into losing territory, they'd all jump in and buy or sell extra contracts to push the price a few ticks my way so I could get out even or at a profit. That was one of the most exciting, unforgettable days of my life.

When it was over, I had traded almost half a billion dollars worth of bond contracts, 4 percent of the total worldwide volume. All by myself. That was a record. I had paid commissions to GNP of $80,000, and my profit was less than $40,000. I would have been just as happy with a loss. I never tried again. It was enough to have done it once.

Months after this, as my core bond position began to sink and I found myself struggling to stay afloat, the craziness began to take its toll. I couldn't sleep for worrying. I was millions in the red, on the verge of being wiped out.

It all came to a head for me one Sunday night. I was wide awake so I decided to go to the office and make myself useful. I sat at my desk trying to figure out how the hell I was going to dig my sorry ass out of this mess. By 9 o'clock that Monday morning I had smoked two packs of cigarettes and swilled two pots of bad coffee, thinking, questioning my sanity, wondering if I could actually be wrong.

Should I fold my tent and take a terrible loss? But I couldn't be wrong! I knew I had it right if I could just hold on. I debated with myself, talking out loud, until I finally settled on a plan. I would not bail out. But how would I stay in? The market was volatile. At least there were big price movements I might be able to work to my advantage. The only way I could see to save myself was to trade my way out, stick with my gut instincts, keep my core position on, but somehow start making $100,000 a day in trading profits to cover my expenses. Otherwise I was toast.

That morning I began. The next time I slept was at 6 o'clock Thursday evening.

First I put on 1,500 put options that cost me $2 million. That was my insurance policy against the end of the world sending bond prices in the crapper. The put options were only good for a short time period, and they would expire worthless unless the bond price had fallen. I had to make $110,000 a day just to cover my put protection. For four days I traded nonstop, twenty-four hours a day, in gold, bonds, stocks, anything, and losing track of reality.

I was staring at financial ruin on one hand and wanting to believe in the power of my convictions on the other. Somehow I managed to stay alive long enough until the bonds finally began to rally, and then they rallied sharply. The price shot up, wiped out all my losses, and before I knew it I was $1.5 million in the black. I had worn myself out, gone through hell, but finally gotten my head above water.

I was so exhausted it didn't even cross my mind that now that I was ahead, I could have bought $1.5 million worth of puts as insurance and let my position ride. If I had been dead wrong, I would have made money either way. Instead I cashed out and disappeared on vacation for two weeks.

The final tally: I had traded tens of thousands of contracts, representing trillions in value. In one year alone I paid $4 million in brokerage commissions, more than my net profit. I had become such a big trader, my brokers charged me a lower commission rate than they charged Fidelity Investments, the giant mutual fund company.

And then, wouldn't you know it, the bonds soared all the way back to par. It was almost a straight line up. At the peak, I had left $60 million on the table!

You don't know how bad that feels until it happens to you. It takes a long time to get over, too.

7

New York Minute

"What's the bottom line?"

When I first moved to Fort Worth in 1966 to study for my commercial aviation certificate, I remember feeling like a bug trying to cross the track during the Indy 500. Driving through Dallas with a U-Haul trailer trundling along behind, my first time on a huge multilane highway in my first big city scared the hell out of me.

By the early 1980s, Dallas was my home in every respect. But, once again, events and curiosity had me looking beyond the borders of my world. For a guy who lived and breathed the markets, the place that held the most opportunity and fascination was New York.

But before I would lay eyes on the Empire State Building and the trading floor of the New York Stock Exchange, the mountain came to me.

Among the brokers I did business with in Dallas was one of the few I've used in my career who was worth his weight in gold. Gerry Guillemaud handled my account for Merrill Lynch. He was what they call in the business a big book broker, handling heavy hitters, active individual traders like myself. Gerry had been an engineer with Texas Instruments before he got the Wall Street bug.

He was the stereotypical high-energy broker, like the character of Bud Fox in Oliver Stone's 1987 film *Wall Street.* You could put Gerry's face in the dictionary next to the word "persistence." He badgered the hell out of me day and night until I agreed to open an account with him.

Before long, I had become such a big trader, generating a rich and steady flow of commissions, that Gerry and the branch office manager arranged for me to directly call Merrill's trading desk in New York and talk to the trader who worked side by side with Merrill's head of all stock trading, a legend named Hugh Quigley. After awhile, I'd sometimes be patched through to Quigley himself.

One day, around the time that the commissions I was paying Merrill passed the $1 million-a-year mark, I got a call from Gerry's boss, the branch manager Mike Crosley.

"Jim, the new CEO of Merrill Lynch, Bill Schreyer, is going to be in town next week," Mike said, a note of excitement in his voice. "His daughter goes to college down here, and he's coming in to visit her and do a little business. How'd you like to have dinner with him?"

I've never been impressed much by titles or position, but Bill Schreyer ran the biggest brokerage operation in the world. I assumed his agenda was a public relations gesture, meeting some of the big accounts coming out of Dallas. But I was glad all the same to have the chance to meet the guy who started his career as a lowly retail broker, and now ran the whole shop.

Schreyer turned out to be charismatic and easygoing, a very comfortable person to pass time with. During dinner we naturally talked about the stock market, and he expressed his appreciation for my business. He told me that if I ever needed anything or had a problem to feel free to call him directly. I'm sure he thought I'd never have a reason.

Schreyer struck me that night as a straight shooter. He talked about the management style of Donald Regan, his predecessor as CEO who recently had become President Reagan's Treasury secretary. Schreyer was the new guy and he was establishing his own style for managing that enormous company.

"A real nuts and bolts guy," Schreyer said of Regan. "A taskmaster." Schreyer gave the impression he wanted to soften that some. We talked about the philosophy of the firm and about what the future held for the markets and the brokerage industry.

Then he said something I've remembered vividly time and again, a prediction that sounded preposterous but proved visionary. He said daily share volume on the Big Board, which was then about 200 million on the busiest days, would soon pass a billion. That was a bold call, one that was hard to imagine coming true. If he'd predicted that volume would double in the next fifteen or so years I wouldn't have raised my eyebrows. But a fivefold increase seemed impossible. History, of course, proved him right.

As we parted that night in Dallas, Schreyer repeated his invitation: "Next time you're in New York, come by and visit. I can show you our new Over-the-Counter [Nasdaq] trading operation. Hugh Quigley can give you the grand tour of the floor. You'll meet the people in New York who really run the firm."

It wasn't long, just a few months, before I took him up on the offer. My "next time" in New York was also my first. Gerry Guillemaud, my Merrill Lynch Dallas broker, chaperoned me to the financial capital of the universe. New York lived up to its best reputation and then some, from the instant I first spotted the jagged, hazy skyline through the window of the plane.

Many people I've known who visited New York for the first time came back wound up with awe and this old cliché on their lips: "I don't know how those people stand living there!"

But when I walked off the plane at LaGuardia Airport, I had the oddest sensation, that I'd just been out of town on business for a few days and was returning home.

Gerry and Merrill Lynch put on the dog for me, rolled out the red carpet. We did the Broadway shows, a Mets game, ate in posh restaurants, rubbed shoulders with the rich and famous, and witnessed the good, the bad, and the ugly of a legendary city.

I finally got to see the New York Stock Exchange up close and soak up the history and the energy of all that capital flowing through one hall. I stopped in and paid my respects to Schreyer, and then met Hugh Quigley. Quigley, who I learned was called Huey by associates, was a big bear of a man, intense and clearly in love with his work. I could relate.

The trading floor blew me away; it was as big as a football field. The faces staring into computer screens at the far end were mere smudges. Several hundred people worked in that huge room. Three sides had no walls, just enormous glass windows looking out on the canyons of lower Manhattan.

All of it fascinated me, but I noted in particular that there were serious opportunities. People responded to me in a way that said I could do business in this town–a lot of business. Time wasters have always annoyed me, which New Yorkers seemed to pick up on. If I had one person tell me this, I've had a hundred: they knew from the first handshake that I was a player. In fact, as I spent more time in the city over the next months and years, that's how people I did business with would sometimes introduce me. "This is Jim Salim. He's a player." Translation: he will not waste your time.

My visit to Merrill and New York got my juices flowing. I had already been a big enough operator to turn the heads of people like Quigley and Schreyer. Same thing with Donegan at Kidder Peabody. Anytime a heavy hitter comes along and his broker starts turning out big commissions, the boys in New York sit up and take notice: Who is this guy Salim? He's the best damn trader we've seen in a long time, and he's making us a lot of money in the bargain.

Back in Dallas, I began to look at situations that previously were too big for me and to think about how to use my newfound contacts and knowledge. I looked at taking big positions in specific companies, rather than trading in a lot of different stocks.

This was the first half of the 1980s, when merger and takeover fever swept the financial markets. The cult of the corporate raider had been born, terrorizing managements and roiling stock prices. It picked up steam in 1981 and 1982 with a flurry of monumental takeovers in the oil business. Oil companies had been printing money for a few years, thanks to $30-a-barrel oil. Big producers were choking on cash. It made sense to go out and buy more reserves and production capacity by gobbling up other companies. It was often cheaper and a whole lot faster to buy oil in the stock market than to look for it in the ground.

There were about four hundred publicly traded independent oil and gas producers at the time, many of them overlooked by the analysts in New York and the market in general. The trick was to find one selling below the appraised value of its oil and gas reserves.

I'd been reading that discovery costs ran about $12 a barrel and that there were a hundred or so companies that would be cheap to buy on that basis. One of these turned out to be May Petroleum, right in my backyard of Dallas. It was selling at 70 percent of its net worth.

May shares had been rattling around in a trading range between roughly $7 and $10. That gave the company a market value of about $75 million to $100 million, not too big a bite for a larger oil producer to swallow. But I needed bankers. You don't bank a deal with Merrill Lynch or Chase in Dallas. You bank a deal with Merrill Lynch or Chase in New York. So I began testing the waters, flying up to the city on a Sunday afternoon to spend a few days making the rounds and talking up my ideas.

Meanwhile, I kept my finger on the pulse of the stock. I began to trade it regularly, doing what I had done before with a stock or other investment that got stuck in a trading range. I rode it up and down the range, making money here and there, getting a feel for how the stock acted day by day, and determining how well the trading desks executed my orders. I crouched, watching and waiting for the perfect moment to pounce.

For May to qualify as a opportunity for me, I needed to know how much stock I could buy without tipping my hand or disrupting the market. If I could quietly load my boat, I'd be in a position to influence the company, maybe provoke a takeover or at least a bid. It wouldn't matter whether the bid succeeded. As long as the attention revealed the true value of the company and boosted the price.

But a couple days in New York now and then wasn't going to cut it if I had serious intentions of getting in on this merger boom. I learned a basic truth about New York business. You're either in the city, or you are not in the city. If New Yorkers think you're not, they just don't take you as seriously as someone who is in the city.

If I was going to step my trading up to the next level, I needed to spend a lot more time there. So, in 1981 Manhattan became my second home. The hotel I chose to live in sat in the middle of the Manhattan beehive. The Park Lane, on Central Park South between Fifth and Sixth Avenues, looked out across the street on Central Park. A few doors east was Mickey Mantle's Restaurant and at the corner reigned the Plaza

Hotel, where the Oak Bar was another Wall Street hangout. The view from my room was one you often see in films set in New York, a big rectangle of green and trees surrounded by a battlement of luxury apartment houses and hotels.

I kept my home in Dallas but spent six to seven months a year in New York City.

I moved to New York with several big advantages. In the same way my status as a good poker player preceded me in Monroe when I was in college, I arrived in New York with a reputation. I had Merrill Lynch to thank and Jim Donegan of Kidder Peabody, who worked out of Los Angeles but who still handled a big chunk of my business. My Louisiana accent, southern manners, New York urgency, and Middle Eastern background combined, I think, to give me an edge.

And I loved it.

From day one the carpets rolled right out. The doors opened on command. The brokerage firms made sure I never got bored, showering me with tickets to sports and entertainment events.

I rented an office just above Times Square on Broadway and set up my trading operation. Sixteen-to-eighteen hour days were normal. I traded stocks and commodities daily and began to find opportunities to exploit the takeover mania. New York was full of deal-makers, and I found that my trading skills not only made me money, it attracted the kind of people who could make things happen on a grand scale.

I had six to seven meetings every day, starting with breakfast at 7:30 each morning in the hotel dining room, which was a Wall Street breakfast hangout. At nine o'clock I'd get in my limousine and head off to my next meeting with brokers, bankers, or lawyers.

Now that I was *in* the city, I wanted a steady car with a driver I could trust to get me where I needed to be when I had to be there. He needed to know New York like his own backyard. That person turned out to be Saverio Pace. Sam, as he preferred to be called, knew everyone in New York who owned or ran the best restaurants and the most popular nightclubs and bars.

Sam had been driving for a limousine service I used and then he bought his own limousine and went into business for himself. He had three customers who kept him busy enough of the time to make it worth his while. The other two were John E. Swearingen, chairman and CEO of Standard Oil of Indiana, and William H. Spoor, chairman and CEO of Pillsbury. Swearingen and Spoor might be in the city only occasionally, but I was there constantly for more than half the year.

Sam was one of the nicest people I ever met and he knew New York *better* than his own backyard. He knew every maître'd in the city. He knew every back street. He knew everybody off Wall Street that I'd ever have a reason to want to meet. He could get choice tickets to the hottest show on Broadway, five minutes before curtain time. Sam played a big role in my life in New York.

Around the same time I met Sam, I was introduced to one of Wall Street's graybeards. Mel Marks had been an investment banker for decades with a big, aggressive brokerage house, Bear, Stearns. Mel retired, got bored, and opened his own office near Times Square. He took on a few clients, to keep his hand in the game—once a deal-maker always a deal-maker.

Mel took me on as a client, and mentored me in the rough and tumble art of high finance. Not only did he know everybody on Wall Street, he'd spent his life as a banker doing big, big deals. He understood how it was done, how to value companies and their assets. Nobody could buy stock on the cheap the way I could. But Mel Marks could put me on the map. We were a good match.

I talked to Mel every day, and sought his advice on nearly every move I made. He saw my skill as a trader, and I knew he'd been talking me up to some of his bigger clients. How big, however, would surprise me.

"Ever hear of a guy named Charlie Bluhdorn?" he asked me one day.

"Yeah," I laughed. "I do believe somewhere I might of heard of someone with a name just like that."

Bluhdorn was the notorious and notoriously successful chairman and CEO of Gulf & Western Industries, a conglomerate he built single-handedly, practically from scratch, by buying up one company after another, more than 150 in all. He ran Gulf & Western with an iron fist. Bluhdorn had a mantra he repeated so often it became a fixture in everyday language: "What's the bottom line?"

"Charlie Bluhdorn is a friend of mine," Mel continued. "I think you guys might have something in common. I can arrange a meeting. Interested?"

You bet I was! Bluhdorn had worked his way up from a $15-a-week clerking job to become master of a $5.7 billion corporate octopus with tentacles into everything from zinc mines to movie studios.

He cut his teeth trading commodities, and became an aggressive stock market operator. G&W, the fifty-first largest company on the Fortune 500 list, served as his home base for speculative plunges in the stocks of other companies. He had a gift for spotting and exploiting opportunity ahead of the pack.

By the time I came along, Charlie Bluhdorn had accumulated an enormous portfolio of big positions in big companies. His raids earned him a reputation as a corporate buccaneer, and his company the nickname "Engulf & Devour." Controversy followed him everywhere, in much the same way it later dogged Microsoft co-founder Bill Gates.

He was a master trader who reputedly managed Gulf & Western's $800 million investment portfolio with two assistants "and his pinky finger." The portfolio included stakes of about 20 percent in five companies; above 5 percent in more than a dozen others; and smaller stakes in many more.

Mel and I went to Gulf & Western's office at Columbus Circle, just a couple blocks down Central Park South from my hotel. We spent an afternoon with Bluhdorn high up in the corporate tower overlooking the park. I found him to be gruff, tough, a man of few words, spoken in a slight Austrian accent. He was no-nonsense, no chitchat. Just, what's the bottom line?

We seemed to click. Like Bluhdorn, my heritage meant something to me. As I'm sure he was in his youth, I was hungry, on the come, a sponge for knowledge, willing to work twenty hours a day. But that wasn't his bottom line. He wasn't expecting to make money with me or do a deal, either. But he did have an agenda.

"The word is you can read the tape better than anybody," he said. "Mel tells me you can accumulate a position in a stock cheaper and better than anyone he's met, without disturbing the market."

"I guess that's what they say," I replied. It was a high compliment coming from a master.

Next thing I knew, Bluhdorn pulled out of his desk a flow chart showing all the positions of stocks in Gulf & Western's portfolio. I saw all the companies Bluhdorn had bought big positions in, percentages above 4.9 percent, which is the point at which a buyer of a company's stock is required to report his ownership to the SEC. That report is required under SEC Rule 13-D, which is triggered whenever a person or entity buys 5 percent or more of the stock in a public company.

In Bluhdorn's case, the target boards of directors sometimes panicked, thinking they were about to be engulfed and devoured. By the time I came along, Bluhdorn wasn't acquiring much. But he explained that he didn't mind when a company would buy their stock back from him at a profit to make him go away. This had become a popular tactic at the time, known as greenmail.

"Why pay a premium for 100 percent of a company when I can buy 20 percent at a discount?" he explained.

Also on Bluhdorn's flow sheet were many positions that did not meet the 13-D rule, and very few people on the Street knew he owned them. It was a great privilege and honor to be taken into his confidence.

"I always have my eye open for new situations," he told me. "But the problem is, when I give the brokers an order to buy or sell a stock, everybody on the Street knows about it in five minutes and they front-run me."

Front-running is a common swindle that Wall Street brokerage firms still practice, taking advantage of the knowledge of their own customers' buy and sell orders. A firm's trading desk will receive a big order, jump in front of their customer, and buy for the house account. That pushes up the price, and then they turn around and sell the same shares they just bought to their customer at a higher price. The same thing works in reverse, when a customer calls in a big sell order.

"Here's what you can do for me, now and then," Bluhdorn said. "You do your work, find situations you like, buy what you want, and tell me about it. I'm not saying I'll buy a single share or buy out the whole company. But if you come up with the right deal, it'll be worth your while."

I never did do a deal with Bluhdorn, but he asked me to be a stalking horse for him on a couple of stocks. This led to other situations in which I was asked to test the market for a stock. Like Bluhdorn, they'd say, "We're looking at this company. What do you think about the stock?"

Most of the time they didn't give me money to go out and do any trading. They just wanted my feel for the tone of the market. The only way to do that is to buy and sell. A smart trader can sit and watch the tape and come to logical conclusions. But until you put in a 100,000-share buy or sell order, you can't tell whether somebody or some group is artificially propping the stock up or it's actually ready to run like the wind.

Sometimes these deals might come from the head trader at a brokerage firm whose client was thinking about buying 10 million shares of a stock. As a favor for a favor done for me or to be done, I'd plunge in the stock, test the market, accumulate a position, and then report back: if you want to buy 10 million shares I can buy it for you. Alternatively, I might report that the stock is thin and it's ready to run. If you're going to make a bid for the company, better make it right now because the tape and the action is telling me it will run away from you.

Near the end of my audience with Bluhdorn he asked me, "What do you think about the market?" I was very bearish at the time. I mentioned the recent comments by some well-followed market analysts and economists that interest rates were going to go back up again.

"Ah, a bunch of crap," he said, waving his hand in a gesture of disgust. "I have no use for Wall Street analysts, or any of the five thousand economists who are constantly revising their forecasts. The market looks cheap to me."

Three months later, the market broke and prices fell sharply. Mel called me one day and said, "Just got off the phone with your buddy, Bluhdorn. He said, 'Tell that kid he was right. I wish I had listened to him.'"

Bluhdorn was also right, in the long run. The bull market began not long after, in August 1982. But early in 1983, as he was traveling in his corporate jet, he died of a massive heart attack. He was only fifty-six years old. I often wonder how my life might have been altered had he lived. I know for a fact that Charlie Bluhdorn would be as rich as Midas were he alive today. He was a trader after my own heart.

Situations like this confirmed Mel as my godfather. In addition to putting me into situations where I could make a lot of money, he knew so many big players that he once saved me from a big disaster.

Earlier I mentioned how hard it is to pick tops and how dangerous short-selling can be. But the urge is often strong, and when I stumbled across a high-tech company in Richardson, Texas, whose shares had soared, my trigger finger got itchy. I didn't know much about Digital Switch, a company that made central office switching equipment for the newly deregulated long-distance telephone business.

I did know that the stock had run from $5 a share to $60, and it was full of hot air just waiting for the pin prick. The same kind of mania existed then as in the dot-com craze. Brokers I knew in Dallas and New York were pumping the hell out of it. The more questions I asked, the more overblown it looked, trading at a ridiculous price-to-earnings ratio. I knew I was right and I began one day to short the devil out of it.

Later that afternoon, I stopped in to see Mel. He was leaning back in his chair talking on the phone. I sat on the sofa and waited. When he hung up I started bragging on myself.

"Well, I'm shorting the dickens out of a piece of garbage I ran across called Digital Switch. Some of my broker friends—."

Mel sat bolt upright and his eyes sprung wide.

"Whoa, Jim. Whoa," he said. "You can't do that!" He grabbed the phone receiver and handed it to me.

"Where's the short?" he said, curtly. "Who's got it? You've got to buy it in, quick as you can. What's the number?"

I was stunned, speechless.

"Jim, one of the most aggressive private banking houses is behind that stock," he explained, holding the receiver out to me. "They'll run you down like roadkill. Now, do as I say. Call and cover that short."

Mel had it dead to rights. Digital Switch doubled from where I shorted it. Ultimately, the stock did collapse and the company disappeared. But I would have been long gone, deep in the red, by then. He saved me a bundle and reminded me that I need to do *all* my homework and quit trying to pick tops!

Although I kept an office on Broadway, I spent most of my days on Wall Street. Thus, my world was the Park Lane and its power breakfasts; Mel's office; the offices of my lawyers, Dechert Price & Rhoads, which were nearby on Madison Avenue; and the watering holes and restaurants where a lot of the trading crowd and hot money hung out. I constantly entertained and spent at least one night a week at a Broadway show.

New York was a nonstop circus. One of the places that became a regular haunt was Sparks Steak House on East Forty-sixth Street. It defined "classy joint" and attracted a broad cross-section of New York's rich, famous, and notorious. It was the sort of place where, on the same night, you might spot Mayor Ed Koch, John Phelan, president of the New York Stock Exchange, and John Gotti, the mobster, along with a zillion Wall Street guys.

The first time I ate there I was the guest of two lawyers, Andy Sidman and David Fiveson. We were looking at the menu when one of them said casually, "Since this your first time at Sparks, you should try the Castellano tartare. It's a house specialty."

"What's that?" I asked. "I don't see it on the menu."

"Well, it never is, Jim. It's on the sidewalk out front."

"Huh?"

My dinner companions burst out laughing.

"Jim, this is where Big Paul got killed. You know, Paul Castellano."

"Oh yeah," I remembered. "That guy used to be head of one of those big New York crime families, right?"

"Right," one of the lawyers said. "He bought the farm right here. They shot him as he got out of his car. Blew his brains out, right in front, on the sidewalk."

Now I burst out laughing.

"Well, holy crap," I said. "Thanks a lot for bringing me to such a nice classy restaurant."

Everything about the city amazed me. It was full of roadrunners.

8

Let The Games Begin

"I knew I was setting up a no-lose situation for myself.
The only question was how big would I win?"

Comfortably settled in New York, Mel Marks and I began to troll for some nice fat fish to fry. A big trend in investment banking in those days was to find poor performing companies with assets that, under better management or some sort of restructuring, could be turned around and made very profitable.

A popular way to finance these deals was a leveraged buyout. In a typical LBO, as the strategy was known, a group of corporate managers with the help of outside investors and banks pledged a company's assets as collateral for huge loans used to buy up all the public stock and take it private. A successful LBO allowed the private investors and managers to get control of an undervalued asset. They'd set about cutting the fat (get it "lean and mean" was the popular phrase), and squeeze out the profits.

The largest LBO in history set off the highly publicized slugfest over control of RJR Nabisco in 1988. A best-selling book, *Barbarians at the Gate*, told the story, followed by a television movie starring James Garner. You don't hear much about LBOs anymore. It was an effective way to dig out hidden assets like real estate or consumer brands that were being poorly exploited or carried on the books at a fraction of actual value. It was all about leveraging assets to "enhance shareholder value."

Mel and I also looked for opportunities for hostile takeovers or for simply filing 13-D positions that might prompt a bid from someone else that would give us a profit in the stock. And, like Charlie Bluhdorn, I would not have complained if a company wanted to buy my shares back for more than I paid.

Thanks to Mel and my other contacts, a steady flow of new people—traders, investors, big book brokers, and others—began to pass through my life. Mel took these people out to dinner all the time. He continually built relationships all across the Street.

I passed many an evening with Mel and his crowd. It amazed me what people would say, the deep corporate and Wall Street secrets they'd let slip after a few drinks and when they thought they were among members of the tribe. Traders and investment bankers are never supposed to disclose who their customers are or what their customers are doing. But the truth is they often do. People have a need to boast and gossip. They can't help themselves.

Mel and I finally found a company that seemed to fit the bill. The business was so far off the radar screen you'd never think there'd even be a way to invest in it—zippers. Talon, a former division of Textron, an industrial conglomerate.

The Talon deal was not strictly an LBO in the sense that we were going to take a public company private. Talon was part of a group of Textron subsidiaries that had been sold off to an investor group. But we were still going to leverage the assets with debt and make it independent.

The deal required an army of lawyers and intricate negotiations. There were serious pollution problems at some of its plants that had to be acknowledged and fixed. There was an employee pension plan that had to be preserved and managed. This was the first time I'd ever gotten involved in a situation where I seriously aimed to buy a whole company.

Mel and I found bankers to put up the money and a great executive to run the company. After stupendous effort and about $1,000,000 of my own cash, the thing was all ready to go.

The guys who negotiated the deal for me were a group of lawyers from Dechert Price & Rhoads, led by Lou Marks. They were good law-yers, terrific businessmen, and ferocious negotiators.

As my bills mounted, Lou would say, "We may charge you a million dollars in fees to do this deal, Jim, but we'll save you $2 million. When we get done beating these SOB's up, it won't have cost you a penny."

In fact, we started with an agreement in principle at about $22 mil-lion. Lou and his team set to work nicking the other side for $200,000 here and $500,000 there, worrying every little detail looking for places to pry off concessions. They got the seller and his lawyers so frustrated they just wanted to close the deal and zip it up. They kept giving in to our demands.

By the time Dechert Price & Rhoads got through with the seller, they had beaten him out of a couple of million dollars.

"See, Jim? We're free!" Lou bragged. I was impressed.

Mel Marks told me I was going to be the next empire builder. I was going to be just like my hero, Charlie Bluhdorn, and the zipper com-pany was going to be my launch pad.

But Talon came with baggage. Before the 1970s, as a Textron divi-sion, it owned 100 percent of the zipper market. But Textron, a con-glomerate with too many fingers in too many pies, had blown its mo-nopoly. A big Japanese concern, YKK, had opened a plant in the United States and was gnawing its way through Talon's market share. By the time the deal came across my desk, YKK controlled 65 percent of the zipper market. Where Talon had been the giant, it now operated in the shadow of another. Even so, the company still had assets, and it still had a business worth owning and streamlining.

As the day approached when we were supposed to close, I began to get a bad feeling in my gut. There wasn't a thing I could put my finger on, but despite all the enthusiasm and all the anticipation of my future on corporate Mount Olympus, something was eroding my confidence.

When I look back on it now, I think it had to do with a habit I developed during the negotiations. I looked at zippers. There were zip-pers on my pants, my luggage, the garment bag, my valise, just every-where. And it seemed as if every time I checked a zipper, it said "YKK." I kept looking for Talon and finding YKK. It became an obsession. If you look at your zipper right now, it's a safe bet it's a YKK.

As I headed out the door the night before the closing, I told Mel I was going to sleep on it one more night. I don't think he had a clue there was anything on my mind but to do that deal. He thought it was just an expression: sleep on it. But in my head, I was kicking tires.

Out on Broadway I found my driver, Sam, waiting in the car at the curb. I opened the door to get in. Just then something, I don't know what, made me glance up. When I did, I saw the biggest billboard in Times Square, lit up like the main runway at Kennedy Airport during rush hour. Emblazoned across it in blood red were the letters "YKK."

That killed it for me. The next day I showed up and told them all how sorry I was, but I had changed my mind. Everyone freaked, even Mel. I was out a million bucks for all the fees I had caused as part of the negotiations. But I never looked back. Maybe it would have been a good deal for me, but sometimes you've just got to go with your gut.

Although I'd invested a lot of time and money in Talon, there were other deals percolating. Soon enough, one sailed my way that ended up yielding a real bonanza.

One day I got a call from an independent investment banker I knew, John McCracken, who was in South Africa and flying back to New York in a couple of days. He had a client who wanted to meet me. I picked McCracken up at LaGuardia and on the way to the Regency Hotel where we were to meet the client and have drinks, he filled me in.

"He's English, old money kind of guy, but lives in Paris. You'd swear he's French, with his accent and all. I think there's a real deal for you here," he said. "He's loaded to the gills. He's a big shooter, buys 100,000 shares at a crack. He claims Goldman Sachs, his broker, has been screwing him, losing him money, and he's very unhappy about it. I told him what a great trader you are and he wants to meet you. He wants to make some serious money."

Over drinks I met the client, Alan Clore, son of a British retailing mogul named Sir Charles Clore. Alan and I were about the same age, but our backgrounds couldn't have been more different. I once read an article that put his net worth at hundreds of millions. He had a reputation for an obsession with secrecy, which may be the reason he lived in France instead of England.

During drinks we agreed to continue the discussion over dinner sometime. Clore casually mentioned that he'd like to go to whichever restaurant at that time was the most famous, exclusive, hard-to-get-into, French joint in New York. I knew the place he was referring to. I also knew that it took four months to get a table.

I got this idea in my head that Clore was testing me, to see if I was as wired as my reputation. I didn't hesitate a second. Bold as homemade sin, I told him in my sweetest, most charming southern accent, "Well, now, if you want to have dinner there, and you tell me when, we'll have dinner there."

He looked at me like I'd lost my mind. And then he threw down the gauntlet. "Very well. I'd love to have dinner there at nine o'clock tonight."

Without missing a beat, I said, "Fine. I'll pick you up."

Clore probably had me pegged as a dumb cracker who stumbled into the big house by mistake. But I knew that Sam could get that table. I went out to the car and told him what I needed.

His forehead crinkled. "Tonight?"

"I don't care what it costs, Sam. Just get me that table."

Sure enough, Sam reported back to me later at my hotel, we were go for the table. It was going to set me back $500. We picked Alan up at his hotel, the Carlyle, and I led the way into the restaurant.

The next thing that happened could only take place in New York. The maître'd, who I had never laid eyes on in my life, the maître'd of the slickest, most exclusive French restaurant in the financial capital of the world, walked up to me, son of a Louisiana crop duster, seized me by the shoulders in a warm embrace, and said, "Monsieur Salim! It is so good to see you. And who is your friend?"

Alan's eyebrows just about flew off his face.

I had to stifle a guffaw. Who is my friend? My friend's practically a billionaire from Paris and his father was a damn knight or something.

When we'd been seated Alan said, "I have never been so impressed in my life. Fantastique!"

And I said, very innocently, "Well, now, I'm just so happy we could get you here, and you can enjoy New York."

Before the night was over we had a handshake deal: Alan Clore would put up as much as $10 million for me to go and do whatever I wanted to make the two of us money trading the markets. For an investment of about a thousand dollars for the evening, voilà! Here's $10 million, Jim. Go, go, go, son. Do it! And tell me if you need some more!

That was one sweet moment.

Clore complained that Goldman Sachs kept putting him into rotten deals. But he was his own worst enemy. He let his brokers trade him to death. He got sucked into money-losing corporate takeovers. He had a sidekick, a French stockbroker who was always with him. Not very bright, this guy was probably feeding him bad advice, or worse. On top of it all, he had expensive hobbies like gambling and horsebreeding. I didn't find out until much later that the SEC had been tracking him on insider trading suspicions.

But none of that had a thing to do with me. He was looking for help, somebody who could make him money and he could halfway trust. We would each put up an equal amount of capital, but I would have total trading discretion. That was the deal.

One sure way to make money with this war chest would be to step up my plunging in May Petroleum. By this time I knew the stock better than the trading desks at the major brokerage firms who made a market in it all day long. I knew the most number of shares any one firm had on hand was probably 100,000. With an average price of about $8 a share, the middle of May's trading range, I could go toe-to-toe with any firm and out trade them.

Meanwhile, I had been keeping a weather eye on the fundamentals of the company. I was still spending about half the year in my home in Dallas, where the company's corporate offices were located. I'd had the chance to meet Charles Ramsey, the CEO. I wasn't getting inside information, just watching my back.

May was badly undervalued by the market, really beaten up. It had good reserves, good properties to drill, a decent balance sheet, smart people running the company. During my first plunge in the stock, it had run from $7 to $8.25. I made the decision that, if I could do it, I wanted to own the whole thing. I waited for it to pull back.

In the meantime, the stock was a cash machine.

It was a bad day if May didn't move at least 25,000 shares for half a point. There were a lot of days when I made $75,000 just day trading. I put together a core position of 300,000 or 400,000 shares around the lows. When it bounced a dollar, I would sell a hundred thousand shares. If it pulled back 75 cents, I'd buy the hundred thousand shares back. It was a real trading stock, not an investment like Houston Oil, where I was betting on a big gas find.

Because I was such an active trader in May shares, and because I had developed a reputation for aggressive plunging, the trading desks had begun to front-run me, just as they had been front-running Bluhdorn. It made me mad as hell. First of all, it's cheating, and second of all, it's illegal. It's insider trading, using the knowledge of my orders to buy or sell in front of me.

But it's impossible to prove most of the time. And for a big player to sue a Wall Street firm for front-running would poison me with the people and firms who could do me the most good. The last thing a trader needs on the Street is a reputation for being litigious.

But with Alan Clore's money to work with, I was in a position to set up a sting operation that would bring some justice to the situation.

First, I quietly opened a new account with all the firms that made a market in May Petroleum. The account had only my name on it. Alan was wealthy and famous. The last thing I needed was for anyone to know about his money being involved. I spread the dough around in six major firms who knew me.

Next, I needed to buy a big chunk of May Petroleum without anybody knowing it. I needed to find an institution or two, such as a pension fund or mutual fund, that wanted to unload a big position. I called the one person I knew who could do that without setting off so much as a ripple. That was Boyd Jefferies, founder of Jefferies & Company, a large Los Angeles-based independent brokerage house.

Boyd was a certified genius, and he hired other geniuses to work for him. He had created a whole trading market that had never existed before. He offered large investors like myself the chance to buy big positions twenty-four hours a day. He seemed to know every stock and every institution that held it, what they paid, how long they'd owned it, and the price at which they'd let it go.

I knew all this because once, when I was trading May, Boyd happened to be in the Dallas office of Jefferies & Company, sitting at the trading desk. My Jefferies broker, Kevin Dann, told him I wanted to buy a large position. Without looking up from the screen of his computer, Boyd asked what I was willing to pay and for how many shares. Then, without making a phone call or turning his head, he rattled off the names of the institutions who owned the stock, how much they held, and which trader to call at each institution. In an hour he'd bought me almost 5 percent of the company, without trading a single share of stock on the open market and without moving the price so much as an eighth of a point.

Boyd Jefferies had helped a lot of big players do their deals, people like T. Boone Pickens Jr. of Mesa Petroleum, a speculator who was to the oil patch what Bluhdorn had been to the rest of corporate America. Boyd wanted to make money, a close aide to Pickens once told me, but he also wanted to please his clients. And he did.

In fact, it was one of the great ironies of the 1980s that Boyd Jefferies was so good he attracted business from Ivan Boesky. Boesky, trying to save his ass from a ten-year prison stretch for insider trading, later ended up fingering Boyd and taking him down with him. For buying and holding stock for Boesky, a practice known as parking, Boyd found himself banned forever from the business. Yet I have watched some of the biggest firms on Wall Street front-run their customers and park stock all the time.

As part of my sting with Alan Clore on the front-running brokerage firms, Boyd found a total of almost 600,000 shares of May at $7^{1/4}$. The trade crossed the tape. I now knew that every trader in May Pete, as the stock was known, had their ears pricked for some kind of action. Who, they were wondering, was accumulating May Pete, and why? I also knew that the block trade report would make them nervous and keep them from selling the stock they owned, or selling short.

Sitting in my office, I clapped my hands together and shouted to my secretary, "Let the games begin!"

I had set up accounts for this operation at firms including Merrill Lynch, Goldman Sachs, PaineWebber, and Kidder Peabody. I had hotlines direct to every one of their trading desks. I picked up the phones two at a time, waited for the traders to come on—unbeknownst to each other—

and barked, "I'm buyin' 100,000 May Pete, a quarter up. I'd like to get it done in the next fifteen minutes. Gotta go!" And hung up.

To those traders, what I'd said meant that if the market price for May was $7^{1/2}$ bid, $7^{3/4}$ ask, and the last trade was $7^{3/4}$, I was willing to pay up 25 cents a share, or \$8, to get the 100,000 shares. It meant I was an aggressive buyer. "I want the stock and I'll pay up for it."

Coming from me, coming after a big block trade, this information put them on high alert.

I did this to every single one of them. And every one put on their trading screens for the rest of the market to see that they had a customer for 100,000 shares of May Pete. All six of those trading desks also were working the phones calling every institution that owned the stock.

Through Jefferies, I had already pulled 600,000 shares out of the bushes. I was going to find out fast if any more stock was for sale. If I got it, I would have bought it. If not, I knew I had a runner, a stock whose price was poised to spike.

A big trading desk can smell a runner, and from what the traders were telling me, there was electricity in the air. My bids for May Pete were all over the place. And just like clockwork, the trading desks all ran out and bought for the house account thinking they were going to skin me, or maybe something was really going on, like a takeover bid.

I knew I was setting up a no-lose situation for myself. The only question was how big would I win? I wanted to own this stock, but I had 600,000 shares to sell if it turned into a stampede. Momentum traders watch every day for stocks that start to act like they are breaking out on the upside, or downside

I waited for the answer, and it wasn't long in coming.

The bid went from 8 to $8^{1/4}$, then $8^{1/2}$, $8^{3/4}$, 9, $9^{1/4}$, all in twenty minutes. I knew for a fact they were front-running me.

Next, I called another brokerage firm where I did not have buy orders, and put in an order to sell at $9^{3/4}$ the 600,000 shares I owned. The dumb traders started calling me back saying, "Jim, looks like you're onto something. We couldn't hardly get you any stock!" Out of all six of those trading desks, where I had cumulative orders for 600,000 shares, they'd bought me only 15,000 shares.

In thirty minutes the market had gobbled up all 600,000 shares I had for sale. Who bought it? You guessed it. The traders did.

In the time it took Alan Clore to get a haircut and a manicure, I'd booked a profit of almost $1,500,000.

But I wasn't done yet! I got permission from Jefferies to short 500,000 shares. By the end of the day I had sold short 350,000 shares at $10^{1/4}$, near the top end of May's trading range. The next day I managed to get off another 150,000 shares at high prices. Now I got back on the phones.

"What do you want to do, Jim?" the poor suckers asked me. "Stock just got away from us."

"Let's see if we can get it to calm down a bit," I told them all. "But if you see a big piece, you give me a call, hear?"

Meanwhile, I was busy selling them more stock. Altogether, I sold the 600,000 shares I bought through Jefferies, and then I sold them another half million shares short.

Now the traders were calling me and saying, "You're looking smart in this May Pete. Something must be up. Look at all the volume. I heard a rumor Boone Pickens is looking to make a run at the company."

And I said, "I don't know. I heard Boone was on a round-the-world vacation or something, isn't he? I don't like what I'm hearing on the Street. The stock is starting to look overblown. I'm picking up some chatter, like management's trying to smooth over some bad quarters coming up. Their numbers might be about to crumble.

"You know what? How much of this dog-crap do I own? Fifteen thousand shares? Let's dump it!"

Now the poor bastards are all sitting there, hundreds of thousands of shares long, at high prices, and the smartest trader they know, the one who is an expert on May Pete, is saying, "Dump it!"

In one of those New York minutes the stock began to tank. The traders rushed the exits, knocked each other down trying to get out the door. Over the next few days, like a rainbow from the sky, the price fell back to $7^{3/4}$. As I covered my short sales, the money poured into my pocket.

In a week I had clipped them for almost $2.5 million, and honored every order that was filled. If those traders had come to me in the beginning with a quarter up on 100,000 shares, I'd have bought it. I'd have bought the whole company for $8 a share. But they reached out in front of me thinking I'd chase the price, or maybe somebody was about to make an offer for the whole company. Maybe me!

I beat the hell out of them, and loved every minute. Not a single trader ever said a word to me about those trades. They couldn't, because they would have to admit that they were trying to cheat me, which would have been like a thief walking out of the bank vault, and ratting out a second thief he spotted going in.

Front-running is one of the hardest swindles to prove because these enormous trading operations have customers all over the world, and they control their own paperwork. They've got a hundred ways to cover their tracks.

That was a crazy week. Between running the sting with May and everything else I had my hand in, I'd been up almost nonstop for two or three days.

I met Clore and his entourage for breakfast to report the results of my trading. They were so wound up by what I told them that they forgot I was there and started chattering away in French, totally ignoring the fact that I didn't understand a word. For all I knew they could have been saying, "This dumbass cracker just made us a million dollars! What the hell do we do with him now?"

I sat there for several minutes of this, too tired to care. Then, all of a sudden, it hit them and they turned to me with looks of horror on their faces and apologized profusely for being rude.

I continued to trade May for Clore for several months, and was getting ready to skin the front-runners again when he called and asked me to buy more stock. I had determined that the time to do that was passed, and it was not our arrangement that he'd tell me what to do. The decisions were to be mine alone.

"Alan, I'm selling, not buying," I said.

"I do not want to sell my shares," he said firmly. "I want to buy."

"I am setting these guys up, again. You're reading the tape wrong. They think I'm buying a 13-D position and they're front-running again. The last thing in the world you want to do is buy a share of stock. What we need to do is distribute to them."

I could tell he wasn't hearing it.

"What is our position," he demanded. At that point we had about 800,000 shares.

"Send me my 400,000 shares and you do what you want with yours."

Now I understood why Alan Clore had been so unlucky. I sent him his stock, and the next day I sold every share I owned. I probably sold half of those shares to Alan Clore. And when he stopped buying, everyone realized they'd been had. The stock collapsed. I made another ton of money and Alan must have lost a ton.

The unhappy epilogue for Alan Clore is that he went on to even bigger and more expensive fiascos. His last disaster went into the record books—an attempt in 1987 to take over KaiserTech, the parent company of Kaiser Aluminum and Chemical. Apparently, everything that could go wrong did. If you believe what you read, he lost more than $100 million, and in the bargain ruined the reputation of his investment banker, David Stockman, President Reagan's former budget director who was then an executive at Salomon Brothers.

Reporting on Alan Clore's crackup in the last article published about him before he disappeared from the investment scene in 1988, a *Business Week* writer observed, "He played the part of the heroic gambler who figured that if he bet enough money and rolled the dice enough times, he would eventually win big. Now he'll be lucky to hold on to whatever he'll have left."

A fool and his money—

9

Money Machine

"The stockbroker's role is to keep your money churning through
his firm's machine. Every time it moves, they get to keep a piece.
You are merely the bee that brings in the honey."

Alan Clore lost his fortune by surrounding himself with takers and idiots. But worse, he listened to stockbrokers. An average investor who thinks the big guys always make the money should remember Alan Clore, and remember some of the painful lessons I had learned up to this point in my career. There were more lessons to come for me, and very painful ones, too.

I had learned a lot about stockbrokers. My opinion hasn't changed in the two decades since I swindled the swindlers on May Petroleum.

There are a few very good stockbrokers in the world. I have been lucky enough to have known some of them: Jim Donegan of Kidder Peabody, Roy Price, the cotton broker at A. G. Edwards, Kevin Dann at Jefferies & Company, and Gerry Guillemaud of Merrill Lynch in Dallas. Another, Dave Mortimer, would play a role later. All honest and good at what they did.

One time Gerry Guillemaud misheard an order I gave him for gold futures, and it cost me about $100,000. Most stockbrokers would try to weasel out of a mistake like that, try to shift the blame, or downright lie. Gerry knew he had it wrong, took the blame, and made it up to me out of his own pocket. That's a good stockbroker.

In March 2000, just as the dot-com bubble was about to burst, a stockbroker I know in Dallas, Jim Hayes with CIBC Oppenheimer, told his customers to "get the hell out of the market." He's been a broker for decades. He'd seen it all. When the bottom subsequently fell out, his customers sent him bouquets of roses. That's a good stockbroker.

If a stockbroker leaves his firm, the competition for you and your account is cutthroat. The firm takes the position that you belong to them. The office manager at the firm where you have an account will be on the phone to you immediately along with your new assigned broker.

Meanwhile, your old broker is on the phone to tell you his sad story of why he left and beg you to fill out the new account forms at his new firm. I once had a broker fly from New York to Maui, Hawaii, where I was living at the time, with the new account forms for his new firm in his briefcase. He took the red eye flight and flew eleven hours just to beat his old firm to the punch.

This baggy-eyed broker arrived in my office and we were talking when the telephone rang. It was his old boss calling. Without letting him know the broker was sitting in front of me, I put the call on the speaker phone.

The guy's old boss proceeded to tell me this long sad story about how the broker was an untrustworthy, unstable, sorry person, and he was so thankful they found out just in time. The man offered me everything but a piece of the firm to keep my business with them.

I told him how flattered I was that he cared so much about my welfare. Then I broke the news to him that the broker was sitting in my office at that very minute with the new account forms from his new firm. I promised myself to try to keep vulgarity out of this book, but you can be sure that in the next thirty seconds the office manager uttered every curse word in the English language.

For every good broker, there are thousands of Bud Foxes. Fox, the ambitious young broker played by Charlie Sheen in *Wall Street*, shares his investment philosophy with a coworker: "Churn 'em and burn 'em, baby!" Followed by high fives and cigars.

Wall Street is a money machine, and the stockbroker's role is to keep your money churning through his firm's machine. Every time it moves, they get to keep a piece. For most stockbrokers, that is the only goal. You are merely the bee that brings in the honey.

The financial expertise required to become a stockbroker is, simply, none. The only thing standing between any idiot on the street and the chance to fool with other people's money is a test required by law and a firm to hire him. The test is fairly simple. About 60 percent of those who take it pass. And almost anyone can find a job as a broker.

To become a licensed stockbroker takes about four months, less than it takes to become licensed to run a beauty salon.

No one I know would get in an airplane with a pilot who doesn't know how to fly. But almost everyone I know gives their money to a stockbroker who has no clue, other than to keep your money moving, to cheer you on when you win, and maybe hold your hand when you lose. The broker makes a commission either way. There is no financial incentive for encouraging you to hold a stock for a long period of time. A day-trading customer is a stockbroker's dream client. Keep the account churning, and watch 'em burn it down. Or worse, help them do it.

Online investing runs on the same principal, except the brokerage firms love it even more. They put their money into software, e-mail spam, and sexy ad campaigns, instead of brokers. This allows investors to delude themselves into believing they have control over their financial future. The truth is, it turns investing into a video game. The more you play, the more they make, the more chances for you to lose. Too often, individual investors discover they have done to themselves exactly what an unethical broker would have tried to get them to do. Churn and burn. The difference is that these customers saved the brokerage house the expense of bricks, mortar, and salaries.

Unless you're a serious player with good instincts, most investors never meet the kinds of brokers I began to deal with when I moved my trading to New York. Called institutional brokers, they service large accounts such as mutual funds and what Wall Street calls high net worth individuals. They deal in large blocks of stock, big sums of money. Most are good at what they do and are well rewarded for it. I've known several who earned more than $3 million a year.

Most average investors deal with a retail broker who works for one of the New York-based wire houses like Merrill Lynch. This broker may

99

have launched his or her career anytime between before you were born and last week. Their life's work is to build a book of customers, roughly 500 if they're successful, and to keep the money moving.

If the firm has a research department, the broker will try to get his customers to buy the stocks they are recommending. He or she can't sell you a stock priced under $5, and you will only be encouraged to buy stocks on the firm's recommended list. The reasons they give may sound compelling, but none of them has anything to do with your financial well-being. Not on purpose, anyway.

The pitches run something like this: "My firm's got a strong buy on Microsoft at $70. Our analyst is going to be on CNBC tonight, and we have a price target of $120 a share. The stock has been oversold because of the government antitrust mess, but we think the momentum guys are sold out, and it's ready to start moving up. You should buy now. Our guy is a five-star analyst and the institutions listen when he speaks."

If you've had a traditional brokerage account for longer than three weeks, you've gotten a pitch just like that or close to it. I begrudge no one an honest living, but the financial advice most retail brokers sell is about as useful as what you'll get from a vacuum cleaner salesman.

The "recommended" stocks may be shares of companies the brokerage firm is financing through its banking division. Maybe the firm has an institutional client that wants to unload a chunk of stock, so they try to get as many retail customers as they can to buy it. Or maybe the firm got caught with a large, losing position in a crappy stock and is trying to foist the loss on to you.

If you had the misfortune to be a customer of Josephthal & Co. in May 1996, your stockbroker no doubt told you a wild story about VictorMaxx Technologies, a small Chicago-based holding company. He or she told you it was going to be the next Gulf & Western, or some such nonsense intended to get you hot and bothered enough to buy the stock.

What the broker didn't mention as part of his "recommendation" was that Josephthal was choking on a million shares of VictorMaxx, showing a loss of almost $4 million. He also left out that Josephthal promised its brokers a staggering 29 percent commission to unload the stock on clients, by any means necessary.

The swindle worked like a charm. Josephthal customers bought every last share at an average of $2.10. Within a month, the stock crashed below a dollar. Four months later, the Nasdaq delisted it.

Unlike many Wall Street swindles, the crooks running this one got caught. But it would take five years to bring some justice to the case. Josephthal settled for $3.3 million in fines and restitution.

There are a hundred reasons why a stockbroker might recommend a stock to you. And there are just as many reasons not to act on it without doing your own homework and research.

If your broker tells you about a rumor, discard it out of hand. You'll be lucky if one in ten turns out to be true. The rest of the time, expect to lose money. And even if the rumor turns out to be true, you still stand a shot at losing your money.

One of my brokers, who I ended up firing, called me one day in 1980 to tell me he had a good source who told him about an oil company that was going to receive a takeover bid the next day. Rumor had it the company would accept the offer.

I thanked him but declined to act. I don't buy rumors or mess with inside information that can get you investigated, or even prosecuted. But I watched the stock the next day. Sure enough, the bid came, and it was for cash, just as he predicted. The company accepted, just as he said they would.

Only one problem: the stock closed at $18 the day before and the bid was at $17. That's what you might call a take-*under*. If I'd bought, that's where my money would have gone, under.

Inside information sounds tempting but consider this. Even if you don't care that it's wrong and illegal, even if you don't care that you might lose any profits, have to pay a fine, and perhaps go to jail, and even if you knew you would never be caught, ask yourself this question: How the hell would a sideshow barker posing as a stockbroker hear actual inside corporate information that isn't available to everybody on the Street? The answer is either no way would he know, or he got it from a real insider, which means acting on that information puts you at risk of civil and criminal penalties. The odds are just as bad as they sound.

Stay away from brokers or friends with rumors and tips. You'll put yourself ahead of the game because the odd one that turns out to be right and makes you a lot of money will never compensate for the money you'll lose on the others or for the legal risk.

There is a third tier of brokers who work for small firms with only one or a few branches. These brokers typically sell penny stocks that are extremely speculative, risky as hell, and sell for no more than a couple of dollars.

They are, as a rule, young people starting out. Their first customers are often family and friends. When they have exhausted that source of business, they ask their friends and family to refer *their* friends and family. These brokers are hungry and with few exceptions know absolutely nothing that will ever be helpful to anyone who wants to preserve and increase their capital.

An accurate picture of the stereotype was portrayed in the film *Boiler Room*, released in 2000. The film is a fictionalized account of a major penny stock scam that operated on Long Island in the 1990s and was finally busted.

If you've spent any time investing, you've stumbled across a penny stock or two. There is an entire industry, much of it corrupt and well organized, and much of it begins in Utah. It fleeces the public year in and year out by selling overpriced shares in practically worthless companies. What these small brokers are selling is a dream, the same one that draws people to slot machines and lottery tickets. Only the odds on slots and lottery tickets are better.

The dream is of a small investment that yields a massive once-in-a-lifetime profit. There are familiar examples of penny stocks that went on to become real companies. America Online was a penny stock. So was Amazon.com. Many successful drug companies started out as penny stocks, raising money to do their research. Early investors became wealthy, and those are the stories you read about in the financial press.

That's where the dream is born, especially in bubble markets like the one that peaked in March 2000. Many dot-coms made the journey from penny stock to big, respectable, hot stock in record time. At the mania's height, you couldn't turn on a financial news channel or read a serious financial publication without running across a perky interview with the latest silicon-aire or internet-aire. American capitalism saluted its heroes.

You rarely hear about the billions of dollars that have vanished, swindled from investors, penny by penny, year after year. It is an easy business to get into and a hard scam for the law to control.

Penny stocks sound cheap. That's the allure, and the illusion. You can buy a penny stock for 25 cents a share, so the pitch is that you can buy so much stock, 50,000 shares, for a relatively small investment. But you'll get a better return paying $100 for a share of General Electric.

The 25-cent stock gives you a share of something that legally is a corporation, but could be lacking products, customers, sales, cash flow, earnings, assets, professional management, and even a telephone number.

If you ask thirty investing friends and acquaintances if they've ever been burned on a penny stock, I'd bet money that twenty-seven of them would say yes, and go on to tell you the whole story.

There are about fifty thousand licensed brokers, public relations firms, market makers, and stockbrokers who are involved in penny stock deals. I've been there. I've seen it. I've been swindled. I've known the biggest penny stock kingpin in New York and seen him operate.

Through one of my good brokers I met one of the sleazy penny stock brokers in 1979. I bought the stock he was pimping and did the same, classic, idiotic thing that everybody else does: I dialed up my twenty best friends to let them in on this great deal I'd discovered. Look at me, I'm a genius! And why don't you just plunge right in, too?

This one was a mining company that held the rights to a newly discovered deposit of coal in Utah. They were going to extract and sell it to utility companies.

Mining has an historic relationship with penny stock scams, especially gold mines. Investors are attracted to the idea of hidden assets just waiting to be dug out of the earth. No manufacturing required, nothing to be invented. Just dig it out and stick it in the bank. More money has been swindled on the basis of mining claims than any other business, going all the way back to the earliest gold rush.

This broker told the story to everyone and anyone who would listen: there had been an appraisal of the coal deposit that found it to be worth $130 million. There were "only" 10 million shares of stock outstanding and the stock was trading at $1. It's simple math: there remained $120 million in unrealized value. The stock simply *had* to go to at least $10! It was a no-lose deal.

He promoted it through other stockbrokers and individuals. They told their friends, they told *their* friends, and so on. It's an easy scam to run because every one fancies themselves a stock plunger. All of a sudden they get to be a player, get to be on the inside of a hot deal–a hidden vein of coal. And the stock's trading at 10 percent of its real value!

It doesn't matter how sophisticated a person might be in other areas of life. I've seen people from auto mechanics to chief executives fall for this scam. Few are immune from having the mark put on them. I've seen it continuously for twenty years.

By the time this coal mining scam played itself out, three hundred suckers had bought 10,000 shares each (it was *only* a dollar, after all), and the broker made off with $3 million. Once the scam was run, the price collapsed. It turned out the appraisal had been inflated, the deposit was on land that was the breeding habitat of an endangered bird, there was a pollution site that needed to be cleaned up, and the chairman of the board had declared personal bankruptcy and disappeared. Finally, somebody took up a collection and hired a lawyer to put the company in bankruptcy so at least we'd get a tax write-off.

The beauty of penny stock scams for the promoters is that each individual's loss is so small nobody bothers to sue. Even if you *didn't* mind admitting in public how you stupidly let your money get sucked into a rat-hole, the legal fees will exceed the loss, which you'll never recover anyway because of the tangle of corporate shells and offshore partnerships these swindles operate behind.

The scams are well thought out and well run. Prosecuting the perpetrators, if they can be caught, is often impossible even if you can find a district attorney, prosecutor, or SEC investigator who has the manpower, the time, the market savvy, and the interest.

When I realized I'd been had on the coal mining scam, the first thing I did was apologize to my friends. The next thing I did was start snooping around this dark business. I discovered that Utah is a favorite spawning ground for penny stock scams, and I kept running into people in the business who told me they were Mormons or worked with Mormons.

This is the basic structure of a penny stock swindle. A promoter creates a shell company in Utah and takes it public. He raises all the initial money within the state, which avoids a lot of annoying federal laws and pesky SEC regulations. The promoter sells the stock to three hundred people who are straw men and women pretending to be public shareholders who bought the stock. This legitimizes the shell as a publicly owned company within Utah. Three million shares of stock are sold at one cent a share. The promoter has—on paper—raised $30,000 for the company, which now has three hundred shareholders of record and three million shares of stock outstanding.

What really happens is those three hundred shareholders immediately endorse the backs of the stock certificates, assigning ownership back to the promoter, for a price of two cents per share. For the use of their names and signatures, the phony shareholders receive a small fee.

Now the promoter has a legal public company with legal stock, ownership of which is technically in the hands of the required minimum number of shareholders, but which is actually all in his hands. He owns the whole box, three million shares. Now the stock can be listed on the Over-the-Counter Bulletin Board, a loosely-regulated, junior version of Nasdaq, a sort of kindergarten for stocks. Once listed there it can begin to trade in the open market.

But it's a shell. It doesn't do anything.

So, the promoter goes shopping. He wants to find a real company, one that wants to go public but can't afford the high fees, or doesn't have a real business quite yet, or has a host of other problems that prevent it from raising capital in an SEC-approved stock offering. But he wants a company that has a salable story, something people will believe, like an unexploited coal deposit.

When the promoter finds a suitable candidate, he arranges a reverse merger. The real company merges into and takes over the public shell company. What survives is the real company, let's call it RealCo Inc., that can now issue additional shares to sell to the public to raise the capital to grow its business: instant credibility.

RealCo Inc. puts together a pretty brochure, hires some Wall Street lawyers, and gets the company listed all shiny and clean with the SEC. Now it can float a legitimate stock offering and raise as much as a couple million dollars at, let's say, 25 cents a share. RealCo manages to sell seven million shares, raising $1.75 million.

Mr. Utah Promoter, meanwhile, is sitting on his three million shares that cost him two cents each. RealCo Inc. is now trading at 25 cents. There are ten million shares altogether outstanding.

The promoter has a paper profit of almost $700,000. If he calls up his broker and says, "Sell three million RealCo at 25 cents," the stockbroker will laugh in his ear. The stock will crash if 30 percent of the whole company comes on the market in one thud.

The promoter has several ways to go. If he wants to keep things clean, he sits on the stock and sells a little here and a little there, as the market can take it, and gets what he can out of the deal over time. The worst thing that can happen is he'll sell enough stock to get his original investment back. He might make a lot of money, but it's a risk and takes time. Most new companies don't survive.

The promoter in this example, however, doesn't want to wait. He knows about the pollution problems. He knows the coal appraisal is inflated. He doubts the company will survive long enough to make money.

He calls in a middleman, someone who has contacts with sleazy stockbrokers all over the country, public relations hacks, corrupt newsletter writers, and chatroom hucksters. The middleman buys the stock from the promoter, some or all of the three million shares, and then he uses his network to get rid of the three million shares, paying everyone off along the way.

While the three million shares are being sold, the word is getting around that RealCo is looking like a hot stock, thanks to the public relations hacks and newsletter writers. The price begins to rise. The volume goes up. Traders begin to notice, and before you know it RealCo shares are soaring, headed toward a dollar. Right around the time the stock hits its peak, the middleman has unloaded all the stock and collected all the money. The hype machine closes up shop, shreds the paper trail, and moves on to the next one.

The stock crashes.

I never ran a penny stock scam, but I did provide financing for a couple of penny stock ventures and ended up making money the clean way. I bought big blocks of stock from Utah promoters, found the private companies that needed capital, did the reverse mergers, raised the capital, and, as the companies began to perform and grow, I sold my stock at a profit.

One of these companies remanufactured television picture tubes. I had never heard of that business before, but they actually made money doing it.

Another had a gimmick called satellite bingo. They beamed live televised bingo games by satellite to people's home dishes. Viewers played with boards that had been mailed to them. The rest of the details escape me, but they had big sponsors like General Motors putting up the prizes.

That stock rose to nearly $5 a share and I made several million dollars. Bingo!

I learned that some promoters were not as flagrant as others. Some kept 60 percent of the stock. The real serious swindlers kept it all. That way they *were* the market for that stock. It was easier to manipulate the sale and the price.

One of the most fascinating people I've known through my trading career was the biggest penny stock scammer of his time. He claimed to have made more than a *billion* dollars doing it. I believe him.

The name he used probably was not the one he got from his mother and father, and I wouldn't be shocked to learn that he met an untimely end in the swamps of New Jersey. But just in case I'm wrong on both counts, I've changed his name to Frank Skinner. He was well known to serious Wall Street players in New York during the early 1980s. He did business with many brokers and other professionals who you'd swear were perfectly respectable and honest.

His crime was highly organized but he was not the mobster portrayed in popular culture. About forty years old, he carried himself like a gentleman, handsome as a movie star, charismatic, with impeccable taste, and bold as brass.

From the beginning of my years in New York, my path frequently crossed Frank Skinner's, all over town, in all the Wall Street haunts. He always had beautiful women with him and wore crisp custom-made shirts and suits costing thousands. He usually had an entourage of sleazy stock-brokers with him.

I got to know him by bumping into him here and there, and then discovering that he also lived in the Park Lane Hotel.

Frank Skinner, I learned through the grapevine, maintained a network of corrupt stockbrokers and hypsters he used to distribute over-priced shares of small, shaky companies. He'd invite a group of these brokers from small firms to New York, take them out to Smith & Wollensky, one the finest steak houses in the city, run them around in a limousine, buy them beautiful whores, and promise them a cut of the shares they sold.

The next day these brokers would be on the phone stuffing hundreds of thousands of shares of Frank's overpriced stock into their clients' accounts.

One morning, after seeing him the night before with a bunch of brokers from a Long Island boiler room operation, I was eating my breakfast at the Park Lane when Frank walked in and took the table next to mine. We exchanged pleasantries and started chatting.

"You sure know how to entertain the troops, Frank. I don't see how Smith & Wollensky could stay in business if it wasn't for you."

He laughed. "Guess how much money I spent last night?"

"I have no idea."

"I spent $5,500 between the girls, the food, the booze, the car, and the hotel rooms.

"Guess how much money I made this morning in the first hour? More than $500,000."

My jaw dropped.

"Frank, why don't you do me a favor sometime? Tell me before you start this nonsense and let me make a little money!"

"Nah. You're too goody two-shoes. You just go on doing it the conventional way, the legal way."

We both laughed.

Frank worked constantly. He never spoke about a family, wife, children, where he was from, nothing. He was like a gray ghost. Like The Great Gatsby, he could have been anyone from anywhere.

He did end up tipping me off about a couple of his deals. I bought early, before they started to run, and made a couple hundred thousand dollars. Then he'd say, "You owe me, you son of a bitch."

So we'd go out and I'd treat him to a $3,000 dinner, with several $500 bottles of wine.

"I like you, Jimmy boy," he'd say. "You're the real deal, a real player."

I would have loved to see his book of business. It became clear to me over time that he had bought people in some high places at mid-level brokerage houses, people in executive positions at firms that could put away a lot of stock.

I encountered Frank at least a hundred times in three years, in all kinds of settings, but mostly restaurants and bars. He picked up the tab almost every time, but I never once saw him use a credit card. At LaGuardia Airport to catch a shuttle flight to Boston one day, Frank and I happened to arrive curbside at the same moment. He reached into his pocket to pay off his driver and pulled out a wad of $100 bills that would choke an elephant. I doubt he even had a bank account or a utility bill in his name.

I finally got a piece of the inside story one boozy night. I was leaving a Times Square theater where I'd just seen a Broadway musical. As I was about to get in Sam's limo, a voice called out, "Would you give a poor bastard a ride?"

It was Frank. He said his car was in the shop.

"Come along, Frank. Where do you want to go?"

"Let's have some drinks," he said.

We stayed up until dawn. As the evening wore on and he got more and more tipsy, he began to open up about how much he made, and how he made it.

"I've done more than three hundred scams," he told me. "I've made more than $1 billion. If I don't pull $5 million on each one, I screwed it up. The worst year I had I only made $75 million because I got lazy and spent a month in the Caribbean.

"If I want to put away a million shares, I can do it with one phone call." Frank owned stockbrokers all over the country, mostly penny stock guys but brokers with big wire houses, too.

"I've never bought a share of common stock in my life," he bragged.

"I've never rented an office or hired brokers. I've never been licensed to do a damn thing but steal!"

Frank Skinner flew so far below the radar that no one in a position to nail him even knew he existed. He was paying so many people off, no one had a good reason to turn him in. He was just too smart and careful.

"Jim, if you're trying to make an easy living, you're sure going around it the hard way."

"Okay. What's the easy way?"

As we bar-hopped our way around town, with interludes in Sam's car, he explained the scam in detail. He had a dozen or so trusted associates around the country who dug up the private companies for the reverse mergers. The finder received 100,000 shares of stock to sell when the scam got running. Frank had stooges who would hold his millions of shares in their accounts for an 8 percent cut of the profits. His name appeared nowhere. Then he had the network of brokers who he courted with New York nightlife, drugs, and women and paid off to hawk the stock.

Each broker received 100,000 shares to unload, and they could keep 10 percent of the shares to sell for themselves. The brokers knew never to put the stock in their own accounts. Instead, they put it in the account of a friend or relative.

Once the deal was teed up, they ran the whole shooting match in two weeks. Volume went from nothing to a couple of hundred thousand shares a day. If the shell had 3,000,000 shares, and he paid his brokers 10 percent, and the finder got another 100,000 shares, Frank had 2,600,000 shares left to sell. His out-of-pocket cost was about $100,000. If he unloaded the shares at an average of $2, then he took in $5.2 million.

He had somebody launder the money, which cost him a few bucks. By the time it was all said and done, he claimed to walk away with at least $5 million per deal.

Frank had nothing but ridicule for the brokers who made him rich. It was from him that I first heard a story all stockbrokers love to tell. Each one has a different version. In Frank's story, he knew a guy from Brooklyn who desperately wanted to be a player. The guy lied to Frank about having lots of customers.

"It turned out the guy had one customer," Frank said. "And he calls him and tells him about the latest piece of used toilet paper we're pimping and gets him to buy 10,000 shares at a buck.

"Next day we've pushed the stock up 50 cents. The clown calls his customer again, gets him to buy another 10,000.

"A few days later, the stock's at $2.50. The prick talks the customer into buying another 30,000 shares. Now the mark is 50,000 shares long. The stock ticks up another quarter and the stupid broker calls him to brag.

"The customer says, 'Okay, sell it all.' "

"And the moron doesn't know whether to shit or go blind. Finally he blurts out, 'Who to?'"

I laughed so hard I almost pissed myself.

"Okay, I understand how you buy the brokers," I said, wiping tears from my eyes. "I understand how you get the fools to buy the stock. But when everybody gets burned time after time, where do the new chumps come from?"

"Are you crazy? Jim, how many people live in New York City?"

"Seven or eight million," I guessed.

"How many people do you think I burn in a deal? Three hundred. There's a sap born every minute, there's another broker for sale, and three hundred more marks sitting out there and so what if they got burned? You know what? There are three hundred more chomping at the bit."

I asked him about the law. Wasn't he worried about getting busted?

"They'll never touch me." He was laughing in the face of the SEC.

As industriously as Frank worked to unload all this worthless stock on the market, he was shocked and dismayed when one of the companies turned out to be the real thing.

An influential private investment partnership had put a ton of money behind a Philippine mining company called Benguet Corp. Benguet started out almost a penny stock but wound up becoming huge, with a stock price to match.

About the same time, purely by coincidence and by no grand objective of his own other than to make his usual $5 to $10 million, Frank found a little copper mining company in South America. He used a guy he'd bought at the American Stock Exchange to get the stock listed so it would look legitimate. Among professionals the Amex had a bad reputation. Any dog company could get listed.

Frank's brokers linked the two companies together in their pitches to customers, and Frank's stock blasted off. He had three million shares. The stock leaped to $10. He sold out, bagging $30 million. He'd made as much as he usually made in five deals!

But wonder of wonders, the stock kept going! It rose to $27 a share. By the time I heard of it, he was furious. His dog crap company turned out to have a major deposit. The banks agreed to lend the money to buy the equipment to dig it out, put up the smelters, and so on.

"Aren't you even a little bit happy for all these poor dopes?" I asked him. "At least you can feel good that you made somebody some money once in a blue moon. And now they'll line up for your next deal."

"Yeah," he growled. "Somebody *actually* made some money. Some sheep-plugger in South Dakota actually made some money buying my shares at $10 and selling at $27. The only thing that happened here, Jim, is I screwed up and left $50 million on the table."

But 99 percent of Frank's deals did not work out that way.

The last I heard of Frank, he'd gotten himself in a bit of trouble with some other, less elegant swindlers.

Frank had boxed the wrong stock. Some mobsters from north Jersey had heard about the company. Knowing it was a bogus deal, they were shorting it at $3. Frank kept his deals tightly controlled, so his brokers were touting the price higher and higher. The mobsters were getting burned, staring at a big loss.

One night Frank got a visit in his hotel room at the Park Lane. The story I heard from someone who swore it was true is that when he answered the door, three goons rushed him. They grabbed his ankles and hung him out the window, thirty floors above the horse-drawn cabs and the sidewalk. While Frank was staring at Central Park South, they persuaded him to pull the plug on the stock in the morning or else.

The most amazing thing about the penny stock swindle is its magnitude and consistency, and the fact that the SEC has only been able to mount a half-hearted effort to shut it down. Arthur Levitt Jr., the SEC chairman who recently retired, came closest to any recent SEC chairman to actually fighting for the small investor. But even he could do little more than wring his hands.

In a town hall discussion in September 2000, Levitt told an audience of individual investors, "When there are so many more people investing, when it becomes so much more easy, the fraudsters come out of the walls. We had a case of someone offering an opportunity to make huge sums of money by investing in an eel farm. In the first place the eel farm didn't exist, and by the time we got to close it down, investors had lost nearly $3 million."

Arthur Levitt seems like a decent man with an honest desire to do the right thing. But I would suggest the SEC throw away the Band-Aids and hire and train some skilled investigators. Only then will the lawmen make a dent. It would be a cinch to strategically plant twenty-five moles in major cities where these scams are concentrated. It's absolutely the easiest thing in the world to infiltrate the business. The promoters are begging people to come work for them. They have recruiters out there looking for bodies. All an investigator has to do is raise his hand.

But I'm not holding my breath that anything will ever be done. Just remember Frank Skinner the next time a broker calls you breathless about some "cheap" stock he's discovered. Ask him how the steaks were at Smith & Wollensky.

10

The Shooter From Dallas

"Wouldn't you love to be in this position,
where you get to make money without taking any risk?"

In the early 1980s the commodities trading I had been doing with Jim Donegan at Kidder Peabody, and our friendship, began to expand. I already had extensive experience trading bond futures. I'd almost lost my shirt and wore myself out trying to save my skin.

When Donegan came to me with a new trading vehicle based on the Standard & Poor's 500 stock index, I was interested but wary. The S&P 500 futures contract allows a trader, for very little margin, to control a basket of all 500 stocks in the index.

I have always loved trading stocks. But the margin requirement is high, 50 percent. Donegan was telling me that now, for only $8,000 in margin, I could control all five hundred stocks. That was attractive, but also presented a greater risk of getting my clock cleaned.

Donegan spent a lot of time convincing me that this was an avenue by which vast fortunes could be made, if you understood the market and understood what a futures contract is all about. I certainly understood the market and the S&P 500 contract was simple. Unlike bonds, the S&P 500 was based on a cash index. The commodity to be delivered was cash, calculated on the basis of the index, the number reported every day in the media.

The S&P 500 index moves point by point. From 200, roughly where the S&P 500 traded back then, the next full point up would be 201. But the futures moved in increments of five. From 200 the futures contract would move to 205. At the time the S&P 500 contract first began to trade, each tick equaled $5. To get the cash value of the S&P 500 futures contract, you multiplied $5 times 500 (number of stocks in the index) times the index itself, 200. In that instance, the cash value of one contract was $500,000.

The low margin requirement gave a trader the incredibly seductive leverage of 63 to 1.

The futures contract traded at a premium to the cash index because, as with all commodities futures, it provided for delivery in the future. Instead of cotton, beans, or bonds, in this case the commodity to be delivered was the cash value.

It had been a tough year, 1984, when the S&P 500 contract first became available. The market had been weak and many pundits were starting to say the bull market that began in August 1982 was all washed up.

I don't remember where I was traveling but I was in an airport about to board a plane when I decided to take the plunge. I called Donegan.

"Jimbo, this market is looking really beat up and washed out," I told him. "I think it's due for a rally. I want to give those S&P contracts a try. Throw fifty cars on there for me." Even though the S&P index isn't delivered in boxcars, traders use the same terminology. My margin requirement was $8,000 times 50, $400,000.

Donegan gasped. "Jim, are you sure you want to do that much for a first trade? That's a big risk. Most of my clients, they're just experimenting with five and ten lots. Are you sure you understand what you're asking me to do?"

He thought I didn't understand the math of the contract and how it worked. He started explaining the numbers, trying to talk me out of it. "That's an awful lot of money to start out."

I listened for a few moments but I knew what my gut was telling me. I understood exactly what I wanted to do. I lost my temper. "Dammit!" I yelled. "I told you to put that on. Now put it on, and don't waste any more of my time. I've got a plane to catch."

"Okay, Jim. No prob."

I boarded my flight without a shred of doubt that I had it right.

The trip included a stopover. I dashed off the plane to call Donegan and see if there'd been any developments. I'd been out of touch for a couple of hours.

"Holy crap, Jim! I've been calling everybody I could think of to make sure you'd call me. The friggin' market took off, just shot straight up. The contract's flying. You're up $800,000!"

"*WHAT!*" I yelled. People at phones all around me turned and glared. "We made how much?"

"Eight hundred thou. What do you want me to do?"

"Do? Take it, for God's sakes! Close it out and take the thing! What are you waiting for?"

That hooked me. I began trading S&P 500 contracts almost every day. On balance I made good money at it. I've always had a good feel for the tone of any market I'm actively trading. In the stock market there are certain bellwether issues I'll watch, depending on what's hot. From them I can often pick up hints of a hidden developing trend. When the bellwethers act contrary to the overall market, my ears prick up. I begin to hear the sound of money falling into my wallet.

One of my biggest profitable trades began with just such an observation. This time my plunging had Donegan's whole office in an uproar. I had been reading the tape closely when the market began to rally. I could tell it was false. The S&P 500 futures contract went limit up, and locked there. Buying built up behind it.

Many investors don't realize that in the S&P 500 only 20 percent or so of the 500 companies are considered technology stocks. But technology within the index has a weighting of 40 to 45 percent. That's because many of these technology companies are huge, but their size isn't reflected in the index. If the market is locked limit up, but IBM and four other bellwether technology stocks are acting weak or look like they're going to break, the rest of the market can't possibly hold up.

I had been watching the market and could see it was trying to swim upstream in much the same way it did when the dot-coms were flaming out in 2000. In this case, when the S&P 500 locked limit up, I was sure it was going to crack.

Nobody I know sells short into a market that's locked limit up. Nobody, that is, except me. It's dangerous. You've got to be right, or you've got to buy calls to hedge your bet. But I didn't need protection. The market was screaming at me to short it.

I called Donegan and told him to sell twenty contracts.

"Jim," he cautioned. "All our clients are buying, and buying like crazy. Nobody's selling into this limit up! It's stuck there, and the pressure is building. Are you sure?"

"Don't you worry about me," I told him. "I've done my due diligence. Sell right into it."

I had a lot of cash in my account, and I added another twenty contracts, and then another twenty. I could tell from the growing worry in Donegan's voice that he thought I might be making a terrible mistake. It was a gutsy trade, but some of my best trades have been gutsy.

The contract just sat there locked limit for about forty-five minutes. Every fifteen minutes or so I sold another twenty contracts. If the market didn't crack, stayed limit up and opened locked limit up again the next day, I'd be staring at a whopping loss of $1 million or more.

Donegan told me later that as my orders were being processed, the Kidder Peabody trading desk in New York noticed the unusual activity. Someone from the head office called his office manager to find out who the idiot was who was selling into limit up. Did I know something, or was I just suicidal?

Donegan's manager came running out of his office, yelling at him, "What the hell are you doing? You're selling in to limit up! Are you nuts? What is this man doing?"

Donegan explained that he had a good client who he knew was a good trader. "He's got the money, and I'm just taking the orders."

Within an hour I was short eighty contracts, representing some $40 million of cash value! And the S&P 500 contract hung in there locked at the high.

Finally, after another hour or so, the index began to show signs of fatigue. Buyers began to pull back their bids. The market came off limit, went back up, and then it broke hard and fast, a violent 3 percent plunge. My profit: $1 million.

How did I know? I'd watched the market run up despite lackluster corporate earnings. Big companies were missing their profit numbers. I looked at the overbought stocks and the oversold stocks. I looked at charts and moving averages. I saw patterns, and all these elements were saying the same thing to me, that the futures contract did not belong where it was. The money was just lying there waiting for me to come along and pick it up. I was happy to oblige.

You may wonder why the New York trading desk of Donegan's firm called his boss to find out why I was selling into an S&P rally. I can assure you they were not concerned about my welfare. They were protecting themselves. Did I have some information that they could use to their advantage? Was I the president's doctor and maybe knew he had cancer? Did I know that IBM was about to announce a huge earnings shortfall, or did I have a cousin on the Federal Reserve Board who had given me a tip on an interest rate increase?

The trading desk of every Wall Street firm is where the rubber meets the road. That is the biggest profit center in each firm, and the way a lot of that money is made is an absolute swindle. You don't have to take my word for it, though. The SEC commissioned a major study that found the same thing. Only they didn't use the word swindle.

In order to understand how it works, you need to understand how stock prices are determined. This is a little tedious, but essential to the rest of the story. Bear with me.

Unlike stockbrokers, traders don't earn commissions. Their money is made working the spread, the difference between the bid and ask prices. All day long at hundreds of trading desks all over the world, stocks are being sought and offered. All stocks, all stock options, commodities, and financial derivatives are quoted on this basis. There is a bid price, which is the price that some trader somewhere has said he is willing to pay for the stock. The ask price is the price at which someone somewhere is willing to sell the stock. These bids and asks are displayed on computer monitors, along with a "last" price, which is the price at which the last trade actually took place. When you go online to check a stock quote, that's what you see: bid, ask, and last.

You've seen, on television, pictures of the New York Stock Exchange floor. Each Big Board stock is assigned to a post where a person called a specialist makes a market in certain stocks. A floor broker can walk up to any post and ask the specialist to buy or sell a stock at a specific price. The NYSE system, two hundred years old, matches buyers and sellers. The specialists make their money by going long or short and profiting like anyone else from fluctuations in prices. They maintain an inventory of stock and broker transactions.

The New York Stock Exchange is the most honest and fair market, and the specialists, many of whom I've met over the years, are some of the smartest people I've ever known.

That's the good news.

The Nasdaq and other markets, on the other hand, are invisible. At trading desks within brokerage firms, the transactions are done primarily on the phone between traders or electronically. There may be as many as forty market makers in a particular stock, and each one posts its own bid and ask on a computer network. Anyone who has stock to sell looks for the high bid. Anyone who wants to buy looks for the low ask, also called the offered price. There may be one firm with the highest bid, or there may be ten. The same thing applies to traders in bonds, stock options, all commodities, and currencies.

All these trading desks at all these firms serve one purpose: to make money for the firm. And you pay the price.

In the SEC study released at the end of 2000, economists proved what every trader and every brokerage firm has known forever: Nasdaq investors consistently get the shaft.

Here's how this swindle works.

Let's say you call your broker and tell him you're thinking about buying WorldCom. He types the symbol into his computer and pulls up a market quote of 36 bid and $36^{1/4}$ offered. The broker quotes you the highest bid and lowest offered prices that all the market makers are showing. The market makers may also show the size, meaning the number of shares sought or offered by each firm's trading desk.

If a firm has lots of capital, it can make a market in almost any Nasdaq stock. Big firms make markets in large stocks. A second tier of market makers, smaller firms, deal in smaller stocks, and sometimes even bulletin board issues like the penny stocks.

Let's say you want to buy 1,000 shares of WorldCom. Your broker quotes you the price, and, in a perfect world, your broker's firm would make a market in WorldCom. If your broker's firm happened to have a customer who wanted to sell 1,000 shares at 36, or even $36^{1/8}$, the trading desk would buy the stock for you, you'd be happy, your broker and his firm would have made a commission, and the trading desk would have performed a service for you.

If you happen to run a major mutual fund such as Fidelity Magellan, or one of the Janus funds, that is exactly what happens.

But God help you if you are a regular investor. If the market shows 36 bid, $36^{1/4}$ offered, let's say you place your order to buy 1,000 shares. You tell your firm to buy the stock for you at the best price it can.

At the very same time someone else gives their broker, at the same firm, an order to sell 1000 shares. The seller tells the firm to get the best price they can for their stock. Both orders land on the desk of the person in charge of trading WorldCom.

What happens? You will pay $36^{1/4}$ to buy, and the other customer will receive 36 to sell. Where did the $250 difference go? With no risk, it went into the pocket of the firm. Nobody told you, you couldn't see it, but you were swindled. And, on top of it all, you still paid the broker's commission.

The trader making a market in WorldCom at your brokerage firm sees every order that comes from his firm's entire system. No other trader ever saw the orders, even though forty firms are making a market in the stock. So, instead of having a real chance to buy the stock at 36 by competing in the open market, your firm's trading desk executed the order in-house. They matched you with one of their own sellers knowing they could keep the "spread," the difference between the bid and ask.

That's the most common swindle.

Now, let's say your firm doesn't have an in-house seller. This time the trader reports that he has sold the stock to you at $36^{1/4}$, immediately raises his bid to $36^{1/16}$, which becomes the high bid in the market and is immediately filled. Now he has stock at $36^{1/16}$ that he has already sold to you at $36^{1/4}$. He just made the firm $187.

Traders see what you will never see: order flow. A Merrill trader not only sees every order in his firm's worldwide system of customers, he sees the other traders' bids and offers to him. He may have just been offered a large block of stock by Goldman Sachs at $36^{1/8}$. He knows there is a 90 percent chance he can buy the stock at $36^{1/16}$, the same stock that he just sold you at $36^{1/4}$.

The trading desk is not there to service you, but to make money for itself. That's it.

When you hit the trading desks at second-tier firms, it gets as ugly as a mud fence. You're now dealing in stocks that are thinly traded and have wide spreads between the bid and ask. If you are trading a penny stock, you cannot force your order to be shown. The market for a stock may be 50 cents bid and 75 cents offered. You give your broker an order to buy 10,000 shares at 60 cents, but the market maker leaves his bid at 50 cents. He doesn't show the rest of the market makers that he has a buyer at 60 cents. He is waiting for a seller to come to him at less than 60 cents. He might hold that order all day, waiting. The moment someone comes in with a better price, he buys it for the firm, then instantly flips it to you at 60 cents. No risk, all reward to his firm, and there is nothing you can do about it.

Trading desks make enormous sums on such thinly traded stocks, as much as a 35 percent profit on your trade, and you never knew it.

I once put in a bid to buy 50,000 shares of a stock at $2, when it showed a bid price of $1.75. The reason I put my order in that way, above the bid, is because it was a large order and I was anxious to get the stock right away. Ordinarily I'd never do that.

The trader refused to show my order. If he had done what he was supposed to, someone would have seen my $2 bid and sold me the stock. Instead, the trader sat there waiting for the stock to come to him at a lower price so he could buy it and sell it to me for $2. I got so angry I threatened to go to the SEC and Nasdaq. The trader told my broker, "Tell him he can go straight to hell. I don't have to show any order I don't want to."

Sure enough, the SEC and Nasdaq told me there was nothing they could do.

Wouldn't you love to be in this position, where you get to make money without taking any risk? Just wait for a seller or buyer, with an order in your hand that no one knows exists.

There are times when traders will actually buy or sell stock short, taking the same risk as their customers. It's rare, but sometimes a large firm may bid slightly above the market because they feel the stock is due for a pop. The trader may buy WorldCom at 36, even though the current bid is $35^{3/4}$. If he's right and the stock goes up, he sells and makes the firm a profit. If he's wrong, he sells his position to you at a quarter point loss. But this hardly ever happens because traders prefer guaranteed profits. Wouldn't you?

I know how it's supposed to work because I've been swindled so many times, buying and selling large blocks of stock, both individually and as part of a small investment group.

The system is stacked against individuals to the benefit of large traders and institutions. Let's say you as an individual trader give an order to your broker, online or otherwise, in a thinly traded stock to sell 50,000 shares at $3 a share. In a thin stock, that's a lot of selling pressure and could cause the price to fall. Your broker gives the order to his trading desk, and since they don't make a market in the stock, they send the order on to a smaller firm that does.

This smaller market maker receives the offer to sell at $3. But first he calls his big customer, an institution like a mutual fund or a hedge fund, and says, "I've got a big block of a stock you own coming on the market. Do you want to sell some of your stock ahead of it?"

They will probably say yes, because they don't want the value of their stock to plunge because of your selling. So, the market maker drops his offer down to $2.95 and sells somebody else's stock ahead of yours. This means the price you will get is less. You've been cheated.

The payoff to the market maker this time is not a trading profit for his firm. But the institution that he tipped off pays his firm big commissions. You never will. The market maker has scratched the back of one of his customers to keep the customer happy and earn a favor down the road.

This is common and it's immoral and illegal. If the SEC could catch people doing it, many firms and their traders would be closed down and sent to prison.

In case you've been lulled by small-sounding numbers like eighths and quarters, let me put the question in vivid context. If the average extra cost to investors of these antics only averages an eighth, or 12.5 cents a share, multiply that times share volume, which is at least a billion shares a day. At least $125 million every trading day, or about $30 billion a year, comes out of our pockets and into the pockets of the brokerage firms who reward their traders for this behavior with fat bonuses.

Here's a side to this swindle that's even more outrageous and less known. Every morning, mutual fund and pension fund managers call up trading desks and tell them what stocks they want to buy and sell that day. These are often big blocks that can affect the price of the stock.

The traders turn around and shop these trades, a process called dialing for dollars: "I've got 50,000 Microsoft for sale at $59^{1/2}$."

If he's having a good day, the trader finds a trader at another firm with an order to buy 50,000 Microsoft at that price or close enough so they can both cheat their customers out of some money. They make a match, the traders carve off their pieces, the customer never knows, everybody's happy.

But what happens if he calls another trader and that guy also has 50,000 Microsoft to unload? First of all, trader number two keeps his trap shut. He now knows there are two orders out there to sell a block of the stock. It might be a good time to buy some put options on Microsoft or sell the stock short.

The moment trader number one hangs up, trader two may do just that for his firm, sell the stock short. He may also call his drinking buddy at an aggressive investment partnership—they call them hedge funds—and let him know there is a lot of Microsoft for sale, "overhanging" the stock.

The reason he calls the hedge fund is not for the great jokes their trader tells at Harry's Bar after the market closes. It's because the hedge fund pays him a higher commission, about ten cents a share. Institutional investors such as mutual funds pay between two and five cents.

The hedge fund is paying more than double in order to "buy a look" at the brokerage firm's order flow. He's buying a phone call in which the trader at the brokerage house pretends he's not giving out inside information as he coyly mentions the names of stocks that he has blocks to buy or sell. "I wouldn't be short General Motors today," he'll say.

By knowing what orders are in the pipeline, a hedge fund trader can make a quick profit effortlessly, front-running the market.

You can be rest assured, in any case, that trader number two will do something to take advantage of the information.

One final example of the way trading desks cheat investors is on initial public offerings. Hedge funds often get the first and largest crack at buying shares of an IPO before the stock begins to trade in the open market. The reason: the hedge fund agrees to split any profits from a quick one or two-day surge with the brokerage house's trading desk. This is illegal. If the SEC caught them at it, they'd be gone from the business forever. But the brokerage firms know how to paper these trades over with legitimate order tickets. It's a common swindle.

Big, respectable brokerage houses deny all day long that they do this, even as they do it. They even deny doing business with hedge funds. But I have this right from the horse's mouth. It's gospel.

Rarely, but every once in a while, the SEC manages to catch a major firm with its hand in the cookie jar. In 1986 an insurance industry analyst at First Boston got a phone call from Cigna Corporation telling him the insurance company was about to announce a huge write-off. The analyst told his boss, his boss told the trading desk, and the trading desk jumped on it like a fly on fresh manure. They shorted Cigna shares and bought puts, based on this inside information that wasn't available to the rest of Cigna's shareholders.

But then the civic-minded traders went on to use the information to scratch the backs of major customers. Michael Steinhardt, senior partner of one of the most aggressive hedge funds at the time, dumped a block of Cigna shares the same day, bragging that he had some "fancy information" about the Cigna write-off.

First Boston paid fines of about $400,000 to make this bad news go away and promised to fire any employees who talked about it to the press.

As I've said, the only honest market in the United States is the New York Stock Exchange.

The most shocking thing about the way trading desks operate is that even though the authorities know about it, have complained and even done something about it, the investing public doesn't seem to understand or care very much.

In 1994 the SEC and the U.S. Justice Department charged that major market makers had been fixing prices to cheat investors out of billions, taking advantage of big spreads. Two years later the SEC, under Chairman Levitt, made it official. It accused the National Association of Securities Dealers, the organization that owns the Nasdaq, with manipulating prices. So much money was at stake that the entire industry came down on Arthur Levitt, trying to discredit and intimidate him. They said the SEC made this stuff up.

But in the end, the SEC stood fast. The Nasdaq member firms knew better than to try to stand and fight a case like that. They paid more than $1 billion in fines to settle.

The SEC also went after the American Stock Exchange and even flushed out a little shady business at the Big Board.

Nasdaq was restructured, some new trading rules were adopted, and spreads on trades narrowed slightly, putting a little money back into investors' pockets.

But none of this stopped the practice. Even if the SEC could stop it, trading desks are always finding new ways to skin customers. The whole brokerage business is like a balloon. Squeeze the air out of one place and it rushes into another. As long as there's money around, Wall Street will chase it.

With the explosion of online trading, the SEC took a look at what effect that phenomenon was having on Nasdaq prices. You shouldn't be shocked to learn that, although orders were filled faster, the prices investors paid or received was worse by as much as 50 cents a share. Since most Nasdaq stocks trade for under $20, that's a big cut for the trading desks.

The Nasdaq folks have been trying to improve their image, pointing out that bid and ask spreads have narrowed. But the practice of front-running and holding orders and tipping off buddies and big customers hasn't changed. Any improvement is a smoke screen behind which the swindle marches on.

Having said all that, there are times when trading desks simply screw up. Some very large firms and funds have blown themselves to smithereens by being on the wrong side of a big market move.

And then there's the story of CRS. One of my favorite traders worked at Bache Securities before it was bought by Prudential. Traders sometimes make markets in many stocks at the same time and they can get confused. But a confused trader usually doesn't last long.

There was a trader on the desk at Bache who could have been Moses' brother, he was so old. He must have been someone's relative, or had been at the firm a long time and they didn't have the heart to put him to pasture.

My friend told me it was not uncommon for this poor guy, whom they called CRS, to totally blow an order. He'd get an order for 10,000 shares and end up buying 100,000. The firm would then have to scramble to sell the unauthorized 90,000 shares. They joked about him around the trading floor when they had his leftover stock to unload: "We've got a CRS for 90,000 shares of Microsoft!"

During the time I actively traded May Petroleum, I called Bache one day and old CRS himself answered the phone. I had never talked to the guy before and I gave him my name. He shouted, loud enough for a hundred traders on the floor to hear him, "It's the Shooter from Dallas on line 14." That was my nickname in those days, the Shooter from Dallas.

Instantly five traders were on the line at once, talking over each other. My friend was one of them, and his voice was full of panic.

"Did you give him an order?"

"No," I said. "What's the big deal?"

"Jesus Christ. Thank God! Don't *ever* give CRS an order for any-thing. Anything! We are constantly having to clean up after this guy." He explained the problem.

I laughed. "All right, I never will. Promise. But tell me something, why the heck do you call him CRS?"

My friend chuckled. "Can't Remember Shit."

11

Showdown

"Gerry, there's something ugly going on down here."

Although front-running is common, it almost never happens that a trader like myself catches the bastards in the act. I did once, and the blowup that followed still gets my juices flowing anytime I think about it.

In 1983 I bought stock in Dallas Federal, an old franchise savings and loan company that had been well run and solid until sky-high interest rates murdered it in the early 1980s. The company got caught with a big portfolio of fixed-rate thirty-year home loans. To stay afloat, Dallas Federal decided to go public, sell some stock, and raise money to restructure its portfolio. Many of the people who were investing in the company were also involved in other banking companies in the Dallas area. It looked like a good deal.

Through Gerry Guillemaud, my Merrill Lynch broker, I bought 4 percent of Dallas Federal at $12.75 in its initial public offering.

Merrill was one of the three big firms underwriting the Dallas Federal public offering. When a Wall Street firm agrees to take a company public in an initial public offering (IPO), it reserves the right to buy an additional block of stock from the company. This stock is called an over-allotment, and the price is set at the same price the initial investors pay, in this case $12.75 a share.

For a brokerage firm, this is a sweet deal. If the stock rises when it begins to trade, as did the price of many IPOs during the 1998 to 2000 market bubble, the firm gets to exercise that option. Let's say an IPO is priced at $10, but when trading actually begins, the price pops to $12. The firm can then say, all right, we'll exercise the right to buy the over-allotment shares at $10, and then sell them into the market at the higher price and keep the profit.

Underwriting firms can also make money on an IPO by selling short when a stock pops. Let's say the stock jumps to $12, the underwriting firm can sell the stock short, and, if it comes back down, as many IPOs often do, cover the short sale and make a profit that way.

There is a practical reason for some of this. It doesn't look good for an underwriting house to take a company public and have the stock jump 40 percent on the first day. The company that is trying to raise the money, like a Dallas Federal, looks at that kind of action and says, "Hey, we left a lot of dough on the table. We could have raised more money, sold more shares."

The investing public doesn't like it, either. You know what I mean if you've ever gotten yourself caught buying a hot IPO at the peak, and watching it crash and lie there.

So, if the underwriter has an over-allotment option to sell into a soaring market for a new stock, that can help damp the rise, keep the price from becoming too volatile, and put a few more bucks into the IPO company.

Selling short has the same effect of checking volatility. And, if the stock falls sharply, the underwriter's trading desk can come in and bid for stock to cover their short position and support the market.

All these opportunities for a brokerage firm to profit on an IPO, by the way, are over and above the banking fees and other commissions and charges that the firm has already billed the going-public company. IPOs are a sensational profit center, and a really hot issue is a gift from heaven, millions in profits and 90 percent of the time at no risk. It's free money and it's legal.

The firms underwriting an IPO are known collectively as the syndicate. The over-allotment option usually lasts for thirty days or so after the stock starts to trade. When all the shares have been sold, the syndicate firms are required to announce that the deal is closed. That's called an all-sold. It is illegal for an underwriter to put out an all-sold and then sell more stock that they've had hidden in the closet.

About three weeks after I bought my 4 percent of Dallas Federal, the all-sold was put out. I got an idea that I wanted to own more of the stock. I thought it might be a good takeover candidate. I let it be known to a number of brokers I did business with that if the opportunity came along, I would consider buying a block of stock that would take me into a solid 13-D position. I said I'd like the courtesy of a telephone call if a block came on the market.

One day, during a visit in my Dallas office from a fellow investor, my mentor, Mel Marks, phoned to say he'd found a big block of the stock, about 500,000 shares. He told me who had it and where to go get it. It was a lot of stock, enough to take me up to 8 percent ownership of Dallas Federal.

I could have given an order for this block to any firm. I deliberately didn't give it to Merrill Lynch because of all the front-running their trading desk had been doing to me. They already knew I had 4 percent because I bought it through them. If I put an order in for another big block, I was sure they'd take advantage of me.

Instead I called another broker, Scott Otey, at Prudential Bache, and asked him to call his head trader to make a discreet bid.

The next thing that happened was one of those quirks of fate. At the time I was trading tens of thousands of shares a day with different firms, getting calls from all over the place all day long—order confirmations, price information, and so on—and didn't even bother most of the time with phone receivers. I just used the speaker-phone.

No sooner did I give the order for the block of Dallas Federal than one of my hot lines rang. It was Bob Tomlin, the head trader at Merrill Lynch, who worked beside Hugh Quigley, the guy who ran Merrill's entire trading floor.

Like an idiot, I blurted, "Bob, you can't believe what's going down right now!"

"What do you mean?"

"I'm buying a block of Dallas Federal that's gonna kick me up to 8 percent," I bragged. "When it comes through, I may want to press the thing further, later today." I meant that I might have wanted to buy some more stock later through Merrill Lynch.

His response would normally have been, "Great!" Instead, he asked, "Jim, where the hell are you finding a block of Dallas Federal?"

I gave him the name.

"Jim, I gotta go," he barked, and hung up.

I didn't think anything about it. I was busy and distracted by my visitor.

A few minutes later, I saw on the broadtape a report of a big block trade of Dallas Federal, more than 300,000 shares. Then another block crossed, the balance of the position I'd been told was available. I figured I had the stock.

Then the phone rang. It was Scott, the Prudential-Bache broker I'd given the order to.

"What the f'ing hell is goin' on, Jim?" he spluttered. "What's the deal? I thought you gave *me* that order for Dallas Federal." On and on, lots of profanity, and no chance to get a word in edgewise.

"Whoa, Scott. Whoa, slow down, buddy!" I shouted.

He took a breath and explained that the first trade I saw had not come out of his trading desk, which meant I didn't get most of the stock.

"Who got it, then?" My temperature started to rise.

"Merrill Lynch," he said.

"Holy ——! Those bastards!" Tomlin and Quigley had front-run me! Only this time I'd caught them with the blood still wet on their hands. A wild rage blew up inside my head. When I told Scott what happened, he went ballistic, screaming that he was going to kill somebody over there. My friend cringed and my two secretaries, who could hear every word, gasped.

I hung up and called Gerry Guillemaud, my Merrill broker in Dallas.

"Gerry, there's something ugly going on down here." I explained the situation, adding, "I didn't give you the order because I've been concerned about this front-running. Well, I feel like somebody has front-run me here, and I feel like that somebody is Hugh Quigley. And if it is, I'm telling you right now I'm going to have his butt!"

A few frenzied phone calls later, Gerry reported that the trading desk in New York admitted jumping out in front of me and snatching that stock away. The next call was from Quigley's sidekick, Tomlin, the guy who spilled the beans. I smashed the button.

"Jim, man, I am just so sorry," Tomlin blurted. "This is a real mess. The block you were trying to buy was not supposed to exist. All three firms in the syndicate put out an all-sold.

"But it turns out Shearson still had stock. I guess they couldn't sell it and didn't want the market to get wind of it. So they put out an all-sold.

"Anyway, it turns out we were short a big block of Dallas Federal. So, we covered our short. I'm really sorry, Jim."

I wanted to break something, shatter a window.

"Sorry ain't gonna cut it, Bobby!" I shouted. "You're gonna make this trade good or else." I wasn't sure what the "or else" was, but I'd think of something.

Tomlin said, "Jesus, Jim. We can't do that. There's no way we can go back and bust that trade. It was a syndicate trade. It'd cause a—"

"I'll tell you what," I said, standing and picking up the receiver so I could talk directly into his ear. "I'll see you face-to-face tomorrow morning. Because I'm gonna charter a damn jet. The next telephone call I'm going to make is to your CEO, Bill Schreyer."

I slammed the phone down.

I next dialed Schreyer, and I guess I scared the hell out of his secretary because she put me right through.

As calmly and politely as I could, I explained the problem and said I wanted a meeting the next day.

"Come on up," he said. He was always such a gentleman. "I'm sure we can work this out."

I called Gerry and he agreed to go with me. He was mad as hell, too. He had a lot at stake.

This was right around Christmas and there was a bad ice storm at the Dallas/Fort Worth Airport. We barely got clearance to take off. Sam met us in the car at LaGuardia. We went straight to Schreyer's office at Merrill Lynch's headquarters across from the World Trade Center.

Quigley was there, and Tomlin. Quigley was scowling and Tomlin had a look on his face like he'd just swallowed a bad oyster. I put on my southern charm and tried to be courteous, exchanging pleasantries with Schreyer.

"Jim," he finally began, "I'm awfully sorry but I'm sure we can work this out."

"I just want to tell you something, Bill," I said. "I've got all of this nailed flat. I've got two secretaries plus an independent third party who heard this whole transaction go down. Plus I've got the broker at Prudential Bache. If I have to bring every single one of them in, plus the SOB who had stock to sell *after* an all-sold, an SEC violation, that's what I'm going to do. This is a gentleman's deal. I asked for this meeting simply to protect you because you're a nice guy and the firm's been good to me.

"But you're gonna make this trade good. And you're gonna pay for my expenses coming up here. And this is never going to happen again."

Quigley, the big old bear, jumped to his feet. "I'm not gonna take an ounce of shit off of you!" he shouted, jabbing a finger at me. "You can say whatever you want. You can put the guy who sold the block in jail, if you want to. But you opened your damn mouth to the wrong trader, and it's my obligation to protect the syndicate's short. That's my job and you can go to hell if you don't like it, and you can take your f'ing business somewhere else."

It got real frisky. I was livid. I threatened to go to the press and the SEC. Dallas Federal had jumped two or three points, which in effect cost me almost a million dollars. But it was more than money. I was giving Merrill Lynch more than a million dollars of commission business a year. And here they were, front running me with wild abandon. They were using inside information from me to cover their short and save them from a loss.

Schreyer did his best to get us all to calm down. Then we separated into different rooms. Before long he was running back and forth trying to negotiate some sort of settlement, suggesting ways to make it up to me.

"Jim, we'll cut you some slack around here. We'll get you in on some hot IPOs. We will make this up to you in some way."

They just didn't want to put anything on the record. They didn't want to do or say anything that would prove what they'd done.

"You will not make this up to me," I said. I was determined to have it my way. "You will make the trade good, or if you don't make the trade good, you can forget another dollar of my business for the rest of my life."

And that's the way it ended up.

I slammed shut my Merrill Lynch accounts, both commodities and stocks. I took it to my lawyers but I didn't sue. The brokerage business doesn't need a thick skin to survive because its got one made of Teflon. If you want to continue to play the game and be treated well, you have to take the bad with the good.

To be tagged a contentious customer would have hurt me more than any benefit I'd have gotten from a lawsuit. As furious as I was at Quigley, it was stupid of me to open my mouth to Tomlin and name the seller. I should have done the trade and then bragged.

Ten other brokerage firms were kissing my behind twenty-four hours a day, guys who would move heaven and hell to get and keep my business. So, that was the end of Merrill Lynch.

No one can say for sure, but if Merrill had made that trade up to me, maybe I would have continued to do a million a year in commissions for them. But, for the sake of saving Hugh Quigley's trading room a few hundred thousand dollars, Merrill Lynch hasn't seen a nickel from me in two decades.

12

Hear No Evil

*"More than life itself, brokers love traders who react to rumors
and recommendations. Brokers will whisper every scrap of gossip
they can pick up, or make up."*

It broke my heart to hurt Gerry Guillemaud. Closing my accounts at
Merrill cost him hundreds of thousands a year. Gerry was so angry at
his firm that he quit. I invited him to my home in Dallas one day to
commiserate and let him know that wherever he ended up, I would give
him as much of my business as I could.

It also broke my heart to lose one of the best stockbrokers I'd ever
had, one who had paid $100,000 out of his own pocket to make up for
that mistake he'd made on the gold trade. When you find great brokers,
you come to trust them with your life. They've got a big chunk of your
assets and often know more about you than your own family. Relationships like that take years to develop.

In my career I have heard every pitch and story in the book. What
I've learned over nearly forty years of investing is that very few brokers
can pick winning stocks. Some can get you great executions on your
trades, at the best prices. Most, however, just take orders and try to sell
their research ideas to you. Nine out of ten haven't a clue beyond that.
They are mainly interested in bagging the next trade for the next commission.

When brokers aren't trying to bag you, they love to bag each other.

Most institutional brokers have offices near the trading desks, maybe in the next room, but always with access to the public address system in the firm. The trading desks, almost without exception, are in New York. Each day the firms continuously broadcast news and updates on trading activity, research analysts' latest opinions, orders to buy and sell blocks of stock, and so on.

Whenever I gave my Jefferies broker an order to buy 100,000 shares of a stock, for instance, he went on the firm's public address system, which reached every other broker in his firm. He'd ask if someone might have the other side of the trade, the sell side. The rest of the market will never see the trade if it can be completed, or crossed, in house. The firm fills both orders and earns the commission on both trades.

It's very difficult for an ordinary investor to get away with manipulating a stock price. But a few people do and, thanks to the Internet, quite a few did during the recent technology frenzy. Even a pimple-faced high school kid did it. The stock may shoot up or down by a wide margin in minutes. But the press finds out right away that there is a hoax and the SEC, FBI, and Nasdaq catch the perpetrator in a few days.

What you don't hear about are all the times brokers scam each other. If a firm gets stuck on the wrong side of a trade, is short a ton of a stock that's running up, and they need to move it down fast, over the squawk box comes the bad news.

"I hear XYZ is going to miss their number big on earnings and revenue."

This is not an analyst, not a preannouncement from the company. Just a dumb broker saying, "I hear . . . ."

The other brokers in the office start jabbering to each other, their customers, and even brokers they know at other firms, drinking pals or old college classmates. This swindle is often done on the eve of a quarterly earnings announcement, during a period when companies legally are not allowed to discuss their financial results until they are distributed to the public. So, they can't even fight the rumor. It's like punching a guy who's got his hands tied behind his back.

When your broker calls you with such a story, take it with a grain of salt. You'd be amazed how often brokers spread rumors. Rumors will get your pocket picked almost as quick as a penny stock. Think about how dumb the idea is to begin with. A broker can be disbarred for life for giving out inside information. Would you risk losing $500,000 a year?

A broker who discloses to you what another customer is buying gets fired on the spot. How would your broker know someone else was going to file a 13-D? Since when would the CEO of Merck tell a stockbroker nonpublic information? Buying on rumors is a game for hardened, risk-taking professionals and other fools.

During the recent market bubble, there were a lot of story stocks. Brokers will push a stock without earnings, telling you, "it's a story stock." I'm not talking about a company that had a bad quarter or even a bad year. I mean companies that have never had earnings, like the latest biotech, Internet, or other technology stock.

If you can't resist playing the game in this kind of trade, buy quick and sell fast, within an hour or two.

Thousands of times a day brokers give each other recommendations and pass on rumors. You would be shocked to know how many times a broker calls his clients with a buy recommendation that came from a broker at another firm. He or she will tell you they are hearing that something good, or bad, is about to happen to a stock.

More than life itself, brokers love traders who react to these kinds of rumors and recommendations. If you actively trade stocks, brokers will whisper every scrap of gossip they can pick up, or make up. They will fight to keep your business until the day you die. For this reason, brokers don't care much for each other.

And they all hate the compliance department, which handles complaints and makes sure the brokers are obeying the law. Nothing ruins the day of a broker like getting a call from the compliance department, or the margin department. The worst days are when the market's crashing and they have to call customers up with the bad news that they've gotten a margin call. The broker talked you into buying the stock, it's crumbled, and now he has to beg you for more cash, or the firm will be forced to liquidate your position at a loss.

Stockbrokers are a colorful bunch. It's part of their job to entertain and woo new customers and keep the customers they have from being stolen. They are trained not to tolerate the word "no."

If you rarely trade and pay between $1,000 and $5,000 a year in commissions, you can expect a Christmas card. If you spend $20,000 a year, you will get a call once every two weeks. If you spend $100,000 a year, expect dinner and drinks once a month. If you spend $500,000 and up, out come the limousines and the front-row tickets.

Good brokers work long hours and work hard to get your orders filled at the best possible price. Kevin Dann, my Jefferies broker, once got me twenty-five trades in a row *below* the bid price. If your broker is actually working for you, he or she will do this often. He will tell you whether he can get you a better price than the market is showing. If he or she encourages you to pay the offer side on a buy, you have the wrong broker. This person only wants to trigger a trade and book a commission.

It saddens me to see how much money investors throw away. If you trade a total of 100,000 shares in one year, a good broker can save you $25,000. You should care about your *net* price, after commissions, and nothing else.

Slick advertising campaigns persuade investors that they're getting a better deal with a discount broker. If the discount broker charges you a low commission for a fixed price order, that's true. A fixed price order must be filled at a price no worse than the one you specify when you place it.

But if you buy at the market—an open order to be filled at the "best" price the firm can get—you will have paid more than you would at a full-service firm. The price will be the best one for the brokerage firm, but not for you.

If the bid is $20, and you got your stock at $19.87 net to you, you've gotten a great execution. If the bid is 20 and you bought at $20^{1/4}$, and paid an $8 commission, you've been hosed.

Never give a broker discretion to trade in your account unless you trust him with your life. A discretionary account gives a broker the power to churn and burn your assets.

Do not nag your broker. You will be treated better if you call only when you really need something. If you call with an order and are told your broker is busy, tell the person who answered the phone, "I have an order pending, and I need to speak to him now."

Your broker will be on the line in ten seconds.

Your relationship with your broker is not a personality contest. If I have to choose between an arrogant jerk who is a superb broker and a really pleasant guy or gal who can't get me a proper fill on my orders, I will choose the jerk. I have met brokers who were sweet as hell and so dumb it scared me to think people actually gave them their money.

A good candidate to become your broker is one who has been at the same firm for several years, who comes highly recommended by someone you trust, and has had some success in the market. If a broker is just starting out, know what you're getting. I'm not opposed to new brokers. Everyone deserves a chance. Just be sure to make your own investment decisions.

Always remember that stockbrokers are salespeople, and rarely come with the financial expertise to make money for you. After all, if your broker could make big money trading stocks, why would he or she put up with being harassed or even abused verbally by five hundred people, five days a week?

Investors get emotional when they lose money. They naturally turn their wrath on the broker who recommended the stock with the nice story about why it was sure to go up. When the stock drops, the broker will blame the analyst, the market, and the management of the company. No one would go through this torture to help his fellow man make a dollar. They do it because they cannot pick stocks correctly. You pay the price whether your broker is honest or a thief, a genius or an idiot.

All major Wall Street firms take their brokers on vacation retreats from time to time. I was vacationing in Maui one year and was invited to attend one of the functions being given by a large firm. This particular outing would have put a Vince Lombardi pep talk to shame. Motivation was the name of the game. I wanted to rush out and buy some stocks, it sounded so good. And this was in the middle of a bear market!

Here are a few facts to warm your heart. Big firms will not allow their brokers to buy a stock and hold it for less than thirty days. The firm will fire them on the spot if they buy a stock in front of you. They will fire them if they take a customer order and call someone else to get them to buy on the advance knowledge of your order. The firm will restrict them from buying in front of the release of nonpublic information.

If you like a particular company and want to verify your own research, you can use a broker for his firm's research department without paying a penny. If you decide to buy, always give the broker a priced order, unless you think the stock is about to take off. All great stock pickers do their own research first.

Brokers are the bottom of the Wall Street pecking order. They are there solely for the purpose of distributing the firm's products and services, their IPOs, debt offerings, and a hundred other investment vehicles. The trading desks need the order flow, the bankers need the power to raise the money. Brokers need you to keep their firm alive, and they need your money to keep moving through the system, leaving pieces of it all along the way.

My biggest mistakes, the ones that cost me millions, resulted from listening to brokers, analysts, and economists tell me I was on the wrong side of the trade. They meant well, but if I had just trusted my own reasoning, I would have been much better off. A customer owes his or her broker nothing more than payment for a trade.

Incredibly, this advice applies also to big players, institutions such as pension and mutual funds. Even institutional brokers swindle their clients.

A friend who worked on the trading desk at a major Wall Street firm once told the story of a broker who called in an order to buy 200,000 shares of a stock for a pension fund customer. The market for the stock was $22^{1/4}$ bid, $22^{1/2}$ offered. My friend told the broker the stock was heavy, meaning a lot of sell orders were around. He could buy it at the bid or lower, but it would take a little time.

The broker said, "Listen, kid, I'm getting ready to go to lunch and I want the commission in my pocket. You just buy the stock at the offer, and I'll hold the phone for the confirm." The trader did as he asked, and off the broker went to lunch having gotten his commission. His client paid $50,000 more than necessary so the broker could get a good table at his favorite restaurant.

Brokers at that level will do most anything to keep business or get new business. Anything. Another friend of mine was playing a round of golf with an institutional broker and the manager of one of his pension-fund customers. The fund manager was giving the broker a lot of commission business, but the broker wanted more. During the round of golf, the pension-fund guy commented on how much he liked the broker's new set of clubs.

When they finished playing, the pension fund manager opened the trunk of his car to put away his clubs. The broker with the nice set winked at my friend and said, "Watch this, sport."

He walked over, placed his clubs in the fund manager's trunk, smiled at him, and walked away.

This stuff goes on every day, and it's a type of swindle. Even if you don't invest, your pension fund is paying the price, which means you'll have less when you retire.

I would bet my life that $25 million a day is wasted in bad order fills because brokers are in such a hurry to get the confirmation and know their commission is locked down. That's about $6 billion a year. It could be the smartest hedge fund, a large mutual fund, or just you. The bigger the account, the more aggressive and reckless the broker is likely to become.

There's so much at stake that brokers will throw punches over clients. I've seen it. I've heard about numerous occasions, especially in the commodities pits. Commodities brokers are rough and tumble, like their markets. Stockbrokers are calm by comparison. New York Stock Exchange brokers are the most calm and orderly, even in a fast market. The commodity folks are loud, waving and screaming at each other all day. I have seen the pit get so frantic that one whole side, a hundred brokers and locals, pushed and shoved so much the whole bunch of them went down in a heap. It's a frisky business.

Final tips: Find a good broker, place your orders to buy on the bid side, and your sell orders on the offer. Call your own shots. Do your own work. Listen to your broker's advice with skepticism.

Remember, it's you versus them.

13

Corporate Raider

*"That's the part management forgets. They forget that it's
someone else's money. They start to think of it as their own."*

The first half of the 1980s took its toll. Almost losing my shirt on the
bond futures, frantically trading in and out of stocks like May Petroleum, the fast-moving S&P 500 contracts, stalking for the Clores and
Bluhdorns of the world, trading gold around the clock, the blowup with
Merrill over Dallas Federal: it all just wore me out.

And then came the avalanche of insider trading investigations and
scandals. When Ivan Boesky rolled over on Boyd Jefferies, I was horri-
fied. Here was a broker, Boyd, who was actually providing a valuable
service to his clients. He was a trader who enjoyed getting his customers the best price, enjoyed beating the great Wall Street swindle at its
own game.

And because he had done for Boesky what every trading desk had
been doing for years for many clients and themselves, the government
drummed Boyd out of the business.

I'm not defending Boesky, or Michael Milken, for that matter. But
the Street started to take on a bunker mentality. I was close to all that
action. I had traded in some of the same stocks that Boesky, Milken,
and other targets had owned or traded. And while Rudolph Giuliani,
then the self-promoting U.S. attorney in Manhattan, was busy grand-

standing with the big "kills," the rest of Wall Street continued to swindle customers day in and day out.

Trading was my first love. I had been told over and over again that I was as good as or better at it than anybody. But I was beginning to wonder if it was worth the aggravation. I had paid millions in commissions, been treated like a king, but courted a lot of risk. I began to see that I was trading just to be trading, because I enjoyed it and the limelight, being the top dog. This was not the way to acquire real wealth.

The bond futures had really set me back emotionally, so far back I never fully recovered. I remember telling Ed Yardeni, an influential and often-quoted economist, and every other person I knew at the time that bonds were going to go back to par, and I would make $60 million to $80 million. Everyone said I'd lost my mind.

It turned out I was right, but early. And then I made the monumental error of bailing out before the real bond rally had begun. An opportunity like that comes along once in a lifetime, and I let mine slip away.

Being an active trader is mentally exhausting, as many online trading addicts learned in recent years. It's a hard way to make an easy living. The lifestyle at my level of activity was seductive. The brokerage firms encouraged that, treated me like a star, the Shooter from Dallas. I found myself in a league reserved for Fortune 500 executives, invited to dinners with Wall Street CEOs.

The experience was rewarding but the price was high. One day I'd make a million dollars on a trade and three days later I'd lose a million. My emotions swung from feeling rich and smart as hell to, "How can I have been so foolish?"

Finally, after a number of people I knew and trusted retired from the business, I'd had enough.

In May of 1985 I packed up my New York operation. I sold my home in Dallas, sold Ross Perot, Sr., almost two thousand acres of investment land I had acquired in the Dallas/Fort Worth area, closed up shop, and moved to Maui, Hawaii. I grew up on the Cane River in Natchitoches, swimming and fishing. I have always enjoyed living near the water, loved Maui, and decided I could afford to withdraw from the field of battle for a while.

I kept track of the markets, of course, and did some trading here and there. But to really stay on top of the game you had to get up at 3:30 in the morning in Hawaii to do business in New York. In any case, I needed to unwind. It was a welcome inconvenience.

But ever the roadrunner, ever restless, I managed to unearth a good real estate deal or two, thanks to John Patterson, a commercial real estate broker with a gift for finding undervalued properties. John brought me a piece of land I was able to buy for $1 million and immediately sold for $7 million. He turned up some other opportunities in the islands to make money selling land to Japanese investors.

In mid-October 1987, the market, which had been on a good bull run, stumbled. The Dow dropped more than 100 points on a Thursday, and another sizable chunk on Friday. I had nothing on the line at the time, so I didn't think much of it. The market looked top-heavy to me, but the economy seemed to be stable.

The following Monday, I rented a yacht and treated a dozen or so friends and acquaintances to a day of deep sea fishing and mai tais. We docked around 4:30 that afternoon. As I stepped off the boat, the man who owned the marina hurried over to greet me.

"Mr. Salim," he said excitedly. "Did you hear what happened today? The stock market crashed!"

Everyone gasped. And then they all ran for their phones and cars.

In New York, it was late evening. I waited until I had gotten home and had a shower before I turned on the TV. I flipped to CNN and caught a live special report. The market had lost 20 percent of its value that day. My ears were pricked.

The *Wall Street Journal* and *New York Times* reach Maui a day late, so I wouldn't have a morning paper to catch me up. I quickly jotted down the price of about twenty stocks as CNN flashed them on the screen. These were big capitalization Dow issues such as IBM and International Paper, solid companies that had been badly mauled. I looked up the price-earnings ratios in the previous day's *Wall Street Journal*.

To reflect the lower prices, I recomputed the ratios for each stock. I felt certain there'd be a follow-through sell-off when the market opened the next morning. I made a list of the stocks I might want to buy.

Working into the night, I looked at the charts to see what the fifty-two-week highs and lows had been, and then at some five-year price charts. The stocks I looked at had been trampled down to between 40 and 50 percent of their previous value, in just three trading days. I knocked off another 20 percent to arrive at a price where I'd be willing to make a plunge.

The market opened at 4:30 in the morning, Maui time. At 3:45 I called my brokers at Jefferies, Bache, and elsewhere. Everyone had horror stories to tell of people who wouldn't pick up the phone, confirmations delayed for hours, big players putting in market orders and getting wiped out.

The trading desks reconfirmed the prices of the stocks I wanted to buy, and from their trading desks I got an idea of the potential opening-price moves. IBM was expected to open down another $4. Everyone anticipated a bloodbath in early trading.

To each broker I gave a few orders. If a stock had closed at $65 the night before, I put my order in at $53, figuring that if the price dipped low enough, there'd be a rubber-band-style snapback that could give me a fast profit.

Out of twenty different stocks I had orders in for, I got fills on six. The other fourteen I missed. About 40 percent of the dollar value of my orders was filled.

And then the market turned. I was bearish on the economy and the market, so I wouldn't have stayed in for a longer haul. All I wanted was to take advantage of an historically oversold situation, a trading rally. As I expected, the market did snap back. I sold everything within four days and in each case made multiple points.

The crash of 1987 paid me almost $400,000. I approached the situation using classic diligence and discipline, placing orders to be filled at bargain prices, or not at all. That way, I vastly reduced my chances of a loss. The next step down was the end of the world.

Had I been living in Dallas or New York, my focus would have been keener and my trading more aggressive. But the market churned so violently I would have had trouble making a big score. The time premium in the S&P 500 index futures had ballooned so much, it would have taken a 200-point move in the Dow just to break even.

The crash caught my attention. Two months later I moved back to the mainland, to Reno, Nevada. Rested, with my war chest at a record level, thanks to some very profitable real estate trades, I was locked and loaded. But instead of trading for the sake of trading or stalking for others, this time out I'd be stalking for myself.

One of the lessons I'd learned from deals like Talon, and from observing role models like Charlie Bluhdorn and Mel Marks, was that managements of public companies often swindle investors worse than Wall Street. I knew from my LBO days with Mel that large profits could be made wresting control of a sickly company away from incompetent managers, and either selling it off in pieces or finding a buyer who could run it more profitably.

Corporate raiders each have an individual style. Some are bullies, some are sneaky, some only want cash flow, others see profit in underexploited brands or other intangibles. My thing is mining hard assets that aren't reflected in the stock price. The hardest asset I know is Mother Earth.

As interest rates began to fall from their historic peak in the first half of the 1980s, construction took off, gentrification kicked in, and land values began to rise rapidly. Companies that had owned land for decades, even a century in some cases, generally carried it on the books at cost. Much of it was the land under useful structures like garages, warehouses, bus stations, motels, and so on. Some of it was agricultural property that the city had grown out to meet.

Greyhound, for example, owned the land under bus stations in nearly every major and medium-sized city in the country. Somebody woke up one day and discovered they were sitting on a gold mine. But the stock price didn't trade like gold because there's no sex appeal in a bus company, not when everyone's driving and flying more.

Another example was Briggs & Stratton, a small-engine manufacturer that owned a huge slice of downtown Milwaukee.

Corporate raiders began to see opportunities to get control of some of these companies at bargain prices. Then they demanded that managements do what they are supposed to do: responsibly and legally reward investors for the risk they took in putting up their money.

It's a simple concept, but you'd be shocked how many CEOs don't get it.

While I lived in Maui, I had a close encounter with management that cared nothing about shareholders. Maui Land & Pineapple was an old Hawaiian firm controlled by the fifth generation of a Hawaiian family, the Camerons. They grew, processed, and shipped pineapple. The company owned thousands and thousands of acres of Maui.

They developed some of their real estate into hotels, condos, and golf courses. The Hawaiian Islands had become a big vacation spot for Japanese tourists. Japanese investors, flush with the profits of their hot economy, followed, paying premium prices for land.

Maui Land & Pineapple owned thousands more acres that could be developed, and that asset had attracted some players. One of these was an old hand at corporate raiding named Harry Weinberg. He lived in Hawaii but had modest immigrant roots in Baltimore. He was a character. In his seventies, he drove a plain Buick sedan, wore gaudy shirts, and kept an office in a ramshackle warehouse. Harry was rich but he thought poor. He'd fly coach back to the mainland and schedule extra stops so he would earn more frequent flyer miles.

He had made a run at Maui Land & Pineapple but hit a roadblock. He bought up 37 percent of the stock. But the Cameron family owned another 43 percent, and they had created an employee stock option trust that owned 11 percent. It was clear that the employee trust was intended to prevent anyone from taking over the company. Weinberg made a tempting offer to the employee trust for its block, but Hawaii shareholder laws prevented him from buying it without the approval of the Camerons.

I had made a small fortune buying and selling land in Maui and started looking at their properties and the price of the stock. It didn't take much figuring to see why Weinberg was so anxious to get his hands on the company. It was cheap. It could easily have been liquidated for $100 a share. But it was trading at about $40.

Colin Cameron was chairman and CEO. Through an intermediary I asked for and got a meeting. Cameron was pleasant, polite, very wealthy, and influential in local politics and business. The family owned the local newspaper.

Once the pleasantries were out of the way, and I had learned twice as much as I ever wanted to know about the pineapple business, I said, "Colin, this might be a sore subject. I know Harry Weinberg's been after you. But did you ever think about selling some of the land?"

I didn't dare say *all* the land. I didn't want to tip my hand about the stock.

"I see some of the land you're growing pineapples on could bring well over $100,000 an acre. How much money do you think you make from an acre of pineapple in a good year?"

Colin guessed about $300 to $400 an acre.

"If you sold the land and put that money in the bank, ordinary interest alone would make ten or twenty times that."

He looked at me with a sour expression, like he'd just eaten an especially tart piece of pineapple. Maybe I was the 350th person to suggest it.

"Well, Jim," he said in a condescending tone of voice we southern boys hear a lot outside the South, "we Hawaiians have a feeling about land. We only have so much, so we don't sell it."

This wasn't going anywhere, so I figured why not just call a spade a spade. "Colin, you're telling me that if someone came in here and busted down the door and offered $100 a share for the company so they could liquidate it and—"

"I'd tell them to turn around and walk back where they came from," he interrupted, putting his palms together. A-men.

Now I have nothing against a person falling in love with a piece of property. The reason doesn't matter, whether it's cultural or business. It doesn't matter how empty the logic. But when you have *public* stockholders, management has an obligation not only to protect the public's investment but to see to it that they enjoy the maximum benefit for the risk they took.

That's the part management forgets. They forget that it's someone else's money. They start to think of it as their own.

In the case of Colin Cameron, as near as I could tell, he was also an idiot. Imagine owning a piece of property worth $100,000 an acre that you could sell, and after paying the gains taxes put the proceeds into short-term government securities—which were paying about 8 percent at the time—and get a better return without lifting a finger. If they had been making millions on the pineapples, I'd have understood. But at the rate they were going, it would take 250 years to earn what they could by selling the land.

No way could Maui Land & Pineapple be taken over in a hostile fashion. Harry Weinberg had proved it. With 37 percent of the stock, the Camerons had even managed to keep the old man off the board of directors, by shrinking the number of seats. Anything to keep from rewarding the public shareholders.

So, I put it in the back of my mind. A couple of years later, I had a chance to buy some of the family stock, 3 percent of the company. The price ran up $10 a share, and I made a $500,000 profit.

More recently, Hawaiian native Steve Case, chairman and CEO of America Online, ended up buying out the Weinberg family with plans to try to preserve the land. Now *he* owns about 40 percent of the company and *he's* stuck with the Camerons.

This is a classic case of a company that was worth two or three times what the stock was selling for, the shareholders were receiving no dividend, and even with all the old owners dead, the family still controlled the stock. If you walked in there today and tried to buy that land, they'd probably laugh you out the door. Yet it's a public company. They're supposed to be looking out for the shareholders.

If the Camerons ever got an uncontrollable urge to do the right thing, they could buy out the rest of the shareholders at a premium and grow pineapples for another 250 years.

By my calculations, Maui Land & Pineapple stock traded at thirty cents on the dollar. If there'd been a snowball's chance of a sale, I would have gone in and bought the hell out of the stock and waited for the rest of the world to wake up.

That's how real money is made in the market. I could read the tape and outtrade everybody. But if I wanted to make the kind of money I left behind in the bond futures, I had to find a situation that was just ripe for picking. With the contacts I had made over the years, I knew I could at worst find a solid backer to bank any moderately sized deal, buy the whole shooting match, and liquidate it myself.

My first chance at this game was with Pic 'N' Save, a California-based closeout retailing chain that had grown to almost $500 million in annual sales. I first heard of the company in Peter Lynch's book, *One Up on Wall Street*. Lynch ran the Fidelity Magellan Mutual Fund for many years and established himself in market legend as a brilliant stock picker.

He told the story of visiting another chain store and happening to notice a packed parking lot outside of a Pic 'N' Save. He had invested in the stock and made a pile of dough. So, the company landed on my general radar screen, along with a few hundred other stocks I had bought or sold or just sniffed at along the way.

It began with a telephone call from a deal maker named David H. Batchelder. David was another well-known figure on Wall Street who crossed my path. He had been a close adviser for ten years to T. Boone Pickens Jr., a Dallas-based corporate raider who controlled Mesa Petroleum. Boone used the company as a platform for stock raids on big oil companies like Diamond Shamrock and Unocal. He was a well-followed celebrity, known for aggressive, winning tactics.

Pickens had hired Batchelder out of a $30,000-a-year accounting job and schooled him in the art of market finance. Batchelder operated much as I had for Bluhdorn and Clore, secretly buying stock or putting together deals with big players on Wall Street, including the infamous Michael Milken.

In 1988, David formed an investment company in La Jolla, California. He intended to get back into the takeover game, on his own terms. David had several smart young people working with him, and they came up with a short list of target companies. I had met David through an investment banker in San Francisco and instantly liked him. He's an easygoing, athletic-looking man with a strong chin and a mane of bright white hair. He created an amazing track record at Mesa. And just before this, he had advised financier Marvin Davis in a failed run at both United and Northwest Airlines.

David invited me to be part of a small partnership he was putting together to do some serious corporate raiding. With his track record, and my careful research and trading sense, I knew this could be a winning combination. The three investors were Dennis Washington, a publicity-shy billionaire from Montana who owned trucking, railroad, and heavy equipment companies; a Canadian billionaire businessman named James A. "Jimmy" Pattison, who grew up poor in a small blue-collar town in Saskatchewan; and myself, a guppy among whales.

David had a new approach to corporate raiding that I was anxious to test out. In the 1980s, if you wanted to get control of a poorly performing company the response was, "Show me the money." You couldn't just walk up to a group of large shareholders and say, "These managers are really bad. Let's kick their butts out and get something better." You had to make a bid for the whole company, an expensive, cumbersome, high-stakes venture.

Those kinds of takeovers often resulted in total disruption of the target company, layoffs, and all kinds of waste and misery.

David Batchelder was on the cutting edge of a new tactic for getting managements off their assets. His plan was to approach a group of large shareholders who controlled a total of 51 percent of Pic 'N' Save stock. These large stockowners were institutions such as mutual funds.

He would say, "This management team does not seem to be getting it done. Shouldn't we change it? The stock is weak, so this may not be the best time to sell the whole company. Let's get the management team out of there and put ourselves in control of the board. Then, we'll get a new management team, fix what's broken, and, if you want, sell the company for what it's really worth."

Believe it or not, that was a radical concept. It was radical for pension funds, mutual funds, and so on, not to just say to a raider, "Why don't you make a bid to buy the whole company?" They didn't want to become involved in a fight with management.

David's approach, he predicted, would become the LBO of the 1990s, although it was no more radical than a good old-fashioned proxy fight in which an activist shareholder or group tries to get enough proxies from other shareholders to win a majority.

Pic 'N' Save was the perfect candidate. The CEO had made a lot of missteps, not the least of which was paying himself a fat salary as the company overexpanded, profit margins shriveled, and the stock price sagged. The board was entrenched, unwilling to make the tough decisions necessary to pull the stock out of its tailspin.

When David started the Pic 'N' Save raid, he told me that one of the pension fund managers who held a block of the stock had told him, "Yeah, the management team is no good. I agree. They suck. But where is *your* management team?"

"It's a chicken-egg deal," David told the fund manager. "How do you entice a new management team without having control? Any good

CEO you'd want is already working. You can't do it that way. You have to force control, and *then* you get the management team."

These were not complicated concepts, but things had been done the wrong way for so long that nobody thought about fixing it.

I was David Batchelder's only active limited partner. I let him know from the beginning, up front, that I was doing the same thing he was: checking out whether this would work. If it did, it opened up a whole new world. You could go fix companies in their public form without having to find bankers and disrupt or dismember the business.

The Pic 'N' Save board, we found out later, truly believed that no matter how bad things got, the major shareholders would leave them alone. The board members didn't own that much stock themselves. It's amazing how few board members have a significant economic interest in the companies they serve. Most are chosen because they're buddies of the CEO, with no real money on the table. That immediately ties their hands. They're not going to start a fight with the CEO, and even if they do, they have no real standing.

So, in most cases the CEO runs the show, and the board tries to stay out of the way and not have to decide anything controversial. All these kinds of directors want to know is: (a) When do I get my check (up to $50,000 a year for nodding yes to the CEO)? (b) Is the officers and directors liability insurance policy big enough, and paid up? (c) Is the next board meeting at Hilton Head or Pebble Beach?

The best boards are made up of seasoned veterans as well as directors with a specific interest or relationship, such as shareholders. The worst board members are those who sit on just one board. They have no reference point, so they don't know how bad they are. If someone doesn't come along and force them to fix things, they'll just roll along. I've seen it many times.

It's a swindle, because shareholders in these companies are being denied the reward they've earned for risking their capital in the stock. Instead, bad managements bleed their companies white or run them into the ground while the directors organize their meetings around expensive golf junkets.

Our group quietly bought about 8 percent of Pic 'N' Save in the open market. We first bought up to just below the 5 percent trigger that requires filing a 13-D. Then we became aggressive and bought the other 3 percent as quickly as we could before the 13-D officially had to be reported to the public. David then met with the ten institutions that controlled 51 percent of the stock and persuaded them to join us.

Pic 'N' Save management rolled out the big guns and declared war. Bankers and lawyers love it when companies fight with each other or a raider. They smell the big fees like pigs can sniff out truffles. Pic 'N' Save hired one of the biggest and most aggressive law firms, Skadden Arps, and one of the biggest and most aggressive investment banks, Goldman Sachs.

But David Batchelder has a brilliant, analytical mind, and I'm a good ol' boy with a no-nonsense attitude. When I get into a deal I'm enthusiastic about it to the exclusion of most everything else. I'll work it day and night, which energizes others and help makes the deal a sure thing.

After many trips to court and an expensive proxy fight, we ended up controlling the board, getting rid of the CEO, and redirecting the company. The stock ran from about $10 a share to nearly $23, then David unloaded a big block.

He told me once, "Jim, you're like that lizard that doesn't look like much when it's just sitting there. But then it gets all riled up and fans out its neck and head, making itself look big and dangerous.

"I'm glad you're on *our* side."

14

Hauling Assets

> "It was clear he was arguing on the phone with Donald Trump.
> [Malcolm] Forbes hung up in a huff,
> gathered up his entourage, and stormed out."

Corporate raiding is a tricky business. Secrecy is one of the most important elements, because target managements will often do anything, even cripple or destroy the company, just to make you go away. Brokers will betray you, traders and others will front-run you.

I have approached many CEOs in my career, offering in some cases to buy the whole company. By being provocative, I hoped they might actually want to do the right thing to enhance shareholder value. With rare exception, however, managements made bad choices that caused the share price to drop well below its true value.

The answer I got was almost always, "We certainly are in favor of increasing shareholder value, but now is just not the right time." Palms together. Amen.

And my answer to that was always, "Really? Well, when exactly *is* the right time?"

What these CEOs were saying is, "Screw the shareholders. I've got a sweet thing going here and you are not moving me away from the trough."

Wall Street on the defense uses every trick and artifice it can think of to stop a raider, as if offering a higher price for a stock is some kind of criminal act. A raider should be admired for helping all the share-holders out of a jam. A raider carries the ball while the rest of the stock-holders get a free ride. They don't get sued, have an injunction filed against them, have to hire a proxy firm, or buy ads telling their side of the story.

Wall Street is at its worst when a stock price is not allowed to rise. When a target company is put in play, anybody should be able to bid for it. But targets use gimmicks like adopting breakup fees attached to a deal that are so steep no one else can afford to make a higher offer. Management gives itself millions in severance-package deals called golden parachutes, the bankers get millions in fees, and the rest of the investors get screwed.

This is an ugly side of Wall Street that seems to worsen steadily. But don't hold your breath waiting for the government to act. Wall Street and corporate America give politicians millions of dollars at election time. Those dollars do make a difference.

Why should a Wall Street banker be able to tell me what I should sell my stock for? What right does a management have to live off you and me? Where the hell is the board of directors hiding? The system is so corrupt, it's almost laughable. Managements can run your stock price into the ground and then squander more money hiring Wall Street bankers and law firms to cover up their stupidity and greed.

The big Wall Street investment banking firms collect their fees no matter what happens, but the fees get bigger when they can persuade a company to stand and fight. Bankers will do anything, as I later found out, to collect those fees. They will even manipulate the facts to achieve a certain result.

When a raider or anyone else makes a bid for a company, bankers on both sides are hired to write what are known as fairness opinions about the proposed transaction. But these fairness opinions are often a joke. They are legal documents that do nothing more than cover the behinds of the participants in the event of a lawsuit by shareholders who discover they've been had.

A fairness opinion says fair value is being paid by the buyer, and the seller is receiving fair value. I have seen Wall Street investment bankers issue a $30 per share value for a company one year, and $8 the next, depending on what the client wanted. This is exactly the same kind of scam practiced all the time in the real estate business, where property must be appraised before sale. The appraiser is often "persuaded" to do what is known as an MAI: Made As Instructed.

A great CEO runs a company in such a way that none of this is relevant. But people like Jack Welch, who helped build and run GE like a well-oiled machine, don't come along often. Most CEOs I've met are good politicians looking out for themselves first, last, and always. And a surprising percentage just plain don't have the sense God gave a gnat.

Managements cost shareholders billions every year, turning away legitimate offers for your shares. You don't even know about it most of the time. I know because I have made such offers and had them rejected. But the companies never told their shareowners. Wouldn't you like to know that someone offered you a 100 percent profit on your stock? Doesn't it seem just a little bit dishonest that the CEO didn't let you choose for yourself? Shareholders should kiss the ground a good raider walks on.

The effort and expense required to unseat entrenched management is stupendous, and there is a personal cost as well. I've had companies hire detectives to shadow me, go through my life, and dig through my garbage.

When I lived in Reno, my home was in a gated community. No one who wasn't invited could enter. During the Pic N' Save fight, I discovered I was being followed. The moment I left for my office, the bank, the post office, a restaurant, there they were, a couple of jerks waiting at the gate in a cheap rental car.

When I mentioned it to one of David Batchelder's associates, Jim Zamthauer, he said he and David also were being followed. We had a laugh about that. But it was annoying and creepy. I thought about what to do and came up with a plan.

One night during a snowstorm, I worked late at the office in Reno. The private detectives were sitting in the car in the parking lot outside the building, my new best friends huddled inside waiting like faithful mutts for their master to return.

I'd bought a box of cherry bombs to keep on hand for the perfect occasion. That night, I decided, was the occasion. The snow covered the car windows, making it difficult for them to see me, and cushioned my footsteps so they couldn't hear me. I sneaked up and crouched behind the car, lit a fistful of bombs, tossed them underneath, and scampered away.

If you've never heard a cherry bomb explode, I can assure you they roar like big guns. In this case, it sounded like a shotgun shoot-out.

Both doors flew open. The two guys leaped out, screaming at the top of their lungs. They ran straight into a deep ditch full of snow and ice water, head first. They scrambled up the far side and sprinted across a boulevard full of traffic. I don't ever remember laughing as hard as I did that night. I never saw those boys again.

Sometimes managements and boards will make deals with raiders to get them to go away. This is called greenmail, and the raider always gets the bad press when it happens. This amazes me. Why would any well-managed company looking out for the best interests of its stock-holders give in to greenmail? And when they do, how is it that the raider becomes the villain? It's the CEO and his team of flunkies that are swin-dling the rest of the shareholders.

Stock prices rise on good growth and increasing earnings, and they fall on sagging earnings and no growth. If you own stock in companies that have good managements and are fairly valued, you're never going to see or hear from a raider. Stocks become targets when the assets of the company exceed the liabilities by an amount larger than the net value reflected in the stock price.

The next target that popped up on our radar was a natural gas sup-plier, Southwest Gas based in Las Vegas. It had several elements that made it attractive, beginning with a deeply depressed stock price, trad-ing at an eight-year low. Along with many other energy companies, Southwest had been clobbered in the 1986 oil crash, when energy prices fell by almost two-thirds. It had a second problem, though. The com-pany owned a savings and loan, PriMerit Bank, which was in a business that also had hit a pothole. After deregulating the savings and loan in-dustry in the early 1980s to help it cope with rising interest rates, the federal government now found itself having to bail out the same banks because the economy by 1990 had stumbled into a recession. The thrifts in particular were choking on real estate loans that had gone belly up.

Southwest had reported some losses and cut its dividend, but the company operated in a high-growth part of the country, Nevada and Arizona. The bank was solvent. You could see a lot of hidden value if you looked close enough, which I did.

So I plunged. I bought a large position, several percentage points, and hired David to advise me. One of the other people I hired was Bob List, the former governor and attorney general of Nevada. I hired Bob's law firm to do my legal work. It turned out he had grown up with Kenny Guinn, Southwest's chairman and a major shareholder. The two had maintained a lifelong friendship.

Southwest had received some bad rate rulings from regulatory agencies, and its bank had been victimized by the real estate bust. David did a leveraged-buyout analysis for me and concluded that the stock was selling at a fraction of the replacement cost of the company's assets.

There is no such thing as a hostile takeover of a utility company, much less one that owns a federally chartered bank. I asked Bob List to arrange a meeting with his friend Guinn to discuss my thoughts on the future of the company.

Like myself, Kenny Guinn was a self-made man. A former teacher, he was a Republican with a reputation for being a maverick. He sometimes supported Democrats. He enjoyed enormous respect throughout the state.

The investment needed to stay friendly and I handled it accordingly.

"My stock holding in Southwest is an investment only," I told them. I was sure they had done their homework and knew I was an aggressive investor. I didn't want them to think I was trying some kind of stunt.

"I'm not interested in a seat on the board, nor do I intend to do anything hostile," I continued. "I'd like to know how the company found itself in its current dilemma, and what is being done to fix the problems."

Guinn took me through every regulatory decision affecting the utility company, the bank's situation, and the reason for the real estate write-offs. He was candid, saying the next few quarters were going to be tough and not to expect earnings to grow rapidly for the next three quarters. An aide then gave me the history of Southwest Gas from its inception. Finally, after two hours, I got to pop the question.

"How do you feel about shareholder value?" I asked Guinn. "Would you entertain a friendly offer from another utility to buy the company if it reflected fair value?"

Guinn leaned back in his chair, looked around the room at his CFO and other executives, and said, "Well, we certainly want to do what's right by our shareholders. I'm a large shareholder myself and we would certainly look at the right offer."

The answer, and the apparent sincerity with which he delivered it, pleased me. They had not been approached by any potential suitors, he said.

After the meeting, I asked Bob List if he thought Guinn was sincere.

"Definitely," he said.

I bought another 200,000 shares, which brought me to 4.9 percent of the company. I didn't want to file a 13-D and attract attention. That would have been in bad taste, to say the least.

Through Bob I was able to arrange a meeting with the company I thought might be a good match, Washington Water Power in Spokane.

The CEO of Washington Water, Paul Redmond, brought his entire senior staff to meet with us. They agreed any deal would have to be friendly and expressed concerns about the bank. We left the question open at the end.

Soon after, we got a call from Washington Water Power. They wanted to move forward. At this point, because of insider trading rules, I stepped aside and stopped buying stock.

It would have been a wonderful transaction for me and all the shareholders. But it never happened.

There wasn't much for me to do about it. It was frustrating. Unless Guinn volunteered to give up control, there was no way to force him. I sold my stock later at a profit, making a good return of 20 percent, but not the double that would have reflected the real value. Such is the world of Wall Street.

Guinn, by the way, ran for Nevada governor in 1998. With his campaign well funded, no doubt in part by his profits in Southwest Gas, he won. The stock rose through the 1990s, peaking just under $30 a share in 1999.

Washington Water Power remained an independent public company, later changing its name to Avista.

Although I avoided breakup situations—where a raider buys a controlling interest and sells the company off in pieces—I found a perfect example in 1990 in a company called Computer Factory. Based in Elmsford, New York, the company had grown rapidly during the 1980s retailing computers. Although it ranked far down the list from top computer retailers such as Tandy and ComputerLand, its sales had grown from $185 million in 1987 to $400 million in 1989.

And then the whole industry just fell apart, much the way e-commerce crashed in 2000. Prices of equipment plunged, and so did stock prices.

Computer Factory had about thirty-five stores spread around the country. I hired Bay Street Group, a San Francisco-based merchant bank led by Phil Gioia, to look the deal over. Phil's analysis found that the inventory was worth $16 million more than the stock value minus its debt. I could buy the company with a premium of 30 percent over the stock price, sell the inventory at cost, and have $16 million in cash left over.

The store leases had to be disposed of, so I hired a real estate firm to look at them, and at the lease for their warehouse. The report came back that all the retail stores were in good locations, and every one could be sublet within three months. The maximum cost to remove that liability would be $2 million.

Now I had to figure out how to get rid of the inventory and maximize its value. We set up a meeting with the CEO of ComputerLand, Bill Tauscher. They could buy the inventory at cost and get rid of a competitor. That would leave just the leases.

We made a deal on a handshake that they would buy the entire inventory if I got the company. I had put myself in a no-lose situation. If I won the raid, I would exercise my plan and liquidate. If I lost, I could make millions selling the whole company to a competitor.

As usual, I plunged, and worked my way up to 8 percent. It wasn't a very big company and the stock traded at about 10 percent of its former peak near $40 a share. Then I got lucky when one of the Fidelity Funds, bailing out of a losing position, sold me a block that took me up to 15 percent ownership.

A company facing a raid does one of two things without fail. They have their bankers and lawyers fight hard to stop you, or they put the company up for sale to the highest bidder. You can try to guess which way they're likely to jump, but you never know until they've pulled the trigger. I've seen CEOs fight when you'd least expect it, and seen entrenched managers step up and do what is right by their shareholders.

Computer Factory turned to fight. A meeting was arranged. Everyone was polite, and the company's investment bank, Dean Witter, as bankers always do, told us right off, "This company's not for sale."

And I made the usual offer, and the next response was the expected, "Your offer is insufficient and does not represent fair value."

But all the posing in the world couldn't ignore my 15 percent and my determination to make something happen. I was not the least bit interested in waiting for a turnaround and told them so.

They let me know they were not going to roll over, and the meeting ended without any resolution. But I could tell how pleased the Dean Witter boys were. I saw them wink at each other. Bankers love the fat fees they get for fighting a takeover and arranging corporate marriages.

The bankers immediately contacted potential buyers to create some competition. As I expected, one of them called me. Avery More, CEO of CompuComp Systems, based in Dallas, wanted Computer Factory and asked if I intended to start a bidding war. He made an offer.

I had two choices at this point: accept his offer with all the other shareholders, or raise my bid, fight for the company, and liquidate it. We looked at the facts, looked at the continued weakness in the economy and in the computer business, and decided we'd better take the money and run. CompuComp acquired Computer Factory for $4.50 a share in 1991. My profit: $3 million.

Although I lived in Reno, I returned to New York frequently. Mel Marks was still there and in business. And Jim Donegan, my broker at Kidder Peabody who handled the S&P index trades out of Los Angeles, had moved to the city to take a job with an old brokerage firm called Thomson McKinnon. Soon after he joined Chase Manhattan Bank.

Jim had been at the center of the 1987 crash because he was selling financial futures to big mutual and pension funds. The institutional investors were using them, based on mathematical models, to hedge their portfolios against market risk.

Jim had been very successful with portfolio insurance, but the crash revealed the flaws. In fact, paradoxically, portfolio insurance was blamed for causing the crash. The whole concept lost favor and Jim had to move on.

At a social event in New York at the end of 1989, I met a banker with Chase Manhattan who told me about a real estate play not unlike Maui Land. This time, however, instead of the middle of the Pacific Ocean, the real estate sat in the middle of New York City. It was a chain of dilapidated, low-end department stores called Alexander's. Donald Trump had purchased about a quarter of the company's stock. Now, he was floating the idea of converting the rundown stores into an upscale chain called—what else?—Trump's.

The situation was like Greyhound in that the operating company was a mess, losing money, poorly managed, and out of step with the times. The stock had crashed from a high of about $90 to around $9.

But hidden under the bargain bins was some of the most attractive acreage in the world. The company's main store sat on Third Avenue at Fifty-ninth Street, a block south of Bloomingdale's, in Manhattan's silk-stocking district. It also owned real estate in some prime shopping centers in the New York suburbs.

When I visited New York I made a point of searching out bankers. In my new game of raiding, I needed to know that if a target company decided to fight, I could bring in some deep-pocket partners. It wasn't hard to put a stock in play as a takeover. But I wanted to make sure I could finance a deal if I had to follow through.

When I got an idea, I would meet with these bankers and try to figure out the cost of doing a deal. Some of these ideas I took to Chase, some I took to Batchelder, and some to other banks just to get some feedback. I was doing my homework.

Trump had invested in Alexander's at much higher prices. By 1990 he'd fallen on hard times. I figured that he would be glad to get out from under his Alexander's stake, which could present an opportunity to grab some prime real estate at a bargain price. Chase had taken the stock away from Trump to guarantee some loans, and the press had been beating the drums about his financial woes. Trump himself acknowledged the pickle he was in, once observing of a homeless person, "At least he's at zero. That puts him $900 million ahead of me."

One day, I invited to lunch the Chase banker who had tipped me about Alexander's, along with Jim Donegan, who, by this time, had joined Chase and helped launch its first retail-stock trading operation. Since Chase controlled Trump's stake in Alexander's, I figured they could give me straight information.

After the pleasantries, I asked this banker, "What do you think about Alexander's?"

"We really can't talk about that," he said. "Mr. Trump is a customer having problems, and I don't think it would be appropriate for me to talk about it."

"In other words, you have the file on Alexander's?" I asked. "You know everything about it, right?"

As he got more and more squirrely, refusing to play along, I became more and more annoyed.

I said, "Listen, all I'm asking you is what's the f'ing real estate worth? What's the big deal about that?"

The banker gave me a dark look and Donegan jumped in to referee.

"Jim is just being direct," he said. But the guy wouldn't give up a single lousy number.

Right after lunch I went to Donegan's boss and said, "I need to see the file on Alexander's."

"I can't give you that," he said. "Why don't you go up and see the head of merchant banking?"

So I went the next rung up. I knew the woman who ran Chase's investment banking operation. I felt comfortable being forward with her.

"I want to buy a lot of stock in Alexander's," I told her.

"You know, we have a conflict here," she said.

"Maria, I just want to buy the stock. I can go out and spend $50,000 and have every one of these properties appraised. I'm not even asking you to show me the appraisals. I think I know what they're worth. I can look at the balance sheet. Now, I'm a good customer. I hope you're not going to make me go spend money to protect a relationship.

"I know you own the stock. It seems to me you guys should be tickled to have somebody get involved with the thing and maybe take it off your hands."

"Well, you know, we're concerned about litigation," she said. "Trump is well known for suing everybody at the drop of a hat."

I knew she was only doing her job but it really ticked me off. And then a most amazing thing happened: as I walked out of her office, I damn near knocked down Donald Trump coming in. We literally crossed paths. And he was not looking too good. His head was hung, his quick step was gone.

Around that time, Malcolm Forbes, publisher of *Forbes* magazine and patriarch of the Forbes empire, had been tearing Trump up in every issue, predicting his demise, practically declaring him bankrupt. Forbes and Trump seemed to hate each other, which was something new. The magazine previously had crowned Trump the boy-wonder of deal makers.

The animosity may have begun one night in the Oak Bar at the Plaza Hotel, a famous watering hole where real men made real deals over real drinks. The Plaza by this time was owned by Donald Trump. It was one of the principal jewels in his crown. He was proud of owning it, protective of its reputation, and had spent a fortune on badly needed renovations.

New York is a paradox on many levels, and perhaps the ultimate paradox is that, in certain subcultures, it's a small town. People in specific social or professional spheres tend to patronize the same restaurants and bars. One segment of the rich, the famous, and the mighty traveled a well-defined circuit that included the Park Lane, the Carlyle Hotel, the Plaza Hotel's Oak Bar, Smith & Wollensky, and Sparks Steak House. It always amazed me how often I saw people I knew or recognized at those places.

Malcolm Forbes was one of those familiar faces. Sometimes he'd have a young man or two in tow, an aspect of his private life that has been well documented in books published since his death in 1990.

One night, I was at the Oak Bar when Forbes entered with a couple of very young guys, teenagers as near as I could tell. He ordered them drinks. The bartender called in the manager, who politely declined, citing state liquor laws that could get the hotel in a load of trouble and rotten publicity as well. How much would the *New York Post* or *National Enquirer* have paid to get *that* story?

Forbes pressed the issue: "What do you mean, you can't? That's ridiculous!"

After a brief and unpleasant conversation, the manager went to the phone behind the bar, dialed, spoke for a moment, then brought the phone to Malcolm. By this point Forbes had turned pink with rage. The bar manager handed the receiver to Malcolm and it was clear to everyone in the place that he was arguing on the phone with Donald Trump. He wanted those kids served. But it was also clear Trump wouldn't relent. Forbes hung up in a huff, gathered up his entourage, and stormed out.

After that, Trump couldn't seem to get a break from *Forbes* magazine.

Soon after I tried to get some guidance out of Chase about Alexander's, I paid a visit to Cushman & Wakefield, a large real estate broker in Manhattan. I wanted to know if anyone in the office had done a workup on the stores. I found one of their brokers who said he had.

"But I can't tell you anything. We have another client who paid to have it done."

"Who are you talking about, Trump?" I asked.

"No," the broker said.

That meant someone had ordered fresh appraisals, which was very interesting. Someone else had the same idea I did. Good news.

"Well, I'm really just looking to buy the stock. I don't have the money to buy the whole company," I explained.

"Why don't you go see your friends over at Chase?"

"I have gone to see my friends at Chase. It's like the Soviet Union over there. The Politburo. Nobody wants to talk."

At that point, the broker closed the door to his office. "Just between us," he said softly, "you'd be a fool not to buy the stock."

Finally! "That's all I'm asking," I said. "Thank you very much. Have a nice day."

I plunged big, loaded the boat. The stock just sat there for a couple of months. This wasn't a quick-fix situation like Computer Factory. But I'd heard that Alfred Taubman, a big mall developer, had been interested in buying the company. And even though New York was scraping along after a real estate crash that followed the stock market crash of 1987, some assets were so underpriced that you could afford to buy and wait for three years. Somebody would make a move on it.

Then, after about three months, the stock started to inch up. And, as I have often done, I sold too quickly. I bought at between $9 and $11, and sold at $22. And then it went all the way back up to its old peak of about $100. If I'd had a five-year horizon, I would have booked a 900 percent profit.

You'd think by this time I would have learned something. But the game just keeps teaching you the game.

15

A Dose of Reality

"When everybody else in the game is taller than you,
you have to find an edge."

Before Jim Donegan landed at Chase, he did a stint at the old-line New
York Stock Exchange member firm Thomson McKinnon. The company
had been around for more than a century, a classic old-money Wall
Street house. Jim described the owners as part of New York's aging
"Irish Mafia," meaning they were politically wired but not all that bright.

When Donegan started with Thomson, I was one of the first people
he called, to see if he could get some of my business. I stopped by the
Thomson offices in Manhattan and found the usual Wall Street beehive
in a slick high-rent building downtown, full of well-dressed men and
women hustling on the phones.

Thomson couldn't do much for me that I wasn't getting from the
twenty other firms where I had accounts. But commissions are commissions. I liked Jim and wanted to help him. His daughter was gravely
ill at the time and needed a lot of medical attention.

I opened an account with a couple of million dollars and started
feeding him some of my business. Jim initially handled my orders, but
as he became more involved in his daughter's care, he handed me over
to a young trader, Dave Mortimer. Dave turned out to a very sharp,
personable kid who quickly won my respect for getting great executions. I
trusted Donegan with my life and quickly grew to trust Dave as well.

After we got to know each other a little, Dave occasionally called me Gordon, a teasing reference to Gordon Gekko, the evil corporate raider who corrupts the ambitious young bond trader in *Wall Street*. Apparently, I had reached an age of experience where a twenty-six-year-old trader like Dave Mortimer saw me as an interesting elder of the tribe.

I'd be talking to him on the phone, watching the ticker on CNBC, and tell him, "Looks like there's some institutional selling in General Motors. What do you hear?"

"Jesus, Jim," he'd say in amazement. "I can't believe you can see all that just from watching television. I'm sitting here with three computer screens full of winking numbers, and guys calling me up every second, and more guys all around me spouting gossip, and I can barely keep track of a few dozen stocks. You seem to know where a hundred stocks are, from the friggin' TV!"

"Bud, the tape doesn't lie," I'd tell him. "It's all there, plain as day."

Dave proved himself a superior trader. He knew the markets intuitively and navigated them well. He kept on top of what I was doing each day. He kept me posted on what was going on and generally acted as my eyes on the Street. He worked orders as good as the best, often buying below the bid and selling above the ask.

While searching for candidates to raid, I stumbled across an opportunity begging to be exploited, but bigger than anything I had ever imagined. I took it to David Batchelder first, to see what he thought: How about a leveraged buyout of International Paper?

Professional investors reading this will snicker out loud, because no matter how big and dangerous I could make myself look, IP was Godzilla. From the Computer Factory deal, which didn't add up to $40 million soaking wet, I now trained my sights on a company with annual sales of more than $12 *billion*. The main attraction, as usual, was a ridiculously low stock price. How could it be, I wondered that an established blue-chip company could trade at less than a third of its sales? You could buy $100 of revenue for $27. How bad could things be in an industry as basic as paper and lumber to justify such a discount?

The answer turned out to be not bad at all. But cyclical stocks like IP were getting hammered because the economy had stumbled into a recession. IP management had made some missteps, but the stock was also being punished along with the rest of its sector, and the market. As with all my investments, however, this wasn't enough to convince me to pull the trigger. I like my plunges to have more than one way to work out. IP did have something else going for it. Once again, it was Mother Earth.

Growing up in Louisiana timber country, IP was a constant presence in our lives. The company had massive land holdings there——pulp and lumber mills, forestry operations, the works. Natchitoches was like a lot of small towns where IP had owned thousands of acres for fifty, sixty, even a hundred years. Over time, the little towns had grown outward until many of them reached the edge of some of IP's holdings.

Timberland that the company carried on its books for what it paid, some of it only cents per acre, was now worth as much as $35,000 an acre. Natchitoches couldn't be the only place this had happened. I was curious to know what those hidden assets were really worth.

IP was trading between $25 and $30 a share. We crunched the numbers on acreage, debt, cash flow, and the rest. When we got to the bottom line, there was so much value hidden in the woods of International Paper that it was equal to the share price, even *after* paying off a mountain of debt! So, at the current price, you could buy International Paper's timber holdings, and thrown in for free you got all the mills, all the equipment, and all the cash flow. It was unbelievably tempting.

For a single shooter like myself, a Computer Factory with movable merchandise and a hungry competitor was a cinch. Here today, in my pocketbook tomorrow. When the asset is real estate, you're dealing with a major handicap: time. It usually takes a lot of it to dispose of land. I had played the real estate game in Hawaii successfully, making some of my biggest profits flipping property.

IP, however, was more than just pineapple fields overlooking the Maui beaches. This was a huge industrial enterprise with sprawling and scattered interests.

When everybody else in the game is taller than you, you have to find an edge. The edge here was the hidden balance sheet. Having banked myself years ago when I started the flying service, I knew my way around

lenders, how they valued collateral and cash flow. The only way I could do a big deal, given my limited financial clout, was to find a big bank.

My pitch would be like so: "The stock's trading at $27 and I've found $32 worth of hidden assets over and above the debt. If you'll loan me the money, I'll liquidate those assets and still have an operating company left over."

Why did I think I could pull off an LBO of International Paper? I had a role model, another client of my mentor, Mel Marks. Former Treasury Secretary William E. Simon turned a $330,000 raid on Gibson Greetings, the card company, into $70 million. He and his partners proved for the first time on a large scale that shareholders could take over an ailing company and make it profitable again. Simon set the benchmark for leveraged buyouts. By the time I started snooping around International Paper, Simon had become a legend and had built his fortune up to more than $1 billion.

The worst outcome I could see from a plunge in IP was that I'd make a lot of money on the stock. Once the company came into play, if I was outbid, I'd still double or triple my money. It was similar to Computer Factory, where I bought the stock at $3 knowing at the very least I'd be bought out at a profit. This is the only strategy I know where you can take a relatively modest amount of capital and play with the big boys.

David Batchelder and I pored over the financials, and, while he agreed that the value was there, he predicted we'd never get the financing.

Chase Manhattan, where I knew people, seemed like an obvious partner. But then I learned that IP's chairman and CEO sat on Chase's board of directors. The Politburo again. It became obvious that this was a pipe dream.

But I had the bug. I decided to plunge and see what happened. IP was a big liquid stock. If I didn't like what was happening, it'd hardly cause a ripple if I wanted to dump everything at once.

I put Donegan on the case, along with Mortimer. I decided to load the boat, as much as it would carry.

"Jimbo," I told him, "I'm going after International Paper." It was time for me to do the lizard thing.

"What?" Donegan barked.

"You heard me. I'm going after IP. I want you to start buying it. They've got hundreds of millions hidden in their real estate. I'm going to put the company in play."

I gave him my orders and hung up. I knew the guys on the trading desk were laughing behind my back. I would have laughed behind my back, too. Here comes little Jim asking to play with the grown-ups.

Every time Donegan or Mortimer phoned me with my order fills, they'd ask, "What do you want to do now, Jim?"

"Keep buying!" I yelled. "I not only want the land, I'll take the whole damn company if I have to. Keep buying and don't stop until I tell you."

We painted the tape on IP, creating the impression that something big was up. Anyone who traded that stock, every analyst, every institutional holder, saw those big trades crossing the tape and they just assumed that somebody was coming after International Paper. Which is exactly what I wanted them to think. In fact, they were right. Jim Salim was coming after the company. He just couldn't finish the deal.

The market soon picked up on what I had seen in IP's assets. The stock got moving and when it popped, I told Donegan and Mortimer to begin selling me out.

"Oh well," I told them. "I didn't want it all *that* bad."

My International Paper trades were hugely profitable. I sold into a good run from $27 to about $50. I was left with 60,000 shares that I used as a core position for day trading. Through no fault of Donegan and Mortimer, the position caused me to do something I had avoided all those years. I had to sue a brokerage firm.

It began on a day when both Jim and Dave were out of the office. I had hedged my position, selling short some call options on an equal number of shares I owned. This meant that if IP fell, the call options would fall, and I could cover my position at a profit without having to sell the stock itself.

If instead IP rose, I could dump the calls and ride the stock up. Which is approximately what happened. The stock had risen, but the calls had lost some of their time premium, so I told the trader who answered the phone to close out the position. "Sell the common and buy in the calls."

I thought nothing about it and moved on to other business.

At that time, a customer had to settle trades, meaning pay for them, within five days. It took about three days for the written confirmation to reach you in the mail. A couple of days after I gave the order to cover the short and sell the stock, Dave Mortimer casually said, "You know, IP is really moving up. You still have these options and they're going against you. I see you sold the stock but you didn't cover the options."

"Sure I did," I told him. "I closed out both the positions at the same time."

"Well, you may have ordered it, but it didn't happen, Jim."

Most trading desks record all phone conversations in the event something just like this happens and there's a dispute as to what was said. We immediately got Donegan on the phone. I gave them the exact time and day of the trades. I told Donegan to play the tapes. The tape would prove me right. In any case, for a trader to claim that I never gave him the options order made exactly no sense: I had matched the stock and the options share for share. I wouldn't have closed out one trade without closing out both.

Well, Murphy's Law was working overtime as IP roared higher, up $2^{1/2}$ points that day alone. I wasn't worried. But then the trader called and asked if I had any IP positions at another firm. Had I possibly gotten confused? I told him I hadn't, and was sure of it.

Then I got a call that sent cold chills down my spine. Thomson McKinnon said they had no taping system. They couldn't find anyone who could confirm my order. Someone higher up in the firm decided there would be no acknowledgment. I was headed for a lawsuit.

I had never had a serious legal dispute in all my years of trading millions of shares of stock. I knew I was right but I had no proof. Donegan and Mortimer stood up for me, vouching to the partners for my credibility. I sent my phone records showing the exact time of the call. But not one trader who was on the desk that day would own up to having received it.

But my complaint was a mosquito bite compared to the blood that was about to be spilled at Thomson McKinnon. It turned out that the partners had been milking the firm dry. They had recently gone on a spending binge, buying out small regional brokerage firms. No sooner had the ink dried than the top producers at these regionals were out the door, lured away by other companies. Thomson had neglected to lock in the big hitters. They ended up having bought some very expensive desks and chairs. The firm unraveled through a tragedy of errors.

Mortimer told me good people were bailing out every day. An institutional trader at Merrill Lynch told me he heard Thomson was filing for bankruptcy. Not even a merger, just a pure bankruptcy filing.

And that's what happened. They plain went belly up. My account was frozen. It took me a few months and cost me $100,000 in legal fees, but I finally got a federal judge to order my money released.

That experience was the opposite of the one I'd had with Gerry Guillemaud. He mistakenly wrote "sell" on a large order I gave him to buy gold futures. He stood up, told the truth, and personally took the loss. No lawsuit, no denials, no hiding behind a big Wall Street firm. That's the way you'd like to think these things will be handled, but don't hold your breath.

Thomson folded overnight and wiped out half of the employees' pension funds to boot. It was a monumental swindle that got very little notice in the press but left a wide path of wreckage in its wake. The bigger houses poked through the rubble, picking up a good broker here or a well-located branch office there. More than a century's worth of history and tradition went up the spout.

Other than the Thomson debacle, my life and my investments seemed to be going my way. I'd bought a spectacular house in Reno that was designed and built by a guy who had made a fortune in whorehouses. Although I don't naturally tend toward showiness, I deliberately chose a place that would make a big impression. I enjoyed an eclectic group of acquaintances: in addition to the brokers, traders, and analysts, there were doctors, lawyers, people in politics, corporate executives, and fellow raiders like David Batchelder. Most people prefer to be entertained in a home than in a restaurant or a nightclub. Why not go for broke?

Once a year for many years, I made a point of inviting a large group of people from around the country to come together for a fun weekend. It would always include a lot of Wall Street folks, but a range of people in other fields as well. I enjoyed creating a relaxed atmosphere. It pleased me but it also served me. When they're relaxed, people will tell you what is really happening in their worlds. In a broad sense, it was an extension of the approach I took in calling on all those cotton farmers. I wanted to know what was going on at the ground level, not what some insulated economist or analyst thought was going on.

I'd invite about fifty couples and really put on the dog. One year, after they'd fled the Thomson disaster, I invited the gang from Chase, which included Donegan, Dave Mortimer, and their boss, John Kelly. I treated them to front row seats for a Liza Minelli performance. I entertained them for a couple of nights and threw a splashy Christmas party complete with members of the Moscow Circus, which was appearing in Las Vegas.

These events cemented great relationships, the kind with people who will tend to look after you. I have had unusually close relationships with the brokers, traders, and other Wall Street professionals I've trusted. My entertaining, which got quite pretentious at times, created a bond that encouraged people who were handling my money to treat me well, think twice before swindling me.

I have enjoyed dove hunting since I was eight years old, so, for a number of years, I arranged dove hunts near Dallas. But in terms of doing my research on life and the world around me, the parties worked the best.

So there I was, at the top of my game, when one day, playing racquetball at a health club in Reno, I felt an odd burning sensation in my left hip. It worsened during the day and before long the muscles started cramping up. I didn't think much about it at first. I was experiencing jet lag from a recent trip to New York and had been working twenty-hour days on Computer Factory and Southwest Gas. Any discomfort I felt didn't surprise me.

A few days later, as I was walking down from the house to a nearby marina, the hip flared up so bad I had to sit down on the side of the road. One of my best friends was Steven Dow, a neighbor who was an orthopedic specialist. The next morning I went in and he shot an X ray. It came back clean, which should have relieved me. But I knew something was wrong.

He agreed to do an MRI. Just by coincidence, that same day I had a long-scheduled appointment for a complete physical at the Scripps Clinic in San Diego. After the scan, I flew down to southern California on a chartered jet.

When I got to Scripps and checked in with the receptionist, one of the doctors came out to greet me.

"Mr. Salim," he said. "I'm sorry for the inconvenience but you need to go to San Francisco right away. There's a car waiting outside to take you back to your plane."

"For what?" I'd just gotten there! He hadn't even examined me!

"We've been in touch with your doctor in Reno and we agreed that you must immediately see a specialist in San Francisco. Everything has been set up for you. The man is an expert in soft tissue tumors, Dr. Jim Johnston."

Jesus Christ.

I worried all the way to San Francisco, wondering what the hell I was going to hear. When I arrived at the specialist's office, he said, "I guess the boys in Reno told you everything about what's going on."

"No," I said. "I don't have a clue. What's going on?"

And the bomb dropped: "You have an extremely aggressive and deadly form of cancer. We've got to get it out of there right away."

My jaw flapped a couple of times.

"Well, I need at least a month to get my business in order."

"No, Mr. Salim. It's not like that," Dr. Johnston said, shaking his head and looking at his watch. "Today's Friday. We're going to take it out on Tuesday. There's no time to waste."

I couldn't believe it. A wave of heat rushed up the back of my neck. "This is impossible. I have too many things going."

Jim Johnston was an older man, much wiser than I. He smiled and said, "They tell me you are a very successful businessman who's made a lot of money. If you were smart enough to make all that money, and smart enough to have accomplished all you've done, you'll be smart enough to get things in order quickly.

"You've got the most lethal form of cancer known. It can spread in a week and kill you. It's in your gluteus maximus muscle, which is your power muscle. And we have to take it out. There is no other option. I'm sorry to be so blunt."

I don't even remember the flight back to Reno. I did what I could over the weekend to organize a few things, arrange to close out some trades, bring David Batchelder up to date on my part of our deals.

The following Tuesday I was on the operating table for eight hours. The biopsy proved the surgeon right. It was malignant as hell. My Reno friend, Steven Dow, would later tell me, "Jim, there was no one else in the world who knew that tumor was malignant other than God and Jim Johnston."

The rest is predictable to anyone who's had cancer or known someone who has. I had to go through radiation and all the misery that comes with it.

But it didn't end there. The doctors told me the cancer had a high incidence of local recurrence, generally within five years. If it didn't come back in five years, it probably wouldn't come back. It was a hell of an ordeal, especially coming in the middle of all that takeover activity.

The recovery put me out of commission for almost two months. Somehow, everything worked out. The deals, my health, the whole thing. As often happens in such cases, I found a new appreciation for life. I had five years to contemplate my mortality and the thought of it weighed on me.

When I was up and around and back in my office, a friend with the Reno fire department stopped by on his annual fund-raising circuit. Christmas was a couple of weeks away, and the firemen ran an annual drive to raise money to buy food and turkeys and receive donations of toys for the kids of families in need. It's cold in the winter in Reno. We got to talking, and he told me something I almost couldn't believe. There were quite a few kids who had no proper winter coats: They arrived at school in the morning in thin nylon jackets shivering with cold.

I gave him a thousand dollars and wished him well. But on the way home that afternoon, I started feeling very guilty. Here I was, living in a 10,000-square-foot mansion, my net worth close to $30 million, and obsessed with deal-making, while children living a few miles away slept in trailers or even cars, didn't have enough to eat, didn't have much to look forward to at Christmas, and, worst of all, arrived at school freezing. That part really stuck with me. By the time I got home, tears were streaming down my face.

The next morning I called someone I knew who was a principal at one of the local schools.

"I need an important favor," I told her. "I'd like you to call your colleagues at other schools and find out how many children in Washoe County need a warm coat. Just counting kids as they arrive at school. I've got something in mind. But I want it to be a real count, not guessing."

Three days later she met me at my office, pulled out a sheet of paper with a list on it, and set it in front of me. I looked at the bottom line and gasped: almost a thousand children! It broke my heart.

That was it. I flew into high gear. I drove down to a local discount department store and looked at coats for kids. They had some quality coats for just under $100, good heavy winter coats that anybody would be proud to wear.

Next, I called up some of my friends in business, people like David Batchelder, and asked them to put me in touch with some top people at Kmart and Wal-Mart.

The first one I reached was a senior merchandising executive at Kmart.

"I want to buy a warm winter coat for every one of those kids," I explained. "And I want to do it as quick as you can find the coats. How much are they going to cost me?"

"That's a wonderful thing you're doing," he said. "We'd be pleased to provide the coats at our cost, which is $30. We can guarantee delivery by December 20, no charge for the freight."

"All right," I said. "Thanks. That's terrific. Let me get back to you."

Then I called Wal-Mart. This was an act of charity, but that didn't stop me from doing my homework.

"That's a fine thing you're doing and we can help you out," the Wal-Mart executive told me. "But you know time is short. When do you need them."

"December 20," I said.

"How about December 15?" he replied.

"Sounds good. How much?"

"We can get these coats for you for our cost, $18."

Now you know why Wal-Mart has been more successful than Kmart.

"Let's make sure we understand each other," I said. "I'm talking about a winter coat that—"

"That anybody would be proud to wear," he interrupted. "It'll be a real good winter coat, Mr. Salim. That's what you'll get."

I fought to keep my voice from breaking.

"Where should I send the check?"

"Don't worry about that. You can pay when the trucks arrive."

Well, I now had saved a ton of money on the coats and learned something useful about retail markups!

"You know, maybe you can help me with something else," I said. "I had budgeted more money for these coats. How much food can I get for $20,000?" Twenty minutes later, he had me on a conference call with a buyer in the Sam's Club division.

This guy's offer was even more amazing.

"We can provide you with $50,000 worth of food for $20,000," he said.

"Done!"

I called the fire department, and the man I talked to was so dumbfounded he could hardly speak. It was an emotional experience every step of the way for everyone I encountered.

Sometime between the phone call to Wal-Mart and the arrival of the coats and food, I learned that they were going to be a few coats short. So I gave the firemen the money and they drove down to a local store to pick up the extras.

A reporter for the local television station happened to be driving past the shopping center and noticed the group of fire trucks parked outside. He stopped to see what was going on. The firemen just blew him off. "Oh, we're just here buying some coats. A local guy is donating a bunch of them for the poor kids in Washoe County."

When the reporter got back to the station, the news director asked him why he was late. The reporter explained that he'd stopped at the shopping center thinking there might be a fire, but it was just some firemen buying a thousand coats for poor kids.

The news director said, "What?"

The reported repeated himself.

"You get yourself back out there right now and take a crew and find those guys. I want that story on tonight."

Next thing we knew, it was on the air. The firemen hadn't given out my name, and I had no intention of taking credit for any of this. The local paper ran a photo of people sorting donations at one of the fire houses. The caption didn't give my last name, but said a local resident named Jim had paid for the coats.

Right on schedule, three big tractor trailers with Wal-Mart signs on the sides showed up. Some two dozen Wal-Mart employees, wearing crisp Wal-Mart uniforms, tumbled out and began unloading. All the food and all those coats were stacked up in the firehouse. Next, the firemen fanned out across the county distributing toys and a month's food for each family that needed it.

Later, when they had finished distributing everything, some of those firemen came by to thank me. They wanted to tell me stories about families living in broken-down cars, kids so hungry they ran past the toys to dive into the food.

One of the principals invited me to come watch the kids' faces as they got their coats. It was again very hard to contain my emotions as these little kids carried on, choosing coats, arguing over them, swapping them, and then showing them off.

We were careful to protect their privacy and dignity. No one pointed me out or made the kids thank me. My heart had been touched in a way it never had before.

Of all the comments that passed during this adventure, the one that really stuck with me was this: "Jim, if all the rich people were like you, there would be no poor people, and everyone would love the wealthy."

16

The Lakes of Arlington

"Real estate has always been good to me.
I shouldn't have been surprised when I got a call
offering me a $5 million profit for a day's work."

The Shooter from Dallas had been plunging in the markets for almost thirty years. For most of that time, I was a workaholic. Twelve hours was a slow day. A regular work week was seven days. I didn't fish anymore. I had outgrown watching football or even going to the stadiums. I quit hunting. My life was all business. I loved the game of making money, but I never enjoyed spending the money as much as I enjoyed making it.

In three decades, I had never developed or created anything in my life. I'd always just bought and sold. I might as well have been a merchant in a store, buying and selling stocks and commodities. There was no value being added to the world. This began to trouble me, especially after having had such a close call with cancer.

By 1992, humbled by a heightened awareness of my mortality and sitting on a mountain of cash, I was wondering what I should do next when I got a phone call from a real estate broker in Dallas. He was pushing a big piece of property, in the Dallas/Fort Worth suburb of Arlington. The price had just been reduced for the fourth time. I was intrigued.

The next day I borrowed a friend's plane and flew from Reno for a look.

The property was a monster, 1,850 acres along the Trinity River between Dallas and Fort Worth. It had been owned by a savings and loan company. Like a host of other thrift banks in Texas and California, Meridian Savings and Loan collapsed during the savings bank debacle that swept the country in the mid to late 1980s. When Meridian blew up, the property was acquired by another thrift institution, Sunbelt Savings and Loan.

The banking disaster couldn't have been worse if it had been conceived and executed by the mob. As a congressional subcommittee would later observe, "The best way to rob a bank is to own one."

A brief history of what went wrong begins in the 1970s. The savings and loan business had been tightly regulated for fifty years. Thrifts were prohibited from paying more than 5.5 percent interest on deposits. But by 1979 inflation had jumped to 13.5 percent. The industry was going broke.

When Ronald Reagan won the presidency in 1980, deregulation came into fashion with a vengeance. It was quickly applied to the thrift industry in such a way that any idiot with noncash assets such as real estate could start a savings and loan company. Then, he or she could finance high-risk mortgages, even to the owners of the bank, with no money down.

And the swindling began.

By the end of the 1980s, after the market crash, the real estate crash, the oil crash, and an economic recession, the chickens had come home to roost. The federal government took over more than six hundred banks with thousands of defaulted real estate loans. The United States Treasury had to bail out innocent depositors at a cost to taxpayers of almost $200 billion. Nearly a thousand swindlers were indicted. More than four hundred went to jail.

A temporary federal agency, the Resolution Trust Corporation (RTC), was set up to sort out the wreckage and get rid of thousands of buildings and pieces of property that these crookedly run banks had financed.

Dallas was ground zero for this mess. Along Interstate 30 northeast of the city, miles and miles of unfinished condominium buildings financed by one of these banks had been left to rot. The fraud was so widespread that the FBI set up a special Dallas bank-fraud task force to document the crimes and convict the offenders.

The property I went to see in Arlington was owned by the RTC, having inherited it from Sunbelt Savings, one of the worst offenders. Sunbelt was run by a swindler named "Fast Eddie" McBirney. McBirney was infamous around Dallas for spending millions of the bank's money on prostitutes, private jets, and lavish holiday parties that featured exotic dishes like grilled lion.

McBirney was a master of the art of the land flip, a procedure by which a single piece of property was sold in the same conference room five or six times in an afternoon through a series of manipulated transactions. The price of the property inflated by at least two or three times. Then, in the same room on the same afternoon, the bank loaned the owners 100 percent of the value as measured by the last sale. The owners and the bank executives and stockholders were often the same group of people.

By the time I arrived back on the scene, the Dallas economy was a smoking battlefield. I would have my pick of properties. There weren't any other buyers.

As disastrous as the thrift crash had been, the RTC's attempts to sort it out were almost as bad. Fraud was replaced by incompetence.

Several years earlier, Sunbelt Savings was appointed to dispose of the remains of Meridian. The property I had come to look at, known as Riverside, was offered for sale at the time. A manager for the property had solicited four offers, ranging from $10 million to $18 million. It had been appraised at one time for $100 million.

The manager, a former engineer with the U.S. Army Corps of Engineers, had worked for Meridian when the bank was trying to develop Riverside for industrial and commercial use. S. J. Stovall, also the mayor of Arlington, later told me, "Nobody wanted to fool with Riverside after the banks went broke.

"I'll never forget the day I dropped those four offers on the desk of the man at Sunbelt who was supposed to sell it. One of them even had a deposit for $500,000, a certified check, too. But he said, 'Don't leave those contracts on my desk. You pick them up and take them with you. I don't even want to know about them.' It was a hot potato."

The real estate broker met me at Dallas/Fort Worth Airport, and we drove out to look at the site, which was only a few minutes away. There was nothing on it but woodlands, prairie, and rolling hills. Years ago it had been leased by a big cement and building-materials supplier, Texas Industries, as a gravel and sand mine.

The property had an out-tract in the center, about 110 acres owned by a man who leased the place to a hunting club and had refused to sell when Meridian assembled the property out of several smaller pieces. An access road had been cut through Riverside to provide access.

The out-tract was the site of an old military outpost known as Bird's Fort, the first Anglo settlement in Tarrant County and the place where a famous treaty between the Republic of Texas and several Indian tribes was signed.

The big problem with Riverside was that it lay in the Trinity River flood plain. In the spring, the river had a habit of cresting and spilling over onto the property. The previous development plan called for building a levee. I wasn't interested in developing it, but I thought I might be able to turn it over for a profit.

Next stop was to see the property manager for the RTC. A kid, no more than twenty-seven years old, greeted me. I looked over his shoulder for the boss, but he *was* the boss.

The kid explained to me that the property had been priced at $21 million, but it drew no takers, so they reduced it to $16.5 million. Now, it was offered for $3 million. I asked him to repeat the price, to make sure I heard him right. Almost two thousand acres of real estate smack in the middle of the Dallas/Fort Worth Metroplex for $1,620 an acre?

"I'll take it!" Incredible, I thought. I've spent more time choosing a pair of shoes.

The kid beamed with pleasure and pride. Now he could tell his boss he'd finally unloaded that white elephant on the Trinity. Giving away this property had made his day.

"Where will you be getting your mortgage, Mr. Salim? Will you be using a local bank?"

"This'll be a cash deal," I said. "No mortgage." The kid's eyes popped. I had the capital and bare land is hard to finance. I knew for a rock-solid fact that I would not lose a penny of my $3 million.

"Cash? Well, let me see. I have to check something about that." He shuffled some of the papers in the folder and found what he was looking for. "Let's see, cash. Right, there it is. For cash there is a 25 percent discount. That would make your price," a quick finger-dance on the calculator, "$2.25 million. Is that all right?"

All right? Pinch me! I whipped out my checkbook. I thought about asking him if they had an extra discount for auto club members, but decided he might not get it.

As the kid fooled with the paperwork, I asked him how long he'd been managing properties for the RTC.

"I started last month, right before Labor Day."

"Where were you before that?" I figured he worked in the loan department at a local bank, or maybe had been a real estate broker.

"Over in the Preston Wood Mall. I was assistant manager at the Kinney Shoe Store."

Go ahead, shake your head. I did, for about a week.

Real estate has always been good to me. So I guess I shouldn't have been surprised when, on the Monday after the Friday I bought the place, I got a call offering me $8 million to sell it. Not bad for a day's work.

What made it especially odd is that the offer came from Texas Industries, which for many years leased the property for mining raw material for its concrete plants. They must not have known that the price fell so low. In any case, I had outmaneuvered them. That gave me increased confidence that I was on to something.

Property transactions are reported almost the next day in the local papers, so word spread fast in the real estate community that I had grabbed this jewel for a song. I received several other offers that I toyed with. But it was just that eagerness on the part of other speculators that convinced me I had something of much greater value than a quick profit.

It took me a while to get focused, but I did two things right away. One was to persuade a friend, R. B. Calhoun, a retired executive, to come in and manage the clearing operation. I had known R.B. for a few years, thanks to one of my Hawaiian land deals. He represented Louisiana Land & Exploration when it sold me a large tract over there. We hit it off and stayed in touch.

The second thing I did was hire a local dirt contractor, Danny Pigg, to dig some test holes with a backhoe, just to see what was there. Danny reported finding a lot of sand and gravel.

This set me thinking. Texas Industries had been hot to get the property. TXI, a Fortune 500 company with annual sales of about $650 million, had suffered during the real estate collapse and the Dallas/Fort Worth depression. Demand dropped off for its concrete and steel construction products. The company's debt was downgraded, and the stock bounced around for a couple of years in a trading range between $19 and $25.

I called the chief of the concrete division to find out if they had any interest in buying just the sand and gravel.

"Hell yes," he answered.

So, I financed Danny Pigg to put in a $750,000 wash plant to clean the sand and gravel, and he began to excavate. TXI took everything we could produce, which netted me about $200,000 a month in royalties. Already the property was a good investment. Two years at that rate and I'd have the land for free.

After only a few months, TXI began badgering us for more. They asked us to put on a night shift. This made me very curious. I'd been meeting quite a few top TXI executives. The next time I bumped into one of them, I asked, "What's going on?"

"We can't meet the demand," he said. "We just can't get enough raw materials for the concrete we can sell."

"That must mean the price of concrete is going up."

He told me that in only four months it had shot from $22 to $37 a yard.

The executives I knew at TXI were professionals. I didn't expect them to blurt out their earnings forecast or slip me inside information. But Jesus, they didn't need to. By any measure, the stock appeared to be trading at a fraction of its real value.

I did some additional research with TXI's competitors. I quickly learned there was a critical shortage in concrete. Prices had shot up for every bit of the product: sand, gravel, Portland cement, finished cement.

TXI, meanwhile, had been making money despite the bad economy, with concrete at $22 a yard. So, if concrete was now going for $37 a yard, $15 additional flowed straight to the bottom line. It was simple.

I asked the guys I knew at TXI how many yards of concrete they sold in a year. The answer: four million. How many shares of stock? Fifteen million. If they make an additional $15 a yard on four million yards, that's $60 million divided by fifteen million shares. These guys were going to make an additional $4 a share. Even at a price-earnings multiple of 10, the stock is going through the roof.

But just to be safe, I looked at the chart and their balance sheet. The chart told me the stock had spent several years putting in a bottom.

I even checked with the state to get a fix on how much money was budgeted to be spent in Dallas and Tarrant counties on road building. This was public information, if anyone wanted to go to the trouble of looking it up.

All signs pointed up. I plunged in TXI in the low 20s and told everybody I knew to do the same. It was money lying on the ground waiting for someone to bend down and pick up. This didn't require X-ray vision, an MBA from Harvard, or friends in high places. Anyone with two eyes in his head who was a road contractor, built swimming pools, or sold reinforcing bar knew there was a concrete shortage and a spike in prices. It was also no secret that Texas Industries was the largest producer in the state. Their profits couldn't possibly do anything but sky-rocket.

In eight months the stock soared to a high of $43.

My property had now paid off in two ways, and I hadn't sold a spadeful of dirt. In the end, TXI paid me a total of $5 million in sand and gravel royalties.

Meanwhile, I picked up a couple of other, smaller properties that bordered mine. Already out of the flood plain, this additional acreage made the property more attractive for development. I now owned about 2,250 acres.

My thinking shifted. If concrete prices recovered, the economy in the Dallas/Fort Worth Metroplex must be recovering, too. What if I could raise the money to develop the property myself? Was this a chance to cancel out the fortune I'd missed on the bond futures? That $60 million was still a little stuck in my craw. You can't help reflecting now and then without thinking coulda-woulda-shoulda.

And there was something else attractive in it, which grew from increased awareness of my mortality. I didn't dwell on that, but it was there. Maybe I could leave something physically substantial. I could remake those 2,250 acres into something of lasting value, something beautiful as well as profitable.

The land seemed ideal for a use other than boring old factories, offices, and apartment complexes. The Metroplex had all those over-built condominiums to absorb. Industrial and commercial development was too easy and wouldn't earn the best return. Someone proposed a Nascar racetrack at one point. But that would have caused huge noise and pollution problems for a large neighborhood of homes just across the river.

Because it lay mostly in the Trinity River flood plain, building on this property required the approval of the Army Corps of Engineers. Wetlands had to be maintained. And the flow of water both upriver and down had to stay exactly the same, even in a once-a-century flood. It had to be designed in such a way that the river would not back up more, or drain faster, than it had in the past. This meant moving the dirt without altering the total volume of space available for floodwater, what hydrogeologists call storage capacity.

The plan Meridian proposed called for a simple levee. They were going the safe route, building an embankment around an industrial park, office buildings, and apartments.

The alternative, raising the land level, would be incredibly expensive and time-consuming. Dirt near the river would have to be dug up and moved back. Part of the property would be lower than it was and more likely to flood, part higher and drier.

An enormous aquifer lay just below the surface. We discovered in excavating sand and gravel that if we dug deep enough, water seeped into the holes from the aquifer. It was as clean as you'd expect from an underground source. But it was unusually clear as well, because it reached the surface only after being filtered through all that sand and gravel.

So, there would be holes filled with beautiful blue water that con-tinuously replenished itself as it drained away through the sandy soil toward the river. The water couldn't stagnate, and there was no muck to cloud it up. Why couldn't someone dig out a series of ponds or lakes, use the dirt as fill to build on, and create a paradise right in the middle of the Metroplex?

Six Flags Over Texas, one of the largest and best-known amusement parks in the world, was just down the street. The Ball Park at Arlington, a major league stadium, was a few blocks farther on. General Motors had an enormous assembly plant nearby, and many large corporations were moving their back-office operations into the region because of its cheap rents and low wages. A corridor of commercial buildings sprouted along Interstate 30, filling with telemarketers, customer-help centers, and high-tech manufacturers.

The ideas began to flow. The first one I made public proposed a park called Arlington Gardens. On 150 acres I would build greenhouses for raising indoor plants. Along winding outdoor paths I would plant indigenous trees, shrubs, and flowers. Next to the gardens, I'd build several wedding chapels to rent out. This would attract attention to the rest of the property and make it more inviting for other uses.

I consulted with David Batchelder and we flew to Victoria, British Columbia, to look at a spectacular garden there as a possible model.

After the gardens were finished, I would gradually develop the rest of the property with other investors or maybe sell off pieces of it for compatible uses. I thought about a water park with lakes and jet ski rentals, an amusement park, theaters, maybe a hotel.

I floated a plan for an entertainment complex called MetroWorld. More than six million tourists a year passed through Arlington, a big audience that could be tapped. Although entertainment projects are hard to finance, if I could push it far enough along, I might take it public and raise the capital necessary to build it out.

Nobody does theme parks better than Disney so I hired a former Disney executive, Skip Palmer, to look at the property and its potential. He wangled an invitation to visit Walt Disney World in Orlando. We had lunch with Dick Nunis, head of Disney's theme parks and the man who, over three decades, built Disney World into the gigantic resort it is today.

Nunis generously made his top executives available to us and, one after another, they amazed me with their intelligence and insight. By the time we finished our tour and fact-finding, I knew there was no way

I'd be able to pull off something as complex and costly as an amusement park. But I also knew that Disney was a well-run company and the stock was seriously undervalued. You can't go wrong buying great management, so I bought a large position in Disney and it paid off handsomely.

This process of sorting out which way to go took a couple of years of thinking and planning, running ideas past potential investors and regulators. During that time I sold my house in Reno and moved back to Dallas full-time so I could devote all my energy to the project.

Finally, in early 1996, I settled on the plan that struck me as the most challenging and rewarding: a community of luxury homes built around a series of lakes—a residential paradise in the middle of the sprawling Metroplex.

And so, The Lakes of Arlington was born.

17

Will They Come?

"He warned me, 'You know this is one of those pieces of property you can easily underestimate.'"

Within a few days of buying the Riverside property, several people who knew about the old project suggested I contact S. J. Stovall, the man who had managed it for Meridian Savings.

Stovall, I was told, knew every inch of the place. He had retired after a long career with the Army Corps of Engineers. He understood better than anyone what needed to be done since he'd already studied the land for the Corps, and later for Meridian.

The icing on the cake was that he had been an Arlington city councilman, the mayor, and a Tarrant County commissioner. He knew his way around, knew the procedures. I called him within a week of buying the place.

"Mr. Stovall, my name is Jim Salim. I've bought the old Riverside property and everyone tells me that you go with the property. I thought I should call and find out exactly what I've bought."

S.J. chuckled. "I don't know where you would have heard that."

"Your signature is all over the paperwork," I told him. "That's got to count for something. And everyone says you're the man to talk to. So, can you help me?"

S.J. said he was happily retired. I promised a generous arrangement if he'd consult for me.

We met at the site a few days later. He explained some of the problems, how they might be solved, and answered my thousand and one questions.

At one point he warned me, "You know this is one of those pieces of property you can easily underestimate. It'll take a lot of money, require moving an unheard-of amount of dirt, and twenty years to build it out."

He was right. But I wanted to prove I could pull it off. I had stars in my eyes, fire in my gut. Once I settled on the idea of arranging everything around lakes, the castle I was building in the sky grew ever more elaborate.

When I finally settled on The Lakes of Arlington plan, my vision became well defined: a pattern of eleven sparkling-clear lakes, aqua-blue water lapping against grassy shorelines, a natural forested buffer along five miles of riverfront, teeming with wildlife. And, of course, tree-lined streets of beautiful homes with waterfront views, an oasis just minutes from town. It was the kind of community I'd want to live in, on the water but near the action.

I kept my options open, as I have done with all my speculations. Even if I couldn't complete the big picture, the property would have more than paid for itself. I could pull the plug anytime and sell out. The Dallas economy continued to improve, so I wasn't worried about getting stuck.

But if I could hang in, I saw a potential profit for myself of about $100 million. From every angle it looked like a win. The city would annex the property, tax revenues would increase, the public would get a new park, the construction would provide jobs for years, the new residents would attract new businesses and growth for the old ones.

What could possibly go wrong?

S. J. Stovall worked with me as we set about redesigning the project, hiring a dirt contractor, and negotiating the way through a thicket of federal, state, and local issues.

The Corps of Engineers permits were a big part of the puzzle, but I wanted to do this project in such a way that the city would get behind it, be my partner. I donated a million cubic yards of clay dirt to Arlington for use as liner for a big landfill just west of my property. Arlington taxpayers saved about $1 million that would have been spent buying dirt, and I saved a lot of money I would have spent hiring a contractor to pick up that million cubic yards and move it.

I also donated more than two hundred acres of wetlands, the largest land gift in Arlington's history. The story ran on the front page of the local papers, and one of them ran an editorial describing it as "a magnificent gesture."

City officials expressed pleasure that I'd made the gift before applying for my zoning permits. Developers typically hold back goodies such as open space to use as negotiating wedges when asking for exceptions to zoning and other rules.

But I wanted to create an atmosphere of cooperation, with a minimum of head games.

The full disclosure of my plans also made the front page. In April of 1996, I officially unveiled The Lakes of Arlington, a luxury development of 644 high-end homes built around a series of private lakes, a country club, a $20 million botanical garden, and permanent wetlands. The lots would be priced between $150,000 and $300,000. Homes would sell for between $500,000 and $2 million.

I estimated that the first house would be finished in a year and a half. My dirt contractor was already on the job, digging out the lakes and grading the land. There would be sailing, upscale restaurants, and a 300-acre green belt along the river.

We estimated the finished project would generate annually about $500 million in additional business activity in Arlington.

Under the headline, "Upscale Lakeside Estates Planned In N. Arlington," the *Arlington Morning News* noted, "The gigantic master-planned community . . . would encompass five percent of Arlington's total land area."

A few weeks later the competing *Fort Worth Star-Telegram* wrote:

"For more than 150 years, a 2,000-acre parcel of land in the Trinity River flood plain . . . has been an ill-fated address.

"The area's first Anglo settlers abandoned it as an inhospitable site in 1842. Even the five who died trying to make a go of Bird's Fort were not allowed a peaceful rest. Their burial site, considered the first in Tarrant County, was mistakenly destroyed by a gravel mining operation in the 1960s."

The article went on to recount the Meridian Savings disaster, adding, "its current owners . . . believe they can buck historical precedent."

I laughed when I read that. No way was I going to be anything less than successful. I had the vision. It would take all of my political and business skills to pull it off, but I never doubted I would. Not for a second.

One of the governmental issues I had to deal with concerned a state highway called Farm-to-Market 157, or FM 157. The highway ran along the western edge of my property. Whenever the river spilled its banks, several feet of water flowed across the roadway.

FM 157 was an important local artery. The river crested several times a year and the detour was long, a nuisance that had grown into a major headache as the area developed. For twenty years local officials had been asking Texas to widen and raise it out of the flood plain. My project added another reason for doing so. I wanted to move the road east into the interior of The Lakes of Arlington, away from the landfill, and closer to the part of my property I'd actually be building on. The project carried a steep price tag of about $13 million and had been put on the back burner. It wasn't even budgeted to begin for another five years, in 2001.

When I first bought the property, neither Arlington Mayor Richard Green nor Governor Ann Richards knew me from a bump on a log. But I thought I might be in a position to accelerate the FM 157 project. Through a state assemblyman I knew in Nevada, Bob Sader, I asked Nevada Governor Bob Miller, a Democrat and someone I knew socially, if he knew Governor Richards, also a Democrat, well enough to put in a good word for me. Turned out he knew her well and agreed to vouch.

Ann Richards was one of the most colorful governors that Texas or any other state has ever had. She was a big presence wherever she went, with her husky voice and white hair. She was often outrageous, and outrageously funny. She may be best remembered for a speech she delivered at the 1988 Democratic National Convention, and for her often biting comments about the way men dominate politics.

"They tell poor women that the country went to hell because they took welfare and stayed home with their children," she liked to say. "Then they tell middle-class women the country is going to hell because they took jobs and left the kids at home." Not since Adam said, 'Eve made me do it,' have women taken the wrath for the world's problems."

With Governor Miller's introduction, and Governor Richards's help, I arranged a meeting with state officials to talk about FM 157. This might have been the only time in my career when I actually asked a politician to do anything. I have donated millions to campaigns, but never once asked a public official for a contract or a job for a relative. As far as going hat-in-hand to the state of Texas, I felt I was as justified as any citizen trying to get government to focus on an important local matter.

In any case, Governor Richards did get the highway people to move the project up. I offered to donate $2 million worth of dirt that would be required to build up the roadbed, and the necessary 1.5-mile right-of-way. Once again, it was a win-win deal. Relocation of the road was important to my plans to attract retail businesses such as restaurants, and everyone agreed that the flooding problem needed fixing. Everyone stood to benefit.

Now I became a public figure in Arlington. Photos of giant earth-moving machines scooping up dirt appeared regularly in the local press, "Will They Come?" asked one headline.

Things were going great guns. I addressed every question from every group that had a concern, whether it was environmental, governmental, or financial. I enjoyed a trusting relationship with city officials, who treated me with respect and expressed appreciation for the straightforward way I conducted my business. No one ever asked me for a bribe or any other compensation to win an approval. It was all aboveboard, something I took great pride in.

At the beginning of May 1996, I got a call from one of the reporters at the *Fort Worth Star-Telegram*, asking to come out and meet me for an interview. By this time there had been dozens of stories in the paper, all largely positive. So, I didn't think anything of the request until I sat down with her and a colleague, and she popped a question that blew me away.

"This is a little awkward, Jim, but could you tell us something about this thing that happened in Natchitoches in 1979?"

My heart sank. A fist squeezed my stomach. I hadn't thought much about Natchitoches in years. I had managed to put out of my mind the circumstances that compelled me to leave and stay away.

Suddenly it all came back in a sickening rush.

When I was young and investing in real estate in Louisiana, I had two financial angels. One of these was R. C. "Pat" Anderson, a wealthy farmer who also sat on the board of a local bank, City Bank & Trust. Pat was a rainmaker. I could take him a deal, and he would lend me the money at a point or so above the interest rate charged by the bank. He would do unorthodox financing but always wanted solid collateral, real estate.

Pat helped launch my career. Over a period of five years, he loaned me about $10 million. He trusted me and treated me like an equal. His handshake was as good as gold. I considered him a friend and a mentor.

Pat was getting older and his health had begun to decline. He looked to be about eighty but was probably ten years younger, the same as his wife.

The Andersons had a daughter and a granddaughter. They also had one great-grandchild, a little boy they adored.

Somewhere along the line, their granddaughter married a man who wasn't the little boy's father. She married someone I knew about from my school days, Charles Rollo. He wasn't in my circle of friends when we were kids. I saw him occasionally around town as an adult, but we never had a reason to speak. He had a reputation for a short fuse, although I had no personal experience. I bore him no grudge.

One day when I popped in at the bank to do some business, the president stopped me on my way out.

"Jim, Pat Anderson is looking for you. He's really upset and it seems urgent. He's in the boardroom."

I found Pat sitting down, pale, trembling, close to tears.

"Jimmy boy, you've got to help me," he pleaded. "You've got to help me. He's gonna kill me. I'm gonna kill him! I don't know what to do. I've got a pistol, just in case. My poor wife, she's falling to pieces. I just don't know what to do!"

Pat had gotten into a terrible fight with his son-in-law, Charles Rollo.

There had been bad blood ever since he married their granddaughter. Things took a vicious turn when Rollo told Pat the Andersons weren't welcome in their granddaughter's home anymore and wouldn't be allowed to see their great-grandson.

Things got out of hand. Pat said Rollo had threatened to kill him, and he had threatened Rollo in return. Pat's wife was having a nervous breakdown over it. He was out of his mind with worry. I had never seen him so stirred up.

"Jimmy, you've got to help me. After all I've done for you, you got to help me this once. Don't you know somebody who could, you know, take care of Rollo for me?"

I gave him a sharp look.

"I don't know what else to do!" he wailed. "I'm afraid he's going to kill me first. Or hurt the boy!"

"Pat, you don't even want to talk that way," I said. "You're thinking crazy. Nothing could be that bad."

I tried to reassure him that things would work out. But he didn't want to hear any of it. He was fixated on the little boy and heartbroken for his wife. He had taken to parking across from the boy's school to watch him play at recess. He was a wreck.

A few weeks later, Pat called and invited me out to lunch. He raised the subject again. He laid on the guilt. To appease him, I said I would ask around. I would see if anyone knew somebody who would do such a thing.

For weeks Pat kept the pressure on. I stalled. I made up forty excuses why I hadn't made any progress. I hoped he and Rollo would calm down, get over this thing.

Pat finally asked me one time too many. Life presented me with one of those moments when a person has a clear choice between doing the right thing and doing the easy thing. The right thing would have been to find psychological help for Pat and his wife, and maybe speak with the granddaughter and Rollo to see if there wasn't some way to work it out. The right thing would have been to call the cops if I really thought Pat or Rollo or the little boy was in imminent danger.

But instead, I did the easy thing—I gave in to loyalty. I have paid for it ever since.

I never met the man who killed Charles Rollo. I made introductions and set the wheels in motion. I deluded myself into thinking that somewhere along the line someone would wake up and realize they couldn't actually go through with it. At the time I was going through a divorce that involved my own children, so I empathized with Pat's frustration and anger.

Like an idiot, I spoke to a man I knew who had done time in prison. In my career, I have rubbed shoulders with all types of low-lifes. This man was just one of those near the bottom.

He apparently knew someone who would murder Rollo for money. And that's what happened. On Easter Sunday in 1979, Charles Rollo was standing in his driveway when someone shot him once in the chest at close range with a stolen shotgun. The coroner said Rollo was dead before he hit the ground.

The killer was an amateur. Several people got his license plate number, and someone spotted him tossing the gun into a bayou as he drove away.

When I found out that the shooter and the guy I knew had been arrested, I turned myself in and was charged with murder and conspiracy. The grand jury wouldn't indict. But the sheriff at the time had an ax to grind, leftover business from a political dispute with me. He was an active Klansman and represented all that was wrong with humanity. I hadn't been afraid to say so, either. He didn't like me one bit.

The sheriff got the case back in front of the grand jury by accusing me of being a Mafia kingpin. By a narrow margin the grand jury indicted. But those charges were later thrown out.

The district attorney then offered me immunity in exchange for testifying against everyone else and that's what I did.

Two men went to prison, and Pat Anderson died soon after in a tractor accident. It was a season of insanity, and I could have stopped it. Instead, a man lost his life, and I made it impossible to remain in my hometown or face my family.

In the years after, my past resurfaced a couple of times. Some people who stumbled across it have tried to blackmail me, threatening to go to the local papers if I didn't pay them some money. I just cursed them and hung up. Once you start with that kind of stuff, it never stops.

The question by the *Star-Telegram* reporter was the first time any newspaper had delved into my past. The reporters said they had known about the Rollo case for a long time. I wondered why they suddenly needed to write about it.

"What has this got to do with anything? I'm not running for any public office. I'm not asking the city to float a bond issue for me."

"We're putting together a feature series on your project," she said. "We want it to be balanced. It's a three-part story."

I made a helluva fuss. I asked for and received a hearing with the paper's editorial board. I hadn't had any experience like this with the press and the whole thing had me baffled.

"What is the purpose of this story?" I asked the editors. "I'm not out here running ads saying 'I'm Mr. God.' What is the significance of this as it relates to a real estate project?"

"Well, you know about the poll?" one of them said.

"Yeah," I said. "I know about the poll."

One day when I was in city hall, someone showed me a piece of paper listing the results of an informal name-recognition poll. The names included Arlington Mayor Richard Green; Tom Vandergriff, a former mayor who is a beloved legend in the city; baseball great Nolan Ryan, who lived in the area; a couple of council members; and a few prominent business leaders who had expressed an interest in running for mayor. My name was on there, but I did not want to run for mayor.

Somehow I had gotten the highest name recognition. Some of these other people who would be contenders for mayor aimed to discredit me in case I had political ambitions.

As I said, I made a helluva fuss, and I'm not bragging about it. I cursed and pounded the table.

"I think it's a cheap shot," I told the editors as I left. "But I can't stop you."

A week or so later, I flew to New York on business. My return flight set me back down in Dallas on a Sunday afternoon. I stepped off the plane, and as I headed away from the gate I glanced at a newspaper rack.

There it was, on the front page:

COMPLEX MAN DRIVES THE LAKES:
DEVELOPER JIM SALIM HAS HIS FANS,
DETRACTORS AND PAST

Past. I didn't have to read the article to know what that meant.

An emotion washed over me like the one I felt the day I found out about the tumor. There was no anger. I was numb. I thought, You have no one to blame but yourself. You gave them a gun, loaded it, pointed it at your head, and told them to pull the trigger.

18

Poor Henry Blodget

"You're better off flipping a coin than listening to an analyst.
The coin is unbiased."

The newspaper series about me and The Lakes of Arlington ran, I got hundreds of telephone calls, and I punished the *Star-Telegram* by not talking to them for a while.

When the reporters and editors got tired of reading about The Lakes of Arlington in the competing *Morning News*, the *Star-Telegram* reporter came to see me again. She said she regretted the paper's decision, and that the editors had been chastised by readers for airing my dirty laundry. Maybe she was just blowing smoke, but the series wasn't all that bad. There were compliments and predictions of prosperity. In the end it had no effect on the development. In a way, it was a relief to get the past out, and then put it truly behind me.

Things moved smoothly through that year. An Arlington planning official told the *Star-Telegram*, "There's no way the city can lose" by annexing my land into the city limits.

Around Thanksgiving, I was driving down Interstate 30 coming up on Texas Stadium when I happened to glance up and almost had a wreck. The *Arlington Morning News* had rented a giant billboard that read:

JIM SALIM SEES A BRIGHT FUTURE IN ARLINGTON

Jim Salim was *hoping* for a bright future, but in the meantime he was working for a bright future, and hard. I was out at the site every day, even on weekends.

The scene looked like a Desert Storm operation. There'd often be eighty or more enormous pieces of yellow construction equipment snorting back and forth, big scrapers that scooped up the dirt into a hopper, D-10 bulldozers, giant dump trucks. And often a plume of dust blowing in the relentless prairie wind. It did look like a military operation, as if we were trying to build a landing strip in record time.

S. J. Stovall tried to get me to be more economical about the way we were shaping the property. But I was not a good listener.

"You need to save some of this dirt that you're moving around," he told me. We had a mitigation area in one corner of the property to compensate for the loss of wetlands in another. This mitigation area had four little lakes on it. I directed the work myself and made those four little lakes into two big lakes. Stovall told me I was hauling more dirt than I needed.

At one point the dirt contractor had forty-five giant scrapers hauling earth. The process of shaping the land was expected to take three years. The Lakes of Arlington covered more than three square miles of land, almost every inch of it needing to be lowered or raised.

The Federal Emergency Management Administration (FEMA) monitored the process closely. The dirt was put down in one-foot "lifts." The scraper dumps the dirt out, the bulldozer knocks it down, the compactor runs across the top of it to tighten it up. Each lift had to be inspected and tested by FEMA to make sure it met a compaction standard so there would be no risk of movement or erosion in foundations when heavy rains came.

I would stand out in the hot summertime in the middle of the property directing the equipment drivers where to dump the dirt. I'm sure S.J. thought I was crazy, and I wouldn't blame him. Here was a multi-million-dollar project and one guy was directing it the way General George Patton leaped down off his staff car to direct traffic during the Battle of the Bulge.

Stovall said to me more than once, "Jim, you could hire an old retired engineer who used to work for the Corps to run this job slick as a whistle."

"I've got to do it on my own," I told him. Then I laughed at myself. "I'm not really a developer, you know. I've never developed anything before."

But I was out there developing.

By 1997, the physical and financial wear and tear of The Lakes of Arlington on me was beginning to show. I had second thoughts. Maybe I should have just cleared it, fenced it, spent the money to get the regulatory approvals, had it ready to go, and then sold it. Plenty of people in Dallas had the dough to develop it from there.

But I'd invested so much money and created so much value that now I was sitting on a piece of property that would take $40 to $50 million just to buy it. After you figured in the cost of basic infrastructure—roads, water, and sewers—and added the interest carry, a buyer would need $75 million to get to the point of actually selling lots and putting up buildings.

In fact, I had floated the idea to some people just to see what the market for it might be. I wanted to know my options. Some very wealthy people tried to raise the money. But they couldn't. It was too big. Just as S.J. had warned, it was an easy project to underestimate.

By 1998 the situation was getting serious. I struggled, feeling really in the soup, spending money hand over fist. My dirt contractor extended me a multimillion-dollar credit line. But even that was getting stretched. One day, Texas Industries called up and said, out of the blue, "We'd like to prepay you six months royalties in advance. We know you're in a jam." They sent over a check for $2 million.

They didn't have to do that. A lot of people did such things, went out of their way to try to help me.

But the money kept going out. The real estate taxes, which at first were based on the $1,200 an acre I paid to the RTC, grew from $60,000 a year to $1.5 million as the value of the property rose.

As I often have, I looked to the stock market for a solution. I found one in Circus Circus, a Las Vegas casino company I knew from my days in Reno. The company had recently launched its Mandalay Bay project, an $850 million hotel casino aimed at an upscale market. The company later changed its name to Mandalay Resort Group.

In 1998 the company was building Mandalay Bay when gaming stocks fell out of favor, the market tanked, and Mandalay crashed. Once traded as high as $50 a share, it fell below $10.

The company's debt had soared at the same time that traffic to Las Vegas was shrinking. There had been a flurry of overbuilding in Vegas as well. Then the company reported that the Mandalay project had a problem with the foundation settling. One of its towers had sunk 16 inches.

Although the company reassured investors that the structural problem was minor, completely fixable, and wouldn't delay the opening, Wall Street clobbered the stock. The *Wall Street Journal*'s "Heard On The Street" column quoted analysts saying the stock "potentially has a long way to fall."

The column quoted Dennis Forst, an analyst with McDonald & Company in Los Angeles, and Bruce Turner, an analyst with Salomon Smith Barney in Tampa, Florida. Turner said, "I'm asking, what makes this stock go up?"

Circus officials argued that the analysts were underrating the company: "The market is saying that Mandalay Bay is going to make zero next year, if you look at [our] valuation," an executive complained.

That got me curious. I knew many people in the gaming industry. I started making calls and asking, "What's the story on Circus?" And they answered, "It's fine. Everything is fine."

I called the gaming analyst at Jefferies. His comment echoed what his colleagues were saying. As a group, the analysts were negative on the gaming industry and especially on Circus.

I flew to Las Vegas for a week and did my own research. Just as I had when I went to visit that Houston Oil rig on the Gulf of Mexico, I put on my blue jeans and drove out to the construction site of Mandalay Bay.

I tracked down the site superintendent, told him I owned stock in the company, and asked him right out, "I'm hearing all these things and wanted to hear it from the horse's mouth. What about these settling problems?"

"We solved that two months ago," he said.

"So the project's on schedule?"

"Oh yeah, no problem."

Company officials had been telling analysts that they were going to get 15 percent returns on Mandalay Bay without a single dollar off the baccarat tables. Baccarat is a high end, high priced, high profit-margin game for the house.

The cash flow looked all right to me. As far as Las Vegas being overbuilt, I'd been hearing that for twenty years. And every time there was a building boom, business marched on like nothing happened.

This was a great opportunity. The stock was at a multiyear low and it was a well-run company with great properties, one of the four dominant players in Las Vegas.

Before I even flew back to Dallas, I plunged big. I bought the stock as low as $8.50. It traded for about a month around $8 and $9. And then it started going up and never looked back. It eventually got into the mid 20s. I sold mine out at around 18.

So, I had doubled my money in the face of a chorus of analysts warning that the stock could go lower.

It's no shock that the analysts got it wrong. They often do. It's unusual when they're wrong on the bear side. Analysts have a strong incentive to hype stocks no matter how bloated the price becomes. Exhibit A is a certified fool who will be long remembered by Wall Street historians. Henry Blodget has become the whipping boy for the dotcom disaster, and he certainly deserves his full share of whipping.

Poor Henry stumbled upon his fame in December 1998, when he worked as an analyst at CIBC Oppenheimer, a small brokerage firm. He predicted that Amazon.com, trading at $243 a share, would soon go to $400 a share. That was Blodget's "target" price, a popular term you don't hear much of since the high-tech bubble burst. That's "target" as in, "Our five-star analyst just got off the phone with the company's chief financial officer and we're raising our target price for the stock to $400."

What in the world does an imaginary share price have to do with whether a company is making a profit, has cash flow, is growing its market share, has a solid product line, and is run by savvy management? The answer is nothing. But it sounds good. It makes people hopeful. In a bubbling market it makes them feel downright greedy, restless, afraid to be left behind. It makes them run out and buy the stock, which is the main thing Wall Street cares about.

"I just bought 100 shares of Amazon at $200," customers bragged to anyone who would listen. "This analyst says it's going to go to $400!" As if the customer had already made a profit.

Blodget announced his prediction just two years after Amazon went public at $18 a share, and the stock was at a record high. Amazon has sold a lot of books, but four years after its Wall Street debut the company still hasn't earned a penny of profit.

Thanks to the feeding frenzy whipped along by Blodget and CNBC's coverage of him, the stock did go to $400 and higher.

Henry Blodget, 33, instantly became a sought-after Wall Street celebrity, despite a scrawny resume that boasted a job as a production assistant for CNN's *Moneyline*, some freelance journalism, and teaching English in Japan. By contrast, I had been investing in the stock market for several years before he was born.

Nevertheless, Blodget's newly discovered genius won him a $4 million-a-year job at Merrill Lynch, which beats hell out of pouring coffee for Lou Dobbs.

Next he landed a hot publishing contract for an untitled book about the Internet that was supposed to predict the future of the business. The publisher declared that Blodget "has a rare talent for explaining why all this market madness actually makes sense."

And then Amazon began to crash.

As Amazon burned, Blodget fiddled. In June 2000, with the stock trading at a presplit price of $150, he slapped a new target on it of $300. But even as he did, he admitted that Amazon might never make enough profit to justify all the money that had been squandered on its shares. "At this point, it is still anyone's guess," he told a reporter.

As I write this, Amazon trades at a comparable price, before a three-for-one split, of about $30. And there's no hope in the chart, just a long slippery slope pointing toward oblivion. So the herd of sheep that followed Henry Blodget off the cliff had as much as 90 cents sheared from every dollar invested.

When I was an active investor during the 1970s and 1980s, analysts were more professional, rational, and independent. There were a number of truly great analysts such as Maryann Keller, who covered the automobile industry and knew it cold. She called a spade a spade. If she thought Ford was going down she would say it, even on television, and in her two books.

Fifteen years ago, the analysts were tough on the companies, and on the markets. Morgan Stanley for decades has had a global market strategist named Barton Biggs who is one of the few commentators who thinks it's his job to tell the truth. Late in 1999, with the Nasdaq soaring and the smell of easy money in the air, Biggs warned investors to lighten up on technology stocks.

He's been quoted and interviewed thousands of times over the years on financial news programs, a frequent and often cautionary voice of wisdom. I remember seeing him on CNBC around the time he turned bearish on the Nasdaq. He was being interviewed by Maria Bartiromo, another former production assistant for CNN's Lou Dobbs, who reinvented herself as a television financial expert.

I couldn't help feeling sorry for Barton. Maria and some of the other hotshot TV talking heads, most young enough to be his children, spoke to him like an old dog that could barely get to his feet anymore, let alone hunt. The Nasdaq continued to soar, rising 46 percent. Barton was spitting into a hurricane.

But each dog has his day. In April 2001, with the Nasdaq back where it stood two and a half years earlier, Barton Biggs got it right.

What changed from the 1970s and 1980s? Brokerage commission rates became competitive, so firms put a bigger emphasis on investment and merchant banking. The banking guys started taking the analysts with them on sales calls. The next thing you knew the companies owned the brokerage firms and the analysts. The word "sell" was stricken from their vocabularies.

Hard proof of this showed up in March 2001 when J. P. Morgan Chase & Co. suffered the misfortune of seeing one of its internal memos published in the *Times* of London. The memo instructed Morgan Chase's analysts to get client companies to sign off on the brokerage firm's reports before releasing them. In other words, forget about objective research on public companies. The goal is to make the investment-banking client happy. The hell with the investors.

In April 2001, Credit Suisse Group, the parent of Credit Suisse First Boston, fired one of its analysts after he warned that SwissAir Group might report a loss for 2000. The analyst sued and Credit Suisse settled out of court.

On Wall Street, as elsewhere, when money speaks, the truth is silent.

If Henry Blodget had been an analyst in the 1980s and tried to make a call like the one he made on Amazon, the public would never have known about it. Whoever was in charge would have summoned the SOB, called him a lunatic, fired him, and had him briskly escorted from the building.

But, during the dot-com bubble, they let these guys get away with murder, and that's a swindle. I blame the brokerage firms and their analysts for the bubble and subsequent disaster.

You have to wonder how someone like Blodget can be so wrong, encourage so many people to throw away so much of their hard-earned money, and get off scot free. And yet, there is an army of such fools and swindlers on Wall Street.

An analyst will brazenly recommend that investors run out and buy a stock from its peak all the way down into the crater. And when the stock is finally scraping bottom, trading for less than the cash the company has in the bank, that's when the analyst will wring his hands and talk about it being a bad time to buy. He won't issue a "sell" recommendation, but he'll call it a "hold," which is the same thing. It's insane.

The time to buy is at the bottom. The time to sell is at the top. They've got it reversed.

If you think about it, big brokerage firms pimp stocks the same way promoters pimp the pennies. One is a well-dressed analyst made up to look like he's got a tan, chanting "Buy! Buy! Buy!" on CNBC. The other is a sleazeball on the phone in a boiler room cramming worthless mining stocks down customers' throats.

It's the same swindle.

You're better off flipping a coin than listening to an analyst. The coin is unbiased. Ninety-five percent of all Wall Street analyst recommendations are buys. At Goldman Sachs, Merrill Lynch, and Morgan Stanley, less than 1 percent of their recommendations are sells. What does that tell you? Analysts are either ignorant or ignoring reality.

If they're ignorant, they fall into that category of analysts who couldn't cut it in an industry, needed a job, and talked somebody on Wall Street into paying them to analyze it.

When they ignore reality, it's because doing so makes their firms more money. If you were General Electric's CEO, would you give your next billion-dollar stock offering to a brokerage house whose analyst told investors to get rid of your stock? I don't think so. Brokerage firms will swindle you with bogus, biased analysis, sacrificing your profit opportunity on the altar of their investment banking fees and bonuses.

What I wouldn't give to see the day when some big firm ran an honest ad in the *Wall Street Journal* that said something like this:

"We are so very sorry we recommended these 100 stocks that lost 50 percent of their value since our recommendation. The analysts have been fired and we sincerely hope this does not happen again to you and your family."

The only real value I get out of most stock analysts is in the numbers they dig out. Like any investor, I can get free research to check out my theories about a stock or an industry.

Analyst recommendations also can sometimes suggest the way the wind is blowing in the market. If analysts recommend a stock and it goes up sharply, we're probably in a bull market. If they recommend a stock and it goes nowhere or down, a bear market is in full swing.

In my opinion, most analysts are flunkies for the companies they cover and the brokerage firms who pay them. If you act on their advice, you face a high risk of financial ruin. I know. It happened to me and not that long ago. As savvy as I sometimes think I am, I have to tell the truth: I have not always heeded my own advice.

I had a good broker at Jefferies & Company who had been on a streak suggesting winning stocks. One day he said, "We've got this guy who covers Recycling Industries. He's an influential analyst. He's pounding the table on the stock, got a strong buy on it."

Recycling Industries was trading around $5 a share. Based in Colorado, the company specialized in pollution control and metal recycling.

It had borrowed or raised almost $400 million and gone on a spending spree, buying up scrap yards around the country. Maybe the stock was bottoming out.

I told the broker, "Let's get your guy on the phone."

During a conference call, the analyst gave me the big spiel about how Recycling's executives were a bunch of ex-Wall Street guys. GE Capital was one of their lenders. They had a rollup strategy, buying up existing businesses in the recycling of steel. The company was well financed, growing rapidly, with excellent management controlling costs, on top of the game, knowing what the hell they were doing.

I told the analyst, "I have friends at Texas Industries. They have a steel division that manufactures beams for construction. They've been saying that steel prices are weakening. How's that going to affect your guys?"

"It'll put a squeeze on profit margins," he admitted. "But they're already cutting costs. They can see this coming. They're increasing productivity to compensate. They'll be just fine."

"Buy me 30,000 shares," I told the broker. I got the stock at $5^{1/4}$. I never did my own research. You'd think that after as many times as I've been swindled and witnessed swindles, I'd know better.

Well, the next thing, the broker left Jefferies to work for a hedge fund. Right about the time he left, I got a new broker who didn't know Recycling Industries from Pets.com. One day I noticed the stock weakening. I called the new broker and asked him if the firm was still strong on the stock.

"Jesus, I don't know a thing about this," he said. "They fired the damn analyst."

Like a jerk I sat there for two months watching the stock burn to the ground and the company go bankrupt. Never listen to analysts, and beware of companies managed by ex-Wall Streeters.

No analyst knows what the people who work in a particular industry know. You don't have to throw a party or stage a dove hunt to find out what's really happening. You don't have to speak to the CEO or anyone in management to get the same information. Anyone can create his or her own network of people representing a broad cross-section of our economy. Listen and observe.

One of the biggest fortunes made in the video game business, back when it was first getting hot in the early 1980s, came after a money manager got curious why his kids begged him every Saturday morning for quarters. He followed them and found they were spending them in a video game arcade. He bought stocks of video game manufacturers and made a fortune.

An independent businesswoman I knew, Roz Newell, told me many years ago that she was selling her Dallas linens store because a big chain called Bed, Bath, and Beyond was too much competition. I bought the stock and it doubled.

A relative works at a Nissan automobile plant in Tennessee, and I have friends who work at a General Motors plant in Arlington, Texas. They know before anyone else how fast the cars are moving out the door and when production is slowing or plants are closing.

Any local realtor will tell you whether business is slow or brisk. If you ask and listen, it's very simple to pick growing companies to wisely invest your money in.

Sometimes, even with all my research, I still manage to screw it up.

One day I was talking to Monk White, a broker I liked who worked for Salomon Smith Barney in Dallas, about a local hotel company that had fallen on hard times. The stock is now known as Wyndham Hotels, but at the time it went by the name Patriot American Hospitality. The stock traded around $8 a share, down from a high of $40. Although it was a Dallas outfit, I'd never paid attention to Wyndham.

Dallas's Trammel Crow family, the biggest real estate developers in the world, started the company. The broker knew James D. Carreker, who had been recruited as president.

"Jesus, this thing has just been beaten to death," I said. "They have some great assets. I'm going to start watching it." He agreed the stock looked cheap.

I finally plunged for 30,000 shares at $8^{1/8}$ and sold two days later at $9^{3/4}$. I walked away with a profit of almost $50,000.

A few weeks later, the bottom fell out and the stock dropped to about $6^{1/2}$. I plunged again, this time for several hundred thousand shares.

At that time I knew a man who was best friends with a member of Wyndham's board. His friend owned 4 million shares of the stock and was taking a bath. That piqued my interest. I pulled everything I could find on the company going back three years, all their financial reports. The reason the stock was collapsing, I realized, was not that cash flow was collapsing, but the company had billions in short-term debt coming due.

Also, the company had several hundred million dollars' worth of equity forward contracts with three major brokerage firms. In an equity forward contract a public company borrows money against its stock. If the stock is trading at $20, and the company wants to borrow $200 million, it gives the brokerage firm or investment bank 10 million shares to hold. At the end of the borrowing period, the company has the option of either paying off the $200 million plus interest or, if the stock has fallen, coughing up enough shares to maintain $200 million worth of collateral.

This is like a margin call, only on a grand scale. If the stock drops to $18, the company must issue more stock to the bank to keep the collateral at $200 million.

Wyndham had all this equity forward borrowing on its books. The lower the stock sank, the more stock the company needed to issue, the more potential stock around for sale, which sent the price lower, and so on and so on.

Clearly, this was a short-term debt problem, I decided. In the course of my research, I found that the company had issued well over $2 billion of debt but with the proceeds bought $5 billion worth of property. Even if they overpaid by 40 percent, the company still should have the right amount of debt associated with the properties.

I became comfortable that the company's liquidation value was way above $6 a share, where it was trading.

The analysts (uh-oh!) estimated Wyndham's breakup value at about $15 a share. If the company could be liquidated for $15, in the worst-case scenario it would be bought out by Hilton, Marriott, or some other outfit that wanted to grab some hotel properties cheap.

I loaded the boat, buying almost a million shares.

The price kept dropping. This must be tax selling, it's the end of the year, I told myself.

But the stock just kept falling, finally bottoming out at a low of

$1.31 a share. The company rejected an offer from Hilton for a capital infusion and the sale of about $900 million worth of property. Never underestimate the ability of management to screw up a company.

The latest CEO became one of my next-door neighbors. I ran into him one day in the elevator and asked him, "How's the company?"

"We're doing great," he said. "But Wall Street hates us."

An important lesson relearned: Just because a stock appears to have hit bottom doesn't mean it's going to go right back up. Once a company loses its credibility with the Street, it can take a long time to rebuild. What goes down doesn't have to go back up.

Even though I tracked what the analysts were saying about Wyndham, I didn't buy on that basis. They were singing "buy" all the way down. PaineWebber, the company's banker, made millions in fees. To no one's surprise, their analyst was flogging the stock as it sank to $5. But he's gone now, along with a lot of customers' money.

I stopped my loss at $1.5 million. Anybody who was in Wyndham got burned alive, even the Crow family, who were billionaires but lost half a billion dollars.

It's not so bad getting screwed when the big guys get it worse than you.

19

Suspender Boys

*"Look, I'm not a developer. I'm a stock market guy.
I've gone about as far as I can."*

Five years after I bought the property, The Lakes of Arlington began to really drag me down.

Although I made some money in the stock market, it was nowhere near the kind of dough I needed to move my plans forward. I raised some cash by selling off some of the extra acreage I'd bought that bordered the original property. But the project evolved into a rolling crisis. As soon as I bought some time, I needed to buy more.

Rex Crim, a local mortgage broker, helped me find short-term loans to keep the heavy-equipment guys working and cover my other expenses. The lender was Beal Bank of Dallas, notorious in the real estate business and notoriously successful. In 2000, Beal ranked at the top of an industry survey, with a five-year average return on equity of more than 50 percent. Even the Mafia can't beat that!

Beal Bank didn't offer checking accounts. It didn't have to. It was known among real estate professionals as a loan-to-own bank, making short-term loans to underfunded but valuable real estate projects hoping, praying, that the borrower would default. Then the bank could swoop in, grab the property for a song, and develop it themselves, or flip it for a profit.

Beal came out of the real estate crash of the late 1980s buying up huge loan portfolios of foreclosed properties and made hundreds of millions in the ensuing recovery. Andrew Beal, the bank's principal owner, was a local character who had made so much money, he started a rocket ship company and threw more than $200 million into it before it folded.

Like a vulture waiting for its prey to die so it can begin to dine, Beal Bank hoped I would fail.

The Beal note was coming due. I needed another financing source, a sale, or a joint venture. Rex flushed a couple of potential partners out of the woodwork, escape hatches in case I needed one.

In a typical residential development, you go in and cut out a piece closest to the road, open it up, put in the utilities, and sell it off. Then you move back into the next section. That way a developer has money coming in to fund the roads and utilities as he moves deeper into the property.

In this case, I had bulldozed myself into a corner. The residential part of the project lay farthest from the road. The commercial lots were in the front. But the commercial real estate wouldn't be ready until Highway 157 had been rerouted, and that project hadn't even started. Until the road had been moved, we couldn't begin to develop the lake community.

We still had to build the basic infrastructure that the city required, including a loop road and all utilities. But I'd already invested a ton of money, and needed a lot more to finish before the first dollar would come back.

I found myself in a tough spot, at least as far as my original vision. Rex worked like a dog to put together financing deals, and caught my fever. He shared the vision. He wanted to live there, too. But it was a constant hustle.

Rex and I huddled and came up with several strategies. In the worst case, I knew I could find buyers who'd be happy to take the residential tracts in a block, and wait for the infrastructure. I would still have come out with millions in profit.

We had two or three other backup solutions, but the situation became a week-by-week vigil.

Rex put together a formal loan proposal and pitched it everywhere he could think of that might catch the interest of a solid, long-term financial partner. We went back to the engineering firms and got cost estimates to finish putting all the basic services in and get it to the point where we could, as they say in the business, start selling dirt. We built into the financial projection about three years of interest carry, just in case.

We calculated that to pay off Beal, finish the lakes and infrastructure, get the road moved, and start selling dirt, we would need $50 million. That was the ideal outcome: find a committed lender without losing too many pounds of flesh. But, if we could raise at least $20 million, we could push things far enough to convince a lender to give us the balance.

Some sharp players in Dallas let Rex know that they'd be happy to help out a poor boy like me who'd got a hole in his pocket. But these offers all came with miles of string. Thinking Rex wouldn't repeat it, they told him, "Salim doesn't know what the hell he's doing. We're smarter than you guys. We've got money to finish the job. We'll back you up, but it's going to cost a big chunk of your ownership. By the way, this offer's only good until Friday. After that it's withdrawn."

The first time Rex brought me one of these I blew my top. He told the others, "I don't think I'm even going to present this to Mr. Salim. He might toss me through a window."

And then, one day, he called with his voice full of genuine optimism.

"Jim, I just got off the phone with a guy from Credit Suisse First Boston, in *New York*. I think they might be interested in taking a look at our deal."

"Credit Suisse First Boston?" A global financial powerhouse. "What the hell do they care about a development in Dallas?"

"I don't know, but I just got off the phone with a guy, Richard Luftig, in their Principal Transactions Group. He sounds like the real deal, Jim."

Rex said Luftig gave him the old New York minute routine: "I'm real busy. Just send the material. We only do big deals. We don't touch anything under $20 million. How big is the deal? Is it big enough? Okay. Send me the book. I'll take a look and let you know."

Rex was impressed. Is it big enough? He'd never worked on a loan deal much over $2 million.

New York suspender boys from Credit Suisse First Boston never impressed me when I lived in New York, so I didn't give the call much thought. But the day CSFB called Rex and invited us to submit a loan application, even I had trouble keeping my hopes from rising just a little.

And then I got a call from Rex that set a whole new string of events in motion. Two investment bankers from CSFB wanted to schedule a fly-down from New York, to look at the property and meet me. They wanted to do it right away.

Rex didn't know what to think. "Are these guys idiots, or do they know something we don't?"

The Lakes of Arlington wasn't a prime deal. Big New York banks prefer deals that are already teed up, highly collateralized, and set to go. Our project needed partners with vision and patience. It was hard to imagine an investment bank in New York seeing anything other than a chance to make a quick buck.

It was a big day for Rex when Richard Luftig and Michael Gough, two CSFB mortgage bankers, flew into Dallas/Fort Worth, a scorcher of a summer day. They wanted to see the project.

I'd been around long enough, and in the right circles, to know that CSFB had a distinct reputation, earned during the 1980s wave of mergers and acquisitions.

First Boston had been a sleepy, white-shoe brokerage firm until two hotshot investment bankers remade the dowager into a gunslinger. The stars who gave First Boston its visibility, Bruce Wasserstein and Joseph Perella, were the most aggressive deal-makers around. They earned huge fees for their firm and themselves by arranging giant corporate mergers and takeovers. Some target companies complained they were too aggressive, that First Boston's team virtually blackmailed them into agreeing to be acquired.

In fact, Wasserstein and Perella would look for an undervalued stock and try to arrange a friendly combination. But if the target wasn't in the mood to go to the altar, First Boston was ready, able, and eager to foment a hostile takeover bid, a bidding war, or force a greenmail payoff.

No matter how the deals turned out, they made money. The more contentious the deal, the more money they made. Peace in the mergers department at First Boston was not synonymous with prosperity. Wasserstein picked up the nickname "Bid 'em up Bruce." He excelled at whipping buyers into paying premium prices for his client companies. Target companies that hired First Boston to defend against a takeover paid through-the-nose fees.

First Boston did well until 1987, when it got hit by huge trading losses. A year later, the merger stars left, complaining their fees weren't big enough. Credit Suisse, a big Zurich-based bank that had owned 40 percent of First Boston for many years, stepped in to guard its investment and swallowed the rest of the firm in 1989.

The First Boston aggressive style remained even after the stars left and the Zurich gnomes arrived. So did disputes over fees and bonuses. In 1992, Credit Suisse First Boston lost a lot of its top talent over complaints about insufficient compensation.

In 1995, the firm hired someone who had plenty of experience complaining about poor compensation. Andrew Stone was a gunslinger who earned his notches in the 1980s, starting as a bond trader right out of Harvard. At Salomon Brothers he learned the art of creating, packaging, selling, and trading mortgage securities. He became a big shooter and played a supporting role in *Liar's Poker*, the best-selling 1989 autobiography by a young Salomon bond trader named Michael Lewis.

Lewis quoted Stone numerous times in his book, including this gem: "The best producers [salesmen] are cutthroat, competitive, and often neurotic and paranoid." Stone, as it turned out, knew exactly what he was talking about.

He left Salomon because they weren't paying him enough. He landed at Prudential Bache in 1987 and left there in 1990, reportedly angered at the small size of his bonus. Next stop was Daiwa Securities America, where he profitably ran that firm's mortgage trading business, creating securities backed by bizarre assets like trailer parks. *Barron's* magazine reported that he earned $15 million in 1992, but that some fund managers were criticizing Daiwa's latest mortgage offering as "the worst . . . deal of all time."

In 1995, Andrew Stone joined the mortgage department at CSFB and became its head man. He was responsible for sending Richard Luftig and Michael Gough to Dallas that miserably hot July day to take a look at The Lakes of Arlington. Stone pulled the levers. Luftig and Gough danced.

Rex picked the two bankers up at the airport and gave them the grand tour.

Luftig was the younger of the two, in his early thirties and slender. Rex wondered how a guy that young got into such a powerful position, handling so much money. Gough was older, around fifty, and stout. Gough was the boss, Luftig the detail man.

Rex drove them around the property in a Jeep, dodging the belly dumpers and the bulldozers, bouncing over the rutted tracks. Luftig took the backseat and spent most of the time on his cell phone, half listening to Rex's spiel. The phone rang almost as soon as he hung up from the previous call. The guy had no manners.

Rex had given this tour many times. He knew the project and he knew all the facts. For two years, The Lakes had been his life as well as mine. He aimed to have a big house on the island that we were building in the middle of the biggest lake. He was a believer.

"We don't need that many people to make this thing successful," Rex told the bankers. "I haven't met a single residential builder who isn't interested in this project. There's no place left in the Metroplex for them to build. They know that the amenities out here are going to be winners. Water, water, everywhere, and all of it aqua blue."

Luftig, in between calls, asked from the backseat, "Aqua blue? What do you mean?"

"This place was mined for years. Anytime you get down near a river, you find large deposits of sand and gravel and you're closer to the ground-water level.

"What Jim's doing is digging down thirty feet in the cut area, below the water table, and raising 850 acres out of the flood plain. Now, we have a unique situation where, when we get down to the bottom, we hit blue shale, a real hard clay, that'll be the lakebeds.

"The lakes just naturally fill up from groundwater seeping in. As water flows underground, it flows toward the rivers, so there's natural groundwater pressure. We've got five and a half miles of frontage on the Trinity."

"Jesus Christ," Gough said. "This goddamn thing is huge!"

"All this water is being filtered through sand and gravel," Rex continued. "So, instead of a muddy sandy bottom, we end up with a bottom that, as the sun goes into that pure underground water, reflects back pure aqua blue. It's blue because of the bottom of the lake and the purity of the water."

"Hard to imagine," Luftig said, dialing a call. "Must be an environmental nightmare, the approvals and all. Sandy, hi. It's Richard. Listen, did Mark call yet?"

Rex was determined to finish his spiel, so he slogged on. At least Gough appeared to be listening.

"It'll be like living in Florida, because of the color of the water, the pristine nature of the water. Jim and the Corps of Engineers got together, and they agreed there won't be any discharge from the neighborhood into the groundwater system. No fertilizer or other kinds of pollutants will be allowed to be used.

"We're not allowing power boats on the lakes, either. Only sailboats. Fishing. We'll stock the lakes, get the state to come in and do it right. We've already got ducks coming in here and cranes and herons. Lots of wildlife."

"Sounds nice," Gough said. "But if you want Florida, why not go to Florida?"

"Well, here you're living in the middle of four and a half million people, on a beautiful aqua-blue lake, three hundred acres of wildlife that you're going to be able to walk through, and you don't have to leave Dallas to do it. We're only eighteen miles from downtown."

It bugged Rex that he couldn't get Luftig's full attention. How could he sell a deal if the prospect wouldn't hear the story? How could he make them see how beautiful it was going to be? Rex was so hooked on the place, he often took his wife and child out there in the summer evenings and had picnics on the island we were building, before there was water in the lake. The island was where Rex and I were going to live when the project was done.

But as the tour progressed, listening to the responses of both men, it began to dawn on Rex that as hard as he was trying to get them to pull the trigger, they were trying hard to sell *him* something.

Gough and Luftig started bragging. They dropped the names of Fortune 500 companies who were their clients. They talked about how many billions they had to work with, how they could make all kinds of miracles happen by snapping their fingers. They were Credit Suisse First Boston, big shooters with a big name.

And then, when they saw the lake beds, they started to get excited.

"You know, we're not going to just come in and make a loan on this thing," Gough told Rex. "What we're going to do is bring development. We'll bring the money to build the buildings, and bring the clients who need the money to build the buildings. We'll make this a success by ourselves."

Rex had a hard time keeping a grin off his face. He'd finally hit the big one. He told me later, "Jim, this may be the last mortgage I ever broker. I'm tired of workin' like a dog!"

Gough and Luftig threw around the names of big hotel companies and anchor stores they could talk into locating along the highway.

"If we do this loan," Luftig piped up, "We have to have a golf course."

That surprised Rex.

"Jim and I, we don't think that's what we need to do here," he said. "There are already four or five public courses within a couple miles, and we've already cut down on the number of acres we can build on, with the wetlands and all. The lakes alone take up eight hundred acres.

"What we plan to do is sell lots. That's the greatest demand in the area, for lots. People will love the idea of living right in the heart of the Metroplex and be surrounded by lakes and wildlife.

"There's a lot of money in the Metroplex. And a lot of very wealthy people who are having to move farther out to find the quality of life they want. People are excited that we're going to have a high-end neighborhood in Arlington."

Luftig stared out the window at the piles of dirt. "I'm a big golfer," he declared. "When I go see my deals, I play golf."

What an asshole, Rex thought.

That night he brought the bankers to meet me for dinner at an Italian restaurant in Arlington.

After introductions, drinks, and pleasantries, I started in. "Look, I'm not a developer. I'm a stock market guy. I've done what probably no other real estate developer could do, or should do, as far as reclaiming this property and getting the approvals and entitlements. I've worked my ass off getting the city and everyone else behind The Lakes of Arlington.

"But it's been almost six years and I've gone about as far as I can. Truthfully, I want to get away from this thing. It's consuming fifteen hours of every day, six days of every week. And I'd like to get my money back off the table."

"We hear you loud and clear," Luftig said. "We've been kicking this around and we have a client that's a public company, a small public company. But we're about to make it a big company. What we'd like to do is have you sell your land to the public company. We'll pay off all your debt, give you your investment back up front, plus 10 million shares of a stock that's trading around $2."

"Okay, you've got my attention," I said. "Go on."

"It's a golf company. They develop residential communities around golf courses. They've got great properties all around the country, Florida, California, South Carolina. All the golf hotspots.

"It's a Credit Suisse First Boston company. It's our company. We're behind it 110 percent. We guarantee that we're going to grow it with $500 million in financing to build out these golf communities.

"We're gonna get our analyst to cover the stock and recommend it. We've got two lawyers working full time getting this company's financials cleaned up, so we can get it listed on Nasdaq and the stock can trade."

"What's the name?" I asked.

"Golf Communities of America. They're in Orlando. The CEO is solid gold, been in the golf business forever. Used to be a golf pro, and he's built, designed, or renovated almost two dozen golf courses. Really knows his stuff. Really knows his golf."

Yes, I wanted my money off the table. I had takers lined up. But if I had the opportunity to pull down a chunk of stock in a company that was going to be backed and grown by a big blue-chip firm like CSFB, that had a lot of upside potential.

But I didn't like the golf part.

"You know, I lived on a golf course in Hawaii, and I can tell you that someone with the kind of money it takes to buy such a place would rather have peace and quiet than listen to some dope out there cursing his slice at seven o'clock on a Sunday morning. And then the ones who are drunk and rowdy in the afternoon."

"We're going to promote the hell out of this thing," Luftig plowed on. "So, instead of waiting five years on a long-term real estate project to get $25 million, you stand to gain $40 million, maybe more, in a year or so."

The pitch sounded solid. I couldn't find a hole in the plan. There was no doubt in my mind that they had the $500 million. Golf Communities had about 45 million shares outstanding, valued roughly at $2, and this monster of an investment bank was talking about dumping half a billion dollars into it. That sounded like a $10 stock easily.

Gough gave the stock a conservative price-earnings ratio of 8, and came up with a $6 price.

I was ready to bite. Except for one thing.

"There's a problem in my past that you should know about first," I said.

"We know about the problem," said Gough.

"You do?"

"We do."

The Rollo business had been in the local papers. Just in case CSFB hadn't turned it up in the background check I was certain they'd done, I wanted to clear the air before we went further.

"Look, I need to know up front. If you're going to have a beef about it, better speak up now. I have three different people who want to buy this thing, real buyers, people like the Pritzkers of Chicago, just to name one.

"You've got to make that call right now. Otherwise, I don't want to waste any more time."

Gough and Luftig asked me to tell them what happened. I gave the short version. When I was done, Luftig said, "Everybody makes mistakes, Jim. Who cares? It was a long time ago and what does it matter to a real estate development? The deal stands on its own."

That sounded good to me. After all, this was Credit Suisse First Boston. The chips don't get any bluer.

We parted with a verbal agreement to go to the next step. I'd have to meet the CEO of Golf Communities, show him the property. If everything looked all right, we'd do the deal.

It looked like my long journey with The Lakes of Arlington was finally going to pay off.

20

Impeccable Timing

"[Investment bankers are] financial termites
. . . a common enemy of investors and business."
—William O. Douglas, Depression-era SEC Commissioner

You'd think that it would have been a red flag for me, but somehow I let it slide that Golf Communities was created out of a reverse merger with a Utah shell. A penny stock with all the bad history of a typical penny-stock scam.

But this was not one of Frank Skinner's crooked brokers. This was an international bank with assets of $350 billion and, most important of all, a reputation it could project and needed to protect.

Warren Stanchina, CEO of Golf, had the same reaction I did, although compared to my experience with the markets he was as innocent as a lamb being led to slaughter.

Stanchina's company was already tied up with a big investment bank called Starwood Capital. Starwood had financed another golf-related company, and they had offered Golf Communities a $50 million investment when Warren received an unsolicited phone call from Richard Luftig at Credit Suisse First Boston.

"We like your company," he told Warren. "We don't have a golf company, and we'd like to put $500 million into the golf industry. We'd like to do it through your company."

Warren was dumbfounded. Half a *billion* dollars, into a little company like Golf whose stock wasn't even properly listed yet?

"Uh, that sounds great," Warren told Luftig, "but I've already go— I'm about to close a deal—with Starwood Capital. We've already negotiated the terms."

Warren didn't say so, but the Starwood deal wasn't as attractive heading into closing as it had been at first blush. The terms had changed, and he didn't like most of the changes. Starwood wanted to merge Golf Communities with the other golf company it had banked. Besides the extra $450 million Luftig was tossing around, Warren was in the mood to be romanced.

Luftig persuaded Warren to bust the Starwood deal. Starwood wasn't happy. Golf was a good catch. Starwood told Warren it would force Golf Communities to cough up the $500,000 breakup penalty that had been written into the agreements. Warren was unhappy about throwing away a half a million dollars on a deal that had changed to his dissatisfaction anyway.

But Luftig reassured him. "Hey, we do deals with Starwood all the time. We don't want to piss them off. So let's just pay them."

"Screw them," Warren said. "They changed the deal. I don't want to pay them a penny. If they want to sue us, let 'em. My lawyers don't think they have a case."

But Luftig was determined. "Look, we'll lend you the money to pay them. It's better that way. This is Wall Street. We don't crap where we eat, you know what I mean?"

Once Luftig had persuaded Warren Stanchina to dump the Starwood deal, CSFB put on a full-court press.

"We can close this deal in ninety days," Luftig predicted in March of 1998. Warren didn't believe him. But suddenly the phones started ringing and kept ringing all day with requests for documents, arranging details, and setting up appraisals of the properties Golf already owned. In three months, they managed to get all the assets appraised. Warren was suspicious of the appraisals. They seemed inflated. But the heat was on to do the deal. Just do the deal, whatever it takes, was the message that came from every mouth and every action at CSFB.

They wined and dined Warren. They introduced him to celebrities, and told anyone within earshot that Golf was *their* company. They were going to take it to the next level. They gave him all kinds of encouragement. "We're going to grow Golf into a $500 million company, Warren. We're going to take the stock from nothing to $10, or even $20 a share."

Warren told me later that the first signs of trouble appeared early, but he didn't heed them. He was blinded by CSFB's reputation and money.

They told him they wanted him to lease a Lear jet for a day of project-hopping. They wanted to go look at golf courses for the company to buy.

"We're going to go and take a look, but we're so busy we have to get there and get out quickly."

Michael Gough explained to Warren that they had access to a Lear jet that was owned by a member of the Credit Suisse loan committee.

"It's his private jet, and the director who owns it likes to keep that jet going. If you'll pay him $10,000 for the day, you can use it."

"I can go rent two Citation prop-jets for $4,000," Warren said, indignant. "I hate Lear jets, anyway. They're noisy. You can't hear yourself think."

"But it's good for your next deal," Gough said. "The guy who owns the jet will look after you when you go before him for final approval on the deal."

Warren paid the $10,000, but it felt exactly like a shakedown.

The jet flew from New York and met Warren in Pinehurst, North Carolina. From there the group flew a short hop west to a small town, a place they could have reached in an hour and a half of driving. What did they do when they got there? Rented a car, looked at a golf course, and played eighteen holes while Warren, a retired pro, gave lessons. The bankers acted like boors, disparaging the course, bad-mouthing the South, arguing about what time they needed to leave to get back to New York in time to catch their helicopters home. And the incessant chirping of cell phones.

A well-known sports announcer was the managing partner of the golf course where they were playing. He joined Warren and the CSFB bankers for a while. The announcer took Warren aside at one point and whispered, "What a bunch of assholes!"

In July 1998, CSFB closed the first deal for Golf Communities, lending the company $87 million. They had several other deals in the works, situations similar to mine where a lot of land needed a lot of capital to get it developed.

One day Gough came to Warren with this news:

"We've got a transaction that we've been working on for several months, and we've come up with a problem where we can't go forward with the borrower. We need to see if we can't save it. We spent a lot of money on it, it's been through the credit committee, and been approved. But we found a problem with the borrower, and we aren't going to be able to do business with him. We would like to see if Golf Communities can buy this deal? It's perfect for a golf course."

"What's the problem?" Warren asked.

"We don't want to discuss it," he was told. "It's confidential. But we'd like you to go to Dallas and meet with this guy, Jim Salim. See if you can convince him to convert his equity in a big land project he has down there into stock in Golf Communities. If you can do that, we'll put the $50 million in to close the deal and another $20 million to improve the property."

The problem was the one I'd disclosed to Luftig and Gough. My guess is that somewhere between the time Luftig and Gough got the initial go-ahead to pursue my project from Andrew Stone, based on the proposal Rex sent up, and the time they walked it upstairs to the loan committee, somebody higher up got a whiff of my past. I can imagine Gough and Luftig being told to go back and find another angle, figure out how to paper this over.

Whatever the reason, Rex received a flurry of urgent phone calls from Gough asking for additional appraisals and other details, and talking up this deal with Golf Communities.

Meanwhile, my hourglass was just about out of sand. Beal was breathing down my neck. I was just about ready to make a deal with another buyer willing to pay enough so I could walk away with a good profit. In fact, I was in conference with these people, ready to shake hands on an agreement, when Rex telephoned and asked a secretary to call me out of the meeting.

"Gough called, Jim. He's ready to go with these golf company people.

He wants you to meet the CEO right away. It sounded like they're ready to rock and roll."

So, I walked from that deal thinking I had almost thrown away the chance to own a big piece of a hot CSFB company.

A few days later, another blistering summer morning, I picked Warren Stanchina up at the airport to give him his tour of the project. At this point I had given hundreds of tours. I could do it in my sleep.

Warren told me the boys at CSFB had bragged about The Lakes of Arlington. They told him, "Let us describe this piece of property for you. If you hired a roomful of consultants to go to Texas and find the best piece of real estate in all of Texas, this is the piece of property they would come up with. It is the very best development opportunity in the entire state."

It was not a good summer to get a sense of that. The ground was cracked, the weather scorching, the lakes dry and dusty. Texas looks mighty grim baking in the heat, flat and brown.

But Warren recognized the value right away, saw the potential. He gave in to the pressure. We all did.

When Warren flew up to New York to walk the deals past CSFB's loan committee, Gough and Luftig discovered they needed to coach his performances ahead of time. During one of his first sessions, he told the higher-ups, "I'm a golf guy. I'm not really a real estate guy."

Warren's handlers just about fell off their chairs. Later they took him aside.

"Jesus Christ, Warren, don't tell them you don't like real estate. Tell them you *love* real estate."

He was called once before the hand of God, Andrew Stone himself. Warren made sure to tell Stone how much he loved real estate. Anything to get the deal done, that's what they told Warren to say and do. Give the numbers that will make it look good. Say what they want to hear. Just get the deal done. We'll fix it all up later.

The guys at CSFB were pushing hard on everyone. Rex was being pressured to advise me to go with Golf. Warren was getting pressure to talk me into swapping my property for his stock. It was push, push, push, a crazy summer. My back was to the wall and, even though I had other options, I kept going back to the stock deal. I'd be getting ten million shares of a stock that a big investment banking house was going to put on the map in a huge way. I could make $50 million, maybe $100 million. I'd hate myself if I accepted a profit of a few million and watched some opportunist rack up the big score in Golf shares.

So, against all my better judgements, all my experience, I bought in to the Wall Street image of the reputable investment bank that keeps its word. I had no experience to the contrary over my thirty-five years of investing. I pulled the trigger.

Golf Communities, with Credit Suisse's financing, would buy The Lakes of Arlington, pay off all my creditors, and issue me $14 million worth of stock, representing my cash equity in the property. From the moment I said yes, events accelerated.

A closing date was set for the end of August and the first couple days of September, just before Labor Day. Warren was in New York for about a week, closing the other deals that were part of the overall financing of the company. It was complicated. The principal attorney for Credit Suisse's law firm, Cadwalader, Wickersham & Taft, slept in his office for three nights straight.

In the final days leading up to the closing, developing events far from New York and Dallas began to shape everyone's future. The Russian economy collapsed, the ruble fell apart, and big hedge funds that had been trading currency futures got hammered. The Dow Industrials cracked and slid more than 4 percent in one day. The U.S. Commerce Department reported the first year-over-year decline in corporate profits in a decade. Stock markets around the world skidded badly.

I took note of these events. The markets looked shaky and I was just about to receive ten million shares of Rule 144 stock I couldn't sell for six months. But other than the general effect a downturn might have on the economy, I didn't link the Russian crisis to CSFB, and certainly wouldn't have predicted the impact on its mortgage securities business. But, in fact, CSFB had a huge exposure to currency futures through its lending to hedge funds. And behind the unruffled, prosperous facade, Andrew Stone's mortgage securities empire slammed into a brick wall.

The closing took place at a forty-foot-long conference table in Cadwalader's headquarters high up in a Wall Street skyscraper. Piles of file folders were lined up in a nice neat rows, with hundreds of pages waiting for signature.

By the time I showed up, Warren had been at it for several days. He was exhausted and worried. I was nervous. Everything had come together so rapidly. We'd only met two months before.

"I hardly know what I'm signing most of the time," Warren confided during a break.

"What about Golf's chief financial officer?" I asked him. "He's here, right? He'll watch your back."

Warren shook his head woefully. "Luftig and those guys, they don't like my CFO. He's a prick. He asks too many questions. They told me, 'When you come to New York to close this deal, leave the CFO at home.'

"I figured Credit Suisse is my partner. Why piss them off?"

So there we were, two fish in a barrel.

Warren told me that news of the Russian economic disaster came in the middle of the closing, and suddenly the mood soured. His CSFB handlers looked troubled. Gough twisted his mustache. He moaned about the collapsing price of Credit Suisse Group's stock, and how bad that would be for their bonuses. They all had long faces.

Warren finally screwed up his courage and asked, "Is this going to be a problem for our deal here? What's going on?"

Gough looked at him meaningfully and replied, "Well, Warren, let's just put it this way. Your timing is impeccable."

"What do you mean by that?"

Gough refused to elaborate, waving him off. "Let's just leave it at that," he said coyly, exchanging a knowing glance with Luftig.

Later, in an unguarded moment, they let slip that by getting Warren's financing closed in September, they'd be certain of receiving fat bonuses on the deal before the end of the year. That's all that seemed to be on their minds, getting the deal done, whatever the deal was. Just get it done, right away, in time for bonus season.

Meanwhile the meter on the legal fees was spinning away, in high gear. Every day one of CSFB's lawyers showed up at lunchtime, but only at lunchtime. He'd show up when the caterers had laid out the food, fill up his plate, and leave.

Luftig explained that the guy was a securities lawyer. He was advising CSFB on the deal, and Golf Communities was being charged $500 an hour for his services. It was part of the closing costs.

Luftig and Gough made a daily joke of it. "Must be lunchtime, Warren. Here comes Lunchtime Lou!" Warren had never met this lawyer before the closing, never saw him anytime except at lunch, and never heard from him again.

When it was my turn to close on the sale of The Lakes of Arlington to Golf Communities, things got ugly. Years ago I had formed a partnership that actually owned The Lakes of Arlington project. Metrovest Partners was a LLC I created in 1992 to buy the land.

When I borrowed the money from Beal Bank, I bought my partner's interest in Metrovest for $8 million. When I began to run short of capital, I borrowed back almost $3 million in cash. So, when we got to the closing, this person was one of the creditors.

We were shoving papers around the forty-foot conference table, reading and signing, when Luftig came in and said, "Jim, I'm really sorry about this, but Andy Stone's being an asshole. He doesn't want to lend Golf the money to pay your partner back. He wants to pay it in stock."

"I know my partner, and I know what I promised," I told Luftig firmly. "This won't fly."

"Well, that's a big problem," he said. "'Cause without taking the stock, Andy has authorized me to tell you we're not going to have a closing. We'll have to walk the deal."

I couldn't believe it, it was so outrageous. Those SOBs! I was spitting mad. They were putting a power move on me they'd planned all along. They knew I was up against a deadline with Beal Bank. It was a setup to get out of having to cough up another $3 million in cash. It was a bold-faced stock swindle.

I had to get on the phone and beg, yell, and badger my partner into going along. I hated doing it and I hated Stone and Luftig for making me feel I had to do it. It was a cram-down. Maybe they really were prepared to walk the deal, figuring they'd end up owning the property somehow anyway. And here I had just blown off all these other buyers for The Lakes of Arlington, pissing them off by dumping them at the last minute in favor of my new partner, Credit Suisse First Boston.

If the closing had been delayed even a few days, I might have had a fighting chance. I couldn't know it but the company had just been nailed for billions of dollars in the Russian debt defaults. CSFB had loaned some hedge funds hundreds of millions of dollars against currency trading positions that fell apart.

Just four business days after the closing, a *Barron's* magazine real estate columnist gave a peek into the black heart of Stone's operation.

> A virtually unimpeded three-year run up of prices in Manhattan's booming office market stopped on a dime in early September with word that the high-flying real estate group at Credit Suisse First Boston had pulled out of the marketplace. The group, which is led by Andrew Stone, has invested billions in real estate across the country in the past several years .... But as global stock markets tumbled in August, Stone and his group found themselves saddled with as much as $1 billion in warehoused loans that could not readily be marketed as mortgage-backed securities.

"'Right now, we can't make adequate returns for our risk,'" Stone told *Barron's*. The article further reported, "his group has closed on some $200 million in loans they were 'legally obligated' to make, but walked away from another $600 million in less-firm commitments."

"Walked away" might not have been so bad. CSFB *fled*. On the evening of Friday, September 3, the start of Labor Day weekend, as Warren signed the last piece of paper, his bankers had already slipped out the door to catch their helicopters home. No champagne, no cheers, no cigars, not even a pat on the back. A secretary helped him drag his luggage to the elevator.

Gough and Luftig always made sure there was a limousine waiting for Warren at the end of each day, to take him back to his hotel. All those days in New York they had paraded him around, wined and dined him, treated him like a king. This is *our* golf company, they told everyone.

But in the final moments, once the deal was sealed and their bonuses assured, they had scattered like cockroaches in sudden light.

Warren was disgusted by the whole frantic experience. He had looked forward to having the transaction behind him, getting into the limousine, catching his flight home, and being reunited with his wife and children.

Like a rape victim, he couldn't wait to take a long hot shower and wash off the feeling of filth.

But when he emerged on the street, no limo. Not even a busted-up yellow cab. On a steamy New York night, sweat running down his forehead and stinging his eyes, he dragged his luggage several blocks to a busier street where he could hail a cab.

21

We Know What We're Doing

"Jim, I'm telling you, something's not right here.
Tell me what the end-game is. I can't figure it out."

The end of my responsibility for The Lakes of Arlington came as a huge relief. I could finally step back and let someone else carry the ball.

It felt good to be back plunging in the stock market. Occasionally, Luftig phoned asking me to have someone or other call Warren about a detail. I was tickled to be out of it.

Part of my agreement with CSFB required that they get the company in full reporting status as a listed trading stock and register my shares in ninety days, so I could begin to sell. They would have their analyst follow the stock. They would call in favors at other major brokerage firms to get their analysts to pick it up and cover it as well.

We were going to have an $8 to $10 stock within a year. CSFB had $500 million allocated to grow the company. They had a rollup strategy that had been approved at the highest levels of Credit Suisse. Everybody was on board, not just Stone's group but everybody, all the way to the top of CSFB. So they told us, over and over.

Aside from the cram-down of stock to my partner, this had been an easy sale. I wasn't worrying about what was going to happen three years from now. I'd told Gough and Luftig I didn't want to hold the stock forever.

"Don't worry," they said. "Once the stock is registered and it's up to

$6 or $8 a share, we can unload it in a few days to a couple of institutions. It's only $60 million, Jim. No big deal."

No big deal? Big deal! *My* big deal. Inside of six months I'd be out, sitting on my score.

Let the good times roll, I thought. I'm out of having to fight the weather, the day-to-day crises, the financial worms eating away at my stake. I began to relax. I took a vacation.

About six weeks after the closing, I got a phone call from Tom Lambrecht, my dirt contractor who was now Golf's dirt contractor. Tom and I had become friendly over the years and we trusted each other.

"Jim, we haven't been paid," he said. "They're into me for about $3.5 million."

I promised to look into it. Probably just a paperwork foul-up.

Twenty minutes later, I got a call from the engineering firm. They hadn't been paid, either.

I phoned Warren. "Nobody's getting paid, Warren. What's up?"

"I know. We're about to straighten it out." He sounded weary. "Luftig is blaming it on Pacific Life, the bank that's holding all the construction funds in escrow. All the bills have to go through there. He's telling me it's just red tape."

I hung up and dialed Luftig.

"Oh, it's just a big screw-up with forms. Stanchina's people got the paperwork all mixed up. Don't worry about it, Jim. Have Lambrecht call me, and the engineering firm, too. Don't concern yourself."

Sure enough, everybody got paid up.

In December, Golf Communities finally began to trade on the Nasdaq. It opened between 75 cents and a dollar. But the volume was negligible. About 90 percent of the stock was restricted, so only a couple of million of the 45 million shares outstanding were available to trade. That's a thin market, not a market for a plunger.

Another six weeks passed, and I got another call from the dirt guy, Lambrecht. We met for lunch.

"I have a bad gut feeling about these guys," he said. "We got paid for the first month, but still haven't been paid for the second. I've had my people call this guy Luftig, and we're starting to get the runaround. Jim, I'm telling you, something's not right here."

"What do you think is going on?"

"Tell me what the end-game is, first," Tom said. "I can't figure it out."

I explained that CSFB had as much to lose as anyone since they owned as much stock as I did. Part of their fee was a hunk of cash, and the other part was 25 percent ownership in the company. Between CSFB and me, we owned 50 percent of the company. They had every reason in the world to make it work, and not a single reason to let it fail.

Neither of us could figure out how a huge bank, eager to back Golf, couldn't get it together to pay its trade bills. I decided to do some homework. I got a copy of Golf's closing statement and read it with a microscope.

The first problem I saw was that all of Golf Communities' projects required extensive development. They weren't office buildings that were 100 percent occupied, worth $50 million with a $20 million mortgage. These situations were just the opposite. Golf had a big mortgage on raw land, land that needed a ton of dough and a lot of patience to develop.

CSFB lent Golf $50 million to buy me out of The Lakes of Arlington. But first, CSFB dragged $11 million off the front end, 20 percent, in bank fees. Cash. They took it from the left pocket and put it in the right.

That left Golf $39 million. But $26 million of that was gone at closing to pay off my all notes and obligations. That left about $13 million for Golf. Yet another $4 million or so had to be paid out for other closing costs and fees.

After all that got carried off, Golf had $9 million left. But the bank required the company to put most of that into escrow accounts for future expenses, insurance, and taxes. There were also a few other fees to be paid.

So Warren Stanchina walked away from closing a $50 million loan on a property needing $20 million of work before he could sell the first handful of dirt with a check for $174,875. And they wouldn't even give him a lift to the airport!

I phoned Luftig for a blunt talk.

"What the hell is going on here? I see where you guys lent this little company $50 million, and then dragged off $11 million in fees. But it's even worse when you add up all the loans you guys made to them. Out of $100 million in loans, you guys grabbed about $26 million in fees, and $25 million worth of stock."

Just saying it caused me to blow my stack.

"My God! That's more than Phillips Petroleum paid you guys to fight a hostile takeover. That was a $7 *billion* company! This is just a damn real estate development that needs every cent it can lay its hands on to get that dirt ready to sell. You're starving the company to death!"

"We know, we know," Luftig blurted. "Arlington is $10 million short to start. We know that. We're just going to pad it back in there. It'll just get lost in the other loans we're going to do. We're going to fund the golf courses so we're going to pad it in there."

"Why the hell do you have to pad anything! You said you were Golf's partner. You sat right across from me at the table at the Arlington closing and bragged for the millionth time that Credit Suisse First Boston had $500 million to throw into Golf. Well, throw it for Christ's sake!"

I hung up in disgust.

Any remaining shred of confidence I had in CSFB doing the right thing blew away. Real bankers from responsible, trustworthy banks that honestly want to make money by partnering and growing a young company don't talk about padding loans. People go to prison for that.

It was clear now that in Andrew Stone's Principal Transactions Group at Credit Suisse First Boston, the principal transaction occurred when the banker banked his fee.

The Lakes of Arlington project needed another $10 million. What was CSFB going to do about that? Luftig kept telling me, kept telling Warren, "Don't worry about it, don't worry about it, don't worry about it. We're Credit Suisse First Boston. We know what we're doing."

You couldn't tell by their actions. Warren received a solid offer for another property Golf owned in North Carolina. The buyer agreed to pay $10 million in cash that Golf desperately needed to survive. CSFB ignored the deal and the buyer went away.

Two months after making the loan to Golf, CSFB resold the mortgage to a bank in Minnesota, an act of betrayal if ever there was one. Warren was furious. It's the kiss of death for a developer when his own bank doesn't want to hold his mortgage. If CSFB really intended to partner Golf's growth, why was it laying off the bet?

Meanwhile Golf was running out of cash. Luftig assured Warren, "We're going to loan you some more money. Keep working. Everybody can wait thirty more days to get their money. It's not a big deal."

CSFB told Lambrecht the same thing: "Keep moving dirt, you'll get your money. We're Credit Suisse First Boston. We know what we're doing."

But finally Lambrecht called me one day and pronounced the patient dead. "That's it, Jim. I thought I'd give you the courtesy of the first heads-up. We're shuttin' it down."

"Are you sure you want to do that?"

"Yeah. The last thing I want is to have to come in with a mechanic's lien behind a $50 million first mortgage, not with those maggots ahead of me. That's a surefire loser."

Overnight everything stopped. The flatbed trailers came and hauled away Tom's equipment. Almost half the dirt work remained undone.

A few months later Warren called.

"Jim, I feel terrible. We're going to have to file for bankruptcy." Just like that, out of the clear blue sky.

"Have you talked to Credit Suisse?"

Warren said he had warned Luftig. "We laid the bait, Jim, hoping they'd finally cough up some cash, at least avoid the public embarrassment of bankrupting one of their own companies. But they didn't bite."

In July 1999, having heard no news, I phoned Warren.

"Looks like we've run out of time, Jim. We're planning to file any day. I called Luftig and told him. He called me back a million times, begging me not to do it. What choice do we have? The bastards never came up with the rest of the money.

"I'm sorry, Jim. You don't deserve this. And I have a whole group of German investors who don't deserve this either."

A few days later, Golf filed for bankruptcy protection in federal court in Orlando, Florida. Six months later, on New Year's Eve 2000, Golf sued Credit Suisse for fraud, self-dealing, and breach of good faith. Warren was convinced the case was strong and had landed on the desk of a sympathetic judge.

I wanted with all my heart to believe him, and to see Credit Suisse hung out to dry financially and publicly.

But four months later, the judge threw Golf's case out and awarded ownership of Golf's properties, including my Lakes of Arlington, to its first mortgage holder, Credit Suisse First Boston.

When it was clear to me that CSFB had decided to welch on a losing hand, I scurried to gather evidence to support the lawsuit I knew I would be filing. I turned a detective agency loose on it. They reported back that a dozen reputable businessmen would be more than happy to say on the record that the bank and its suspender boys had repeatedly promised to invest $500 million in Golf Communities. No jury would ever doubt they'd said it and that Gough, Luftig, and their cohorts worked damn hard to get all of us to believe it.

With my proof in hand and all my ducks in a row, I took it to my lawyers, Don Godwin and George Carlton at the Dallas law firm Godwin White & Gruber. It was an open and shut case against an outfit with bottomless pockets. It was a near certainty that they'd settle out of court after a single phone call.

So you can imagine my shock when Godwin greeted me at their offices saying, "I'm afraid we've got some very bad news, Jim."

He slid a two-inch-thick document to me across the conference table, opened to a page that had a paragraph highlighted in yellow. It said, in effect, that I had agreed I could never sue CSFB or anyone at the firm for any reason anytime until the end of the world.

Godwin, one of the top trial lawyers in Texas, said, "Jim, this is one of the most onerous documents I've ever seen."

"I never signed this or anything like this."

"Look at the signature," Godwin said. "Does it look like yours?"

I couldn't be sure. So we called in a handwriting expert. But before the handwriting expert rendered his opinion, I remembered something that made my stomach flip-flop. At the closing, the CSFB attorneys asked me to sign two blank pages, telling me these belonged to documents that were being copied and would be attached later. But they assured me this would have no effect on the deal.

"Just boilerplate. Routine stuff," I was assured.

It was clear that one of those signature pages had been stapled to this document I had never seen before. I don't think I've ever felt so foolish or enraged.

The swindle was complete.

Compared with what it could have been, The Lakes of Arlington is a worthless piece of property today. If CSFB hired a developer to go out there and finish the project, it would lose $80 million. Whoever touches it is likely to go bankrupt. If they gave the property back to me today, and the money to finish it, I wouldn't take it.

No one will ever know what the end-game was. The end result was that Credit Suisse First Boston and its mortgage bankers trapped and suffocated Golf Communities. By its deception and inaction, the bank destroyed a valuable project.

There are a lot of people who are keeping their knives sharp for Credit Suisse First Boston. I pity the first CSFB property manager who turns up at Arlington City Hall looking for a permit.

The body count:

Warren Stanchina lost his company, and all of Golf's investors lost their money.

Rex Crim, my mortgage broker, took his fee in stock and lost it all when Golf went bankrupt.

Arlington, Texas, and all its citizens lost the economic and aesthetic opportunity of a generation.

Andrew Stone, who'd been paid an estimated $20 million a year at CSFB, quit after reportedly demanding a $100 million severance package.

Gough and Luftig left CSFB.

In one fell swoop, Deutsche Bank hired nearly the entire staff of CSFB's asset-backed securities group, wiping it out. Rumors circulated that morale was low.

Morale was low in Dallas, too.

I lost $14 million in cold, hard cash on The Lakes of Arlington, along with the economic opportunity of my lifetime. The project set me back financially and cost me precious years. But what really broke my heart was that I had contributed to letting down the people in Arlington who had opened their doors to me and shared my dream.

I made a mistake, but mistakes have been my best teachers. The game taught me the game, as Edwin Lefèvre wrote, and didn't spare the rod.

I've never lost faith in my judgment for long, though. That's what it means to be a plunger. You do your homework, and then go with what you know. Read the tape, study conditions, take your position, and stick to it. That's how the big money is made. It's a lesson I'm still learning.

In the same way that I went toe-to-toe with cancer and survived; traded my way back from ruin in the bond futures; started over after Natchitoches; disco danced my way back from the brink of bankruptcy; woke up in the nick of time flying autopilot—with that same spirit I'm back in the market now, crouching like a cat, stalking, watching, waiting for the right moment to pounce.

Just the other day, for instance, I plunged in the new crop of cotton at 44 cents. I will buy on dips, too, averaging down. I'm going with something I know—it costs that much to grow it. Banks won't lend against 50-cent cotton. Farmers will plant something else this spring. Soon enough there will be a cotton crop forecast that's smaller than everyone expects. The price is a cinch to jump.

It's money lying on the ground, waiting for somebody to bend over and pick up.

22

It's Not The End

"Listen, at least I had a chance. You never had a hope in hell."

As the millennium came to an end, I found myself meeting builders, decorators, clerks, people in all walks of life who had never been involved in the stock market, suddenly plunging and bragging. A broad sector of society that had never done any real trading jumped on the Internet and started buying the "new economy" hype. So many people tried to tell me that it's different this time, a revolution. The world isn't round anymore.

My wife had a friend, a jewelry designer, who joined us for dinner one evening early in 2000, just before the air started to leak out of the dot-com bubble. Adam knew I was a market player and proceeded to tell me the hot stocks I should be buying. I owned no computer nor did I have any direct experience with the Internet. He was going to do me a favor and tell me where I should invest my money.

"Jim, it's just amazin'," he gushed. "I'm buyin' everything on the Internet now—Ebay, Amazon, Priceline. Airline tickets, books, computers. You can even buy your friggin' groceries online. And the stocks are just goin' up and up and up. Why, only 10 percent of the population is using the Internet, so when ever'body starts buyin' online, these companies are gonna make a fortune!"

It was a shame to stick a pin in it, but I couldn't let him go on like that.

"Very interesting, Adam. How long did you say you've been investing?"

"Oh, a *long* time. Almost two years! I've made a ton of money, too—$80,000 in 1998 and $150,000 last year. This year I'm really steppin' up to the plate."

"Uh-huh. Do you read, Adam?"

"Yeah, I love to read, Jim. I buy a couple books every week from Amazon. They deliver right to your door. Why?"

"You should go to Amazon and buy a book about the history of the stock market," I said. "Do you know how many automobile companies went public in the United States in the first three years after Henry Ford rolled out his Model T?

Adam shook his head.

"About a hundred fifty.

"Do know how many railroads Cornelius Vanderbilt and the rest of those guys took public back then? About two hundred."

Adam rolled his eyes.

"Do you know how many U.S. automobile companies there were before Daimler-Benz bought Chrysler, the number of automobile companies that *survived* since Ford started his company? The answer's three, Adam."

He sighed impatiently.

"And did you know that out of those hundreds of railroad companies that used to exist, you could count on one hand the number that exist today?

"That's about how many big Internet companies are likely to survive the long haul. It's the same thing, only a hundred years later."

Adam made a face.

"Oh, Jim," he said, "I know you're one of the best traders around. But this time is *different*." He threw his hands forward in a dismissive gesture. "You're just not with the program! The Internet is changing everything. You need to get yourself a computer. Then you'll understand."

"All right," I said. "We'll see."

Not long after, we went out to eat one night and ran into an older woman we know. We had heard that her husband had died suddenly, leaving her a substantial inheritance. We knew that Adam had befriended this woman, so we weren't surprised to learn that he had rushed to her side during her period of mourning.

"Adam has been so helpful," she told us. "He's even handling my money now, investing it for me in the stock market. He's done very well, you know."

"Adam? *Adam* is investing your inheritance for you?"

"Yes. He's found all these new companies that are going to make a lot of money on the Interweb."

You never know what's the right thing to say in a situation like that. If she'd climbed into an airplane with a pilot who I knew couldn't fly, I'd say it right out: Don't. If she stepped in front of a runaway bus, I'd grab her arm and pull her out of harm's way.

I said calmly, "I think that's an unwise thing for you to do."

She looked at me with real fear in her eyes. "Why, Jim? Do you think he's a crook?"

"No, no. It's not that at all. I just think he's a fool to be messing in the market. He has no experience. You should let him make you some beautiful jewelry. But that's it."

Six months later, the stock market had begun its grinding decline. The Amazons, Ebays, Pricelines, and WebVans crumbled and, in some cases, imploded.

One night at our favorite restaurant, we spotted Adam with our widow friend. She waved us over to join them. But poor Adam would hardly raise his head. He looked, as we used to say in Louisiana, like he'd been shot at and missed, but shit at and hit. I recognized the expression on his face. I've been there.

The moment we sat, he broke down and wept.

"Oh, Jim, I lost *all* my money. How can I have been so stupid not to listen to you? I feel so bad."

I knew just how he felt, although I don't get quite so emotional about these things.

"Listen, Adam, I lost $1.5 million last year on Wyndham Hotels. I lost $14 million on The Lakes of Arlington. And I dropped another million on a little high-tech piece of crap whose CEO couldn't tie his own laces.

"But at least I had a chance. You never had a hope in hell. Go back to making your money designing jewelry. It'll take you two or three years and then you'll get on your feet again having learned from your mistakes."

"It just makes me feel so stupid," Adam said. "I didn't want to sell and admit I was wrong. And then I'd lost everything."

That's the classic pattern after an overblown market erupts and collapses. People hold on all the way down, first because they cling to hope of a rebound. Sometimes they even buy on dips. When the cash is all gone, and hope has faded, denial sets in. People stop checking the price. Denial slips into paralysis. And then one day the stocks have become so worthless they won't even fetch the commissions it would cost to sell them.

Anyone who understands better than 50 percent of the trading I've described in this book now has an unofficial master's degree in the art of speculation. You know that there are no rules more important than the one that tells you to do your homework, and go with what you know.

Beyond that there's often no rhyme or reason to market behavior. I've made $800,000 in a couple of hours on a hunch. And then I spent a month researching, poring over documents, and talking to people all over the country in the hotel business before plunging in Wyndham Hotels, and got hammered.

From its dot-com peak of 5000 in March 2000, the Nasdaq fell in one year to as low as 1615. Even the old, reliable Dow Jones Industrials shed a thousand points in just six trading days. Fear finally replaced greed.

There is no new economy, nor is there an old one for that matter. Companies just have to earn money to justify the price of their stock. It's that simple.

Here's the good news. Just as I tried to teach Adam, my message to anyone I meet these days is that markets always go to extremes. The markets blow up and the markets will hit bottom. And when they do, once-in-a-decade opportunities present themselves.

With a working knowledge of market history, you will spot clear parallels to the 1972/1974 market that almost wiped me out. There was no sudden 1929-style crash then, just thousands of nicks over time that added up to the equivalent of a crash.

In the bear market that began in 2000, many investors lost half the value of their portfolios. Bear markets are painful, they produce panic, and they end when the last paralyzed investor finally bails out.

Where the bottom is and when the market gets there is always anyone's guess. But there are clues that professionals recognize as signs of a bottom, signs that it may be time to strike.

A key barometer is the performance of brokerage stocks. They are always one of the first groups to lead the market back. Brokers know when business is getting better sooner than anyone else, and they're the first to take advantage of it.

Pay attention to big, established companies that begin to talk optimistically about better earnings down the road. When this is repeated by several companies in different industries, the time to buy is approaching.

Pick ten or so stocks of companies you've wanted to own but thought were overpriced. Remember how I chose my stocks after the crash of 1987, when I lived in Maui. It's the same process. Judge all stocks by their price-earnings ratios, against historical price-earnings ratios. Do *all* your homework.

Watch these stocks you've chosen for signs that they have quit falling. If the market has a bad day, for example, but your stock doesn't fall, that's a good sign.

Right now, in June 2001, it appears we are in a long ride down in valuations until we reach more historically normal levels. If I'm correct, investors will be presented with tremendous opportunities to buy solid assets at huge discounts. There have only been three such moments in my life. In 1974, when the stock market bottomed out; when cotton soared to $1 a pound and I shorted it; and when Treasury bonds were yielding 15 percent interest, guaranteed by our government.

My late friend Mel Marks used to say, "The difference between a rich man and a poor man is that the rich man never makes the same mistake twice." That's an exaggeration. A rich man makes the same mistake but differently, learning something profitable from it each time.

Here's another old Wall Street saw that every investor should write down on a big piece of paper, frame, and set where they'll see it every day:

Bulls make money.
Bears make money.
Hogs get slaughtered.

Here are a few final tips to keep in mind:

- The analyst who told you to buy a stock at $50 with a price target of $200 is the same idiot who tells you to sell at $5. Never wait for an analyst to tell you when to sell, never sell just because an analyst said so. Assume that the analyst is compromised from the beginning. If you are lazy and obey him, you increase the chances of getting clobbered. Having someone else to blame doesn't get you off the hook.

- Brokers don't make a penny unless you buy or sell a stock. You owe a broker nothing else. You take all the risk and pay a commission for the execution. You buy and sell when you choose to, without regard for the broker or the firm. You can have great relationships with brokers. Just don't forget, it's a cold-blooded game of them against you.

- Most of the time, market orders are for fools or people trading on inside information. You are going to get swindled if you give a broker, or place online, an order to be filled "at the market." Make the firm work for you. Use limit orders. Never buy the ask, never sell the bid. Have more than one account. If you aren't getting good executions on a timely basis, let your broker know you can take your business elsewhere in the time it takes to dial a phone number or log on to a website. They need you. You don't need them.

- Never buy stock in an initial public offering for a company without a record of solid earnings.

- Talking heads on television often promote the idea of long-term investing. That scares the hell out of me. With few exceptions there is a time to buy and a time to sell. Nothing goes up forever. There are plenty of examples of stocks that are worth less today than they were twenty years ago. That's a long term, but not much of an investment.

- Penny stocks will ruin you. Brush off anyone who tries to sell you on them. The biggest swindle on Wall Street, it's run by the scum of the earth. Spend the money on a Las Vegas vacation instead.

- There are times to be aggressive and times to back off. Don't trade just to trade. Stocks don't go up in bear markets. They get cheaper, until a real opportunity presents itself. Then plunge with a vengeance.

- A paper loss is a real loss. Averaging down in a bear market is the deadliest of sins. You have to let the bear run its course and that means don't fight the tape. The market knows more than you ever will. Listen and it will speak to you.

- The toughest call, even for professionals, is knowing when to plunge in a stock that has compelling value above its price, but the market is in bear territory. Wait until the stock refuses to fall even as the broad market continues to decline. If the fundamental business of the company is solid, buy and be prepared to wait weeks or even months before you get a move up. If you believe you're right, act like it.

- The Internet will continue to enhance business efficiency. Companies are better run today than ever. Once we hit the next bottom, growth and earnings will explode. If your timing is right, you should be able to double your money without margin in eighteen months owning good, solid companies at fair prices.

- Watch for the signs and be patient. Then plunge with everything you can afford because you will not get the chance again for a long time.

- If you remember nothing else, remember this, the most basic rule of all investing: buy in a bull market, sell in a bear market.

INDEX

EG&G, Inc. 10, 11, 12

F

Federal Emergency Management Administration 200
Fettinger, Mike 8
Fidelity Funds 159
Fidelity Magellan. *See* Peter Lynch
First Boston 215, 216
   Cigna analyst leak 124
Fiveson, David 84
Forbes magazine 163, 164
Forbes, Malcolm 153, 163, 164
Forst, Dennis 202
Fort Worth Star-Telegram 191, 193, 197, 199
Fussell, Tommy 30

G

General Electric xv
George W. Bush xvii
Gioia, Phil 159
Giuliani, Rudolph 141
GNP Commodities 68, 69, 70
Godwin, Don 237
Godwin White & Gruber 237
Gold 57, 62, 67, 68
Goldman Sachs 53, 88, 90, 92, 120, 152, 207
Golf Communities of America
     220, 221, 222, 223, 225, 227, 229, 233, 234, 237, 238
Gough, Michael
     215, 216, 217, 218, 219, 221, 224, 225, 226, 228, 229, 230, 232, 237, 238
Green, Arlington Mayor Richard 192, 197
Greyhound 145, 161
Guillemaud, Gerry 73, 75, 97, 127, 130, 134, 172
Guinn, Kenny 157, 158
Gulf & Western Industries 16, 79, 80, 81

H

N

Natchitoches, Louisiana
   1, 2, 13, 17, 23, 24, 27, 28, 30, 36, 40, 41, 42, 142, 168, 193, 194
Natchitoches Times 2
New York Stock Exchange
   8, 11, 26, 65, 70, 73, 75, 84, 118, 119, 124, 140, 166
Newell, Roz 209
Northeast Louisiana University 5, 6
Northwestern State University, Natchitoches 24
Nunis, Dick 187

O

Otey, Scott 129

P

Pace, Saverio 78
Pacific Life 233
PaineWebber 92, 211
Palmer, Skip 187
Park Lane Hotel, New York xx, 77, 84, 108, 112, 163
Passman, U.S. Cong. Otto 37
Patriot American Hospitality 209
Patterson, John 143
Pattison, James A. "Jimmy" 149
penny stock 50, 102, 103, 104, 105, 106, 107, 109, 111, 112, 121, 135
Perella, Joseph 215
PerkinElmer. *See* EG&G, Inc.
Peter Lynch 10, 16, 148
Pic 'N' Save 148, 149, 150, 151, 152, 155
Pickens, T. Boone Jr. 92, 94, 149
Pierson, Ed 34
Plaza Hotel 78, 163
Polaroid 16
Price, Roy 53, 54, 56, 97

Starwood Capital 222, 223
Stone, Andrew 216, 225, 226, 227, 229, 230, 232, 235, 238
Stovall, S.J. 181, 189, 190, 200
Sunbelt Savings and Loan 180, 181
Swearingen, John E. 79
SwissAir Group 206

T

Talon, divison of Textron 86, 87, 145
Tarrant County, Texas 182
Taubman, Alfred 164
Tauscher, Bill 159
Texas Industries 182, 183, 184, 185, 201, 208
The Lakes of Arlington
The Wall Street Journal xvi, 202
Thomson McKinnon 160, 166, 171, 172, 173
Tomlin, Bob 129
Trinity River xviii, 180, 182, 186, 191
Trump, Donald 153, 161, 163, 164
Tsai, Gerry 16
Turner, Bruce 202

U

Utah, penny stocks 104

V

Vandergriff, Tom 197
Volcker, Paul 58, 66, 67

W

Wal-Mart 176, 177, 178
Wall Street Journal 2, 3, 4, 8, 9, 11, 64, 143, 207
Wall Street Week with Louis Rukeyser xv
Washington, Dennis 149
Washington Water Power 158, 159

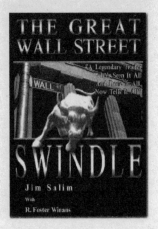

Where writers become authors.

To Order Additional Copies:
Call Toll Free: 1-866-XLIBRIS (954-2747)
Email: WallStreet@xlibris.com

Online: http://www.xlibris.com/TheGreatWallStreetSwindle

Title	Edition	Qty		Unit Cost	Total
The Great Wall Street Swindle	Hardback		x	$28.95	$

FREE SHIPPING/HANDLING

I will be paying by:

❏ Check (made payable to Xlibris)
❏ Money Order (made payable to Xlibris)
❏ Credit Card (fill in and sign the form below)

Cardholder Name _____

Street Address _____

_____

CC# _____ Exp. Date _____

Signature _____

Mail or Fax this form to: Xlibris Corporation
                                   436 Walnut St., 11th Floor
                                   Philadelphia, PA 19106
                                   Fax 1-215-923-4685

Please allow one week for each shipment to arrive within the continental United States.